THE
VICTORY TIPS
PROGRAM

GAIN VICTORY OVER ANXIETY AND DEPRESSION

No part of this publication may be reproduced, distributed, or transmitted in any form or by any means, including photocopying, recording, or other electronic or mechanical methods, or by any information storage and retrieval system without the prior written permission of the publisher, except in the case of very brief quotations embodied in critical reviews and certain other noncommercial uses permitted by copyright law. Bible verses excluded.

All Bible verses used in this version of the program
are from the King James Version of the Bible.

Join our conference calls to see how best to use this program. For times and phone numbers to call in, call 213-426-8223 (US) & 289-723-2420 (Canada),

Copyright © 2019 by Vincent J. Beyer

Faith and Love Publishing
95 Church St., St. Catharines, Ontario, Canada, L2R 3C7
"The only thing that counts is faith expressing itself through love." Galatians 5:6 NIV

ISBN 978-1-7752298-2-7

www.victorytipsprogram.com

Table of Contents

(The format for our support meetings begins on Page 155.)

Introduction 3
Testimonies..4

Happiness Tips

1) "Fly By The Instruments" 6
2) Stop. And Be Still 10
3) Admit You Have A Problem 14
4) Disarm the Shame... 18
5) Form a Support Team 23
6) Guard Your Thoughts 27
7) Speak Right Words... 31
8) Make Right Choices 39
9) Develop Your Faith 42
10) Respond Rather Than React........................... 46
11) Know Yourself.. 55
12) Don't Judge.. 59
13) Be "Good Ground" 62
14) Develop a Conqueror Mentality..................... 64
15) Eliminate Wasted Thinking 69
16) Develop a Disciplined Lifestyle..................... 79
17) Develop a Life of Holiness 82
18) Become an Optimist....................................... 88
19) Eliminate Anger 94
20) Practice Humility 98
21) Collect "Grace Doors" 102
22) Volunteer 105
23) Conquer the Addiction................................... 111
24) Have a Vision for Your Life 117
25) Be Thankful 121
26) Welcome "MLC's" 124
27) Resolve Delayed Maturity 129
28) Sing... 137
29) Join a Church 144

Happiness Basics

1) Meeting Start Page 155
2) Happiness Speaker 155
3) Strong Speaker 158
4) Knowledge Speaker....................................... 161
5) Word Speaker 162
6) Faith Speaker... 165
7) Truth Speaker... 166
8) Love Speaker... 166
9) Affirmation Speaker 168
10) Slogans Speaker... 169
11) Beliefs Speaker.. 169
12) Hindrance Speaker... 170
13) Gospel Speaker 170

Practical Tools

Affirmations

1) I Do Not Fear... 173
2) I Am Strong 176
3) I Flow In Harmony and Love 179
4) I Only Speak Right Words 181
5) I Only Think Right Thoughts 183
6) I Am Happy Because..................................... 186

Core Beliefs

1) God Loves Me and I Am Valuable 195
2) Christ's Crucifixion Paid For My Sin 199
3) God Wants Me to Live in Perfect Peace 204
4) I Have an Enemy - Satan............................... 208
5) I Have another Enemy – Fleshly Appetites.. 216
6) God Wants Me to Enjoy Good Health 218

A) Types of Abuse... 222
B) Author's Message... 224
C) Message to the Strong 225

Welcome to The Victory Tips Program

Since 2004, we have been helping people rise above anxiety and depression. Over the years, many of the people requesting help have been Christian. Thus, we have published this manual that helps people find wholeness using scripture. We want Christians to plainly see that God wants them well, and that He has provided guidance in the Bible on how to be well. For those who are not Christian, we suggest they find a mature Christian to walk them through this manual. We would be happy to help them find such a person in their area. Our contact information is provided below.

The "Toolbox"

We think of the Bible as a toolbox. But if we don't know how to use the tools in the toolbox, the toolbox will have no value to us. Because many people do not have experience using the "toolbox" (the Bible), we have written the Victory Tips Program in simple terms so it can be easily understood, and be helpful to as many people as possible.

The Program

The Victory Tips Program has three main sections, the 29 Happiness Tips, the Happiness Basics, and the Practical Tools section. The program is written in a recovery group format. This means it can be used to lead a recovery group. People with little understanding of mental health knowledge can use this program to make a difference in the lives of those around them.

An important benefit of the Victory Tips Program is access to daily support. Daily contact through conference calls and one-to-one support calls enables individuals to quickly learn recovery truths that will help them heal emotionally. Having contact with others who are journeying toward wellness, offers another benefit, that of, making new friends.

The Version

This particular version of the program uses Bible verses from the King James Version of the Bible. For a Victory Tips Program using other Bible translations, or for a program translated into other languages, please visit our website at www.victorytipsprogram.com, or contact us: 213-426-8223 (USA) or 289-723-2420 (Canada), or email us at victorytipsprogram@gmail.com.

The Impact

To get the most out of this Bible-based program, we suggest you invite the "Author" of the Bible, Jesus Christ, into your reading time. You can do this by praying this prayer. *"Jesus, I invite you into my reading time. Please teach me how to live my life free of all anxiety and depression. Amen."*

Please Note

The Victory Tips Program is a peer-to-peer, personal networking and group recovery tool, and is not intended to take the place of professional counseling or medical treatment.

"But thanks be to God which gives us the victory through our Lord Jesus Christ."
1 Corinthians 15:57

Testimonials

"When I first contacted Victory Tips, I was angry, sad, and inconsolable. To say I was difficult is an understatement. I felt cheated and robbed of what had been a happy life. But they more than hung in with me, offering compassion, understanding, and solutions so I could go on…….. Today, I am self-employed which is something I thought I could never do. I can't thank them enough for saving my life and giving me the tools and insight to regain control of my life. They helped me realize there is life after suffering." - Beth (2007)

"My needs as a wife and mother were not being met, and I felt hurt, betrayed, neglected, and at times like I didn't matter. I began shaking and jerking on my left side due to the depression and the medications. I wanted the pain to stop…….. I am now in a church that provides help and support….. For many years I felt like damaged goods. I am being restored. It is by the relationship I have with God that is allowing this to happen. Situations and circumstances are going to come up. I need to remember that I can do all things through Christ who gives me strength." - Lindsay (2006)

"I got back an email that said, "I want to talk to you." I was very hesitant, but unconsciously I must have emailed them back. Then another email came saying that God's will is that you enjoy life. It was as if God himself was speaking to me through those words…….. The things that helped me so much were the Affirmations. I read them every day without fail. Sometimes I read them repeatedly. I apply the Affirmations to my everyday life….. With a whole heart, I gladly endorse the wonderful knowledge and topics that you will find in this program. I trust it will do for you what it did for me. I pray that you give them a chance to help you. Remember that you are not alone. The best is yet ahead of you! The Holy Spirit will embrace you and restore you!"- Lori (2004)

"I found Victory Tips through a telephone prayer line; they were my last hope, I had called every single prayer line listed on the Internet and prayed with thousands of them. My husband of 14 years (17 years of being together) had kicked me out and had replaced me with a girlfriend half his age. We have three children; we had a beautiful farm, everyone thought we were as in love as I thought we were, it crushed me…. This program, the group members, the Lord Christ, God JEHOVAH, saved my life and taught me how to have faith in God and rely on Him to get me through trials, there aren't enough good things I can say about this program." - Sarah (2015)

"My husband and I went through tough times with my family. We also had very stressful financial problems and health problems…. It is a huge blessing of God to have this kind of support that helps me to understand that my real family is my brothers and sisters in Christ… I have received so much love from this program and group that every day I feel so full of the love of God, and that is all that we need to live in Victory. The Victory Tips program itself can heal you, transform you, and change you for the better."- Maribel (2017)

Testimonials

"I don't know of anything else that could have helped me through such sorrow as well as this Holy Spirit led program. Victory Tips is amazing. Because of their dedication and diligence, this program lifted me to a higher place in my Christian walk and pulled me out of the loneliness of depression. It also brought much restoration in my family and a closer relationship with Our Lord."- Catherine (2014)

"I was at an ultimate low in my life when I came to the Victory Tips Program. I had just recently tried to harm myself and was told I needed help. My daughter had found the Victory Tips program online. It was then I decided to try this program. As I began to study this course, I began drawing closer to God after being estranged from him for sooo long. I felt an indescribable PEACE set in. I highly recommend this program to anyone and everyone. This program gives you exactly what the title says, "Victory Tips" on how to cope with life and its challenges !!!! While bringing you closer to God."- Connie (2015)

"On reflection, it had been a very brief courtship, and on the day we married my husband's personality immediately appeared to change...He became extremely angry, moody, abusive and at times threatening and violent to me. I knew he had problems, but did not know the extent of them or the possible repercussions...During this desperate time, I became aware of the existence of Victory Tips prayer ministry. We had daily discussions, which probably kept me alive and kept me praying. They linked me with other similar girls on the program with shared prayer calls; this was also supportive to me... I found the Victory tips program literally to be a lifesaver."- Deborah (2015)

"As I explored churches over a period of some 42 years, I was amazed that in the face of the Great Commission, the practical value of making disciples was nearly totally absent. Searching for something to fill that gap in my life I turned to the Victory Tips program. There I found that in the context of the lesson was how to be a disciple of Jesus Christ. The Great Commission must be completed, and discipleship is the first step. "Do your best to present yourself to God as one approved, a worker who does not need to be ashamed and who correctly handles the word of truth (2 Timothy 2:15)." In His love and Service." - David (2019)

"Thirteen years ago I prayed to God to send me someone I could talk to but found no one. I was desperate and did not stop crying. I asked God, "Why?..." all the time. My family thought I had left the best thing that had ever happened to me, and they did not come around. My friends had left because of the man I was with. I searched for help....I found Victory Tips. They understood and listened to me while I cried. They prayed for me, talked to me. They encouraged me to get back to church. I did not want to trust anyone in church again. I listened, and found a church. I changed my thinking.... They were active in my steps to recovery. The Victory Tips Program was the basis of finding the Love of God who heals all of the sorrows in this world. I felt like God would not ever love me as I had been such a sinner. I had to step out in faith and seek His love. Our Lord is faithful to His Word." - Hope (2017)

TIP #1

***

"Fly By the Instruments"

***

1A - Flying by the Instruments is a term used when aircraft pilots are unable to see ahead of them because of precipitation, darkness, or cloud cover. In these conditions, pilots rely on their instruments to guide them safely to their destination. We thank God for instruments in an aircraft because they can mean the difference between landing safely, and crash landing. So it is in our lives. Life can become so difficult that we can no longer "*see where we are going*". We end up losing inner peace and happiness. At these times it is vital that we know how to "Fly by the Instruments."

Question 1: Can you remember a time when you needed help to get through a problem? If so, would you like to share with us briefly what happened?

2A - What are the "instruments" we can "fly" by? The scriptures give us principles we can hold onto when life gets tough.

"Instrument No. 1" - <u>God Loves Us.</u>

During most times in our lives, the fact that God loves us may be an unquestionable truth. Here are some scriptures about God's love for us.

a) **John 3:16** "For God so loved the world, that he gave his only begotten Son, that whosoever believeth in him should not perish, but have everlasting life."

b) **Ephesians 2:4** "But God, who is rich in mercy, for his great love wherewith he loved us,"

c) **Titus 3:4** "But after that the kindness and love of God our Savior toward man appeared,"

2B - However, when we are under severe stress, the simple truth of God's love can seem foreign to us. It can tempt us to believe that God is mad at us, and is showing His dissatisfaction toward us by allowing the negative circumstances in our lives. This is a common occurrence and needs to be addressed; otherwise we lose precious time in needless stress.

2C - Some of the hard times we experience can come because of poor choices we have made. The hurtful results of these choices cannot be blamed on God. The good news is, when we are His child, we have only to confess our poor choices to Him, and repent of them, and He instantly forgives us. God's mercy is so great. Following, are some Bible verses about God's willingness to forgive us.

a) **Isaiah 1:18** "Come now, and let us reason together, saith the Lord: though your sins be as scarlet, they shall be as white as snow; though they be red like crimson, they shall be as wool."

b) **Isaiah 55:7** "Let the wicked forsake his way, and the unrighteous man his thoughts: and let him return unto the Lord, and he will have mercy upon him; and to our God, for he will abundantly pardon."

c) **1 John 1:9** "If we confess our sins, he is faithful and just to forgive us our sins, and to cleanse us from all unrighteousness."

2D - God's Grace

Along with forgiveness, God promises to give us grace to get through the tough times. Below is a well known Bible verse about God's grace that carries us through such times. The Apostle Paul wrote it. Paul was troubled with an affliction, and he wanted Jesus to give him relief from it. However, this was a special kind of affliction. The affliction came to him because he was given a vast amount of knowledge about Jesus Christ. Jesus felt it was necessary to keep Paul humble and allow him to somewhat suffer, so he would never lose sight of the job that was given him to do. The following verse gives us some details about this situation.

2 Corinthians 12:7 *"(Paul speaking)* And lest I should be exalted above measure through the abundance of the revelations, there was given to me a thorn in the flesh, the messenger of Satan to buffet me, lest I should be exalted above measure."

2E - Paul asked for relief from his affliction. See underlined text, below, so read how Jesus responded to his request.

2 Corinthians 12:9 "And he said unto me, My grace is sufficient for thee: for my strength is made perfect in weakness. Most gladly therefore will I rather glory in my infirmities, that the power of Christ may rest upon me."

2F - Above, Jesus told Paul, *"My grace is sufficient for thee: for my strength is made perfect in weakness."* In essence, Jesus told Paul that, "No, I will not relieve you in the way you are asking. I will help you in another way." That way is called grace. Paul had to learn that there is a special place in God where His grace carries us through the difficult times of our lives. It is a place of resting and trusting in God. We find that place by meditating on God's Word.

2G - When difficult times come, for whatever reason, it's not that God wants us to feel long-lasting shame and regret. God is all about welcoming us when we do wrong. The truth is, God has a plan for us that is filled with peace and blessing. If we've failed God, or failed ourselves or failed those around us, no problem – we simply go to God in humility and faith, to receive pardon for our sins through Jesus Christ. God will forgive us, and give us a "Plan B" to follow, to get back to God's blessings. That is what makes the Christian life so amazing. We are always only one sincere prayer away from a new beginning!

For more scriptures that show us how much God loves us, read the bible verses in Core Belief #1 – God Loves Me.

"Instrument No. 1" is God Loves Us!

Question 2: Can you think of a time when God showed His love to you?

3A - "Instrument No. 2" - <u>People Love Us</u>

There are people in our lives who honestly love us, and want to help us. If our family and friends cannot help us, surely people from a nearby church will help us. The mandate of the church is to go out to the "highways and bi-ways" of life and compel people to come to Jesus Christ their Savior. Jesus wants to show them how to have their lives transformed by His love and His truth.

3B - Granted, not every church can help with financial needs, but a good church, for sure, will help with friendship and spiritual guidance.

Why would a church want to help people who are struggling? A good pastor knows the value of helping someone who is suffering. Once that person is brought to a place of faith and peace, they become the best person to reach out to others who are suffering.

Here are some scriptures about the church reaching out to help people.

a) **Matthew 25:35** "For I was an hungred, and ye gave me meat: I was thirsty, and ye gave me drink: I was a stranger, and ye took me in:"

b) **Romans 12:13** "Distributing to the necessity of saints; given to hospitality."

c) **Galatians 6:2** "Bear ye one another's burdens, and so fulfil the law of Christ."

"Instrument No. 2" – <u>People Love Us</u>!

Question 3: Can you think of a time when God used people to help you?

4A - "Instrument No. 3" – <u>We Were Created to Win</u>

When we are overwhelmed with the stresses of life, it's great to know that we were created to win! It may feel like we could never win, but that isn't the way God created us to be. When we receive Jesus Christ as our personal Lord and Savior, we enter a community of people who are "overcomers" in all aspects of life.

4B - We read in Genesis 1:26 that God created Adam to have dominion over the world. See Genesis 1:26 below, and other "overcomer" scriptures.

a) **Genesis 1:26** "And God said, Let us make man in our image, after our likeness: and let them have dominion over the fish of the sea, and over the fowl of the air, and over the cattle, and over all the earth, and over every creeping thing that creepeth upon the earth."

b) **Psalm 8:4-6** "What is man, that thou art mindful of him? and the son of man, that thou visitest him? ⁵ For thou hast made him a little lower than the angels, and hast crowned him with glory and honour. ⁶ Thou madest him to have dominion over the works of thy hands; thou hast put all things under his feet:

c) **Psalm 115:16** "The heaven, even the heavens, are the LORD's: but the earth hath he given to the children of men."

4C - The New Testament also has scriptures on how man was created to win.

a) **Matthew 10:1** "And when he had called his twelve disciples to him, he gave them power over unclean spirits, to cast them out, and to heal all kinds of sickness and all kinds of disease."

b) **Acts 1:8** "But ye shall receive power, after that the Holy Ghost is come upon you: and ye shall be witnesses unto me both in Jerusalem, and in all Judaea, and in Samaria, and unto the uttermost part of the earth."

c) **Romans 8:37** "Nay, in all these things we are more than conquerors through him that loved us."

Question 4: Can you remember times in your life when you were winning? If so, can you tell us about any of them?

5A - Now that you have found out the truth, believe it!

"Instrument No.3" – <u>We Were Created To Win</u>!

"Instrument No. 4" – <u>We Have a Weapon</u>

When everything about life seems so chaotic, it is good to know that God doesn't leave us defenseless. Ephesians Chapter 6 talks about the armor of God that every Christian needs to have on, at all times. One of the pieces of armor is the Sword of the Spirit.

Ephesians 6:17 "And take the helmet of salvation, and the sword of the Spirit, which is the word of God:"

5B - The Sword of the Spirit is the Word of God. It is what Jesus used to defend Himself when Satan tempted Him in the wilderness during a 40 day fast. At one point, the devil tempted Jesus to turn stones into bread to feed Himself. However, Jesus told him, *"It is written, Man shall not live by bread alone, but by every word that proceedeth out of the mouth of God."* (Matthew 4:4) The devil also tempted Jesus to jump off the temple peak, by saying "If thou be the Son of God, cast thyself down: for it is written, He shall give his angels charge concerning thee: and in their hands they shall bear thee up, lest at any time thou dash thy foot against a stone. But Jesus told him, *"It is written, "Thou shalt not tempt the Lord thy God."* (Matthew 4:7) Satan kept tempting Jesus, and each time Jesus defeated the devil with the Sword of the Spirit, the Word of God.

5C - We notice in the above story that Satan also knows the Word of God, and he uses it to try and deceive us. That's why we need to have a good understanding of the scriptures. So, the question for us is this: Are we going to let Satan beat us up with his lies and deceptions, or are we going to stop Satan in his tracks with the Word of God? The choice is ours.

Question 5: Do you have any experience in using weapons to protect yourself?

6A - The rest of this manual teaches us how to use God's Word to keep us in a state of peace and happiness.

"Instrument No. 4" – <u>We Have a Weapon</u>!

When life seems out of control, we can take back control of our lives; starting with, "Flying by the instruments."

Contact us today to get help on your journey toward peace and happiness. Clear skies are just ahead!

213-426-8223 (USA) or 289-723-2420 (Canada)

* * * * * * *

TIP #2

Stop, and Be Still

1A - We can all agree that life can be challenging. When we get to a point where we've been trying so hard to make life work but things aren't going well, sometimes it is good to just stop.

But what does the average person do? They keep trying and trying until they exhaust themselves physically and emotionally. Life was never meant to be so difficult, but we make it so because of our ignorance.

1B - <u>What Does "Stop" Mean?</u>

When life gets hard, and we stop, we're not quitting, we're just pausing to assess our strategies. What does 'Stop' mean to you in your situation? It may mean to stop actions leading to a divorce or a job resignation. Maybe it means cutting back on commitments or working fewer hours. Whatever it may be, we're going to have to stop and take time to learn strategies that can help us win in life.

1C - <u>"Stopping" in the Scriptures</u>

One incident in the scriptures of a person feeling the need to stop was Mary, the sister of Martha. In Luke Chapter 10 we read how Jesus went to Mary and Martha's house to visit and teach them. Mary chose to stop and sit at Jesus's feet to hear Him teach. When Martha complained to Jesus that her sister wasn't helping her prepare food for His visit, Jesus told Martha, that Mary had chosen the right thing to do, to stop and hear him teach. Mary chose to "stop and be still," and it gave her favor with Jesus.

Question 1: What is your favorite place in your home where you can stop and be still each day to learn from the scriptures?

2A - <u>Saul of Tarsus</u>

Another time in scripture of a person feeling the need to stop was Saul of Tarsus. In Acts Chapter 8 and 9, we see that Saul was living a passionate life for God. Saul was strictly following the Jewish teachings of the day. He even imprisoned and killed people who were a threat to the Jewish ways of living, including followers of Christ. Then one day Jesus got his attention with a bright light that blinded him. He then heard an audible voice, saying, *"I am Jesus whom thou persecutest: it is hard for thee to kick against the pricks."*

That caused Saul to stop what he was doing. How did Saul "become still"? Scripture tells us that he neither ate nor drank for 3 days. He waited to receive direction for his life. Saul later became the great Apostle, Paul, who wrote most of the New Testament. Saul chose to "Stop, and Be Still," and it helped him become a renowned leader for the Church of Jesus Christ.

Question 2: Have you ever had a time in your life where God used circumstances to stop you suddenly to get your attention? Can you tell us about it?

3A - The Apostles after the Resurrection

Another occasion of people "stopping and being still" occurred after Jesus had been crucified. He arose from the dead and showed himself to His followers. He gave them these instructions, *"And, behold, I send the promise of my Father upon you: but tarry (wait) ye in the city of Jerusalem, until ye be endued with power from on high."* (**Luke 24:49**). In obedience, the followers of Christ met in a large upper room and began praying. They were "stopping," and as they did, God's Holy Spirit came down from heaven and filled them all with God's power. **Acts 2:2** describes what happened; *"And suddenly there came a sound from heaven as of a rushing mighty wind, and it filled all the house where they were sitting."* From then on, the Apostle's began preaching and teaching the Word of God in great power. The 120 people in the upper room chose to "stop, and be still" and it transformed their lives!

Question 3: Have you ever attended a spiritual retreat or set aside a block of time to focus on God? Did God help you or direct you in some way?

4A - When Anxiety Comes - "Stop"

"Stop" can also be used whenever we feel anxiety coming on. When this happens, we can stop what we are doing and pray a short prayer, such as: *"Dear God, anxiety is building up in me. Please show me what is causing it so I can disarm it and go back to a place of peace and calm."*

If anxiety has become such a close companion to you that you don't even notice it when it tries to come on you, ask God to help you recognize it in its early stages, and then confront it with the above prayer.

4B - "Be Still."

It can be helpful to take time each day to "be still" from activity. The goal of taking time to be still in our actions is to learn how to be still in our thinking. Being still can also help us spiritually, for when our hearts are at rest, we are most able to sense God's guidance in our lives.

4C - Ways we can become still in our actions

Bible Reading

It can be helpful to develop a consistent time of Bible reading each day. In the Happiness Basics, we learn about the importance of knowing God's Word. This is what we use to help ourselves during difficult times.

2 Timothy 2:15 *"Study to shew thyself approved unto God, a workman that needeth not to be ashamed, rightly dividing the word of truth."*

4D - <u>Prayer</u>

We can also consider developing a consistent time of prayer each day (See Daniel 6:10 below). We can make a list of our prayer requests, and bring them to God every day. When we pray, it is good to pray with faith and thanksgiving. God wants us to believe that He is answering our requests.

Daniel 6:10 "Now when Daniel knew that the writing was signed, he went into his house; and his windows being open in his chamber toward Jerusalem, he kneeled upon his knees three times a day, and prayed, and gave thanks before his God, as he did aforetime."

4E - Another good habit is to take time throughout our day to invite God into our situations.

Taking time to "be still" and pray, will help us have more peace as stated in the scripture below:

Philippians 4:6-7 "Be careful for nothing; but in everything by prayer and supplication with thanksgiving let your requests be made known unto God. [7] And the peace of God, which passeth all understanding, shall keep your hearts and minds through Christ Jesus."

4F - <u>Study</u>

Another good habit to do is to stop and take time to study God's Word. In the Happiness Basics, we have a section that teaches us about the importance of seeking knowledge. Here are two verses that bear this out.

a) **Proverbs 4:7** "Wisdom is the principal thing; therefore get wisdom: and with all thy getting get understanding."

b) **Proverbs 16:16** "How much better is it to get wisdom than gold! and to get understanding rather to be chosen. than silver!"

4G - <u>"Being Still" in Our Speech</u>

An important way to become "still," is in the amount of speaking we do. Throughout the Book of Proverbs, it cautions us to be careful how we speak. Our words have creative power in our lives either for good or for bad. We go into more detail about this in Tip # 6 – Speak Right Words.

4H - <u>Become "Still" in Our Goal-Reaching</u>

Another way we can practice being still is in how we reach for our goals. Sometimes we get a goal in mind, but we try too hard to control events and people to achieve our goal. Doing so can take away our peace of mind. Instead, it is better to become a person who is flexible. Progress may not always happen as quickly as we want, but if we leave our setbacks in God's hands, we'll find God gets us to where we should be in due time.

Question 4: Do you know someone who can be overly goal-driven?

5A - <u>"Being Still" in the Scriptures</u>

In the Book of Exodus, in the Ten Commandments, we read a Bible command for us to "be still":

Exodus 20:8-11 we read: "Remember the sabbath day, to keep it holy. [9] Six days shalt thou labour, and do all thy work: [10] But the seventh day is the sabbath of the LORD thy God: in it thou shalt not do any work, thou, nor thy son, nor thy daughter, thy manservant, nor thy maidservant, nor thy cattle, nor thy stranger that is within thy gates: [11] For in six days the LORD made heaven and earth, the sea, and all that in them is, and rested the seventh day: wherefore the LORD blessed the sabbath day, and hallowed it."

In our fast-paced lifestyle, it is easy to stay busy seven days a week. But that isn't good for us. God recommends that we take one day out of seven to "be still."

Question 5: Do you have one day each week where you do very little but rest?

6A - Verses Related To "Being Still"

a) **2 Chronicles 20:17** "Ye shall not need to fight in this battle: set yourselves, stand ye still, and see the salvation of the LORD with you, O Judah and Jerusalem: fear not, nor be dismayed; tomorrow go out against them: for the LORD will be with you."

b) **Psalm 4:4** *"Stand in awe, and sin not: commune with your own heart upon your bed, and be still. Selah."*

c) **Psalm 46:10** "Be still, and know that I am God: I will be exalted among the heathen, I will be exalted in the earth."

d) **Isaiah 40:31** "But they that wait upon the LORD shall renew their strength; they shall mount up with wings as eagles; they shall run, and not be weary; and they shall walk, and not faint."

6B - Hindrances To Stopping and Being Still

There can be hindrances to stopping and being still. With this in mind, we can start being sensitive to the things that upset us, things that prevent us from being still. These are the *triggers* we can focus on in our recovery. Thankfully, we can learn how to disarm them so they no longer control us, and we find a place of peace and calm in God.

Question 6: What do you think will get in the way of you practicing Tip #2 - Stop, and Be Still?

* * * * * * *

TIP #3

Admit You Have a Problem

1A - This can be a difficult step because it requires us to admit we have a weakness in our life. However, weaknesses can be blessings in disguise. When we conquer a weakness, we increase our self-esteem and we gain the ability to help others who struggle with a similar weakness.

1B - One of the more challenging aspects of this Tip can be facing the extent of our damaged emotions. Most of us do our best to present a positive image to the people we interact with each day. But if we've only learned a few "tricks" to barely get through everyday life, it won't take many life problems to overload our capacity to manage them well. Eventually, the challenges can overpower our cobbled defenses, and we see the true extent of our damaged emotions. This is the risk we take by not dealing with our issues. Now is the time to decide what we want to do. Do we remain a "just-getting-by" person, or do we work at becoming a healed person, someone who genuinely embraces and enjoys all aspects of our life?

Question 1: Do you know people who are "just-getting-by" or "healed and at peace"?

2A - <u>Forced To Learn</u>

Sometimes we don't have the luxury of being able to choose which of the above groups we want to be in; life has already conquered us, and we are forced to learn new ways to win at life. Thankfully, there are benefits to being "down and out".

For one, we have no image to live up to. People have already seen us at our worst, so there's no having to try hard to hide our mental health challenge.

2B – Two, we become a tangible example of recovery to those who know us. Our friends and colleagues who know of our challenges can now watch us as we emerge from pain and loss, to love and life. These people will be like those in the crowd 2,000 years ago who were watching Jesus heal blind people, lepers, and invalids. We become proof that Jesus is alive and still healing men and women of their illnesses. Do you recall what the individuals did after Jesus healed them? They went far and wide telling the world the amazing things Jesus had done for them. That can be our experience as well!

Question 2: Do you know people who use their healing to point people to Christ?

3A - Another benefit can be is that we learn how to be humble. Humility can be a great stress-reliever. For more on this topic, read Tip #20 – Practice Humility.

3B - Another benefit to hitting rock-bottom is personal awareness. Most of us think we are healthier than we are. Some of us, who have had to face our emotional weaknesses, look back and see that the state of our emotional health was different than what we thought. That is painful, but valuable! It leads us to truth. Knowing and accepting the "true us", as ill as we are, better equips us to help ourselves get well.

Question 3: Have you had to see and accept how injured your "heart" is? How did it affect you?

4A - Medication

Thankfully there is medication that can offer some relief from symptoms of anxiety and depression. Some people are judgmental toward those who take medication for a mental health condition. But it is never good to judge others.

4B - For one thing, we don't know what a person is struggling with. It could be that they have suffered great personal injury, and their pain is manifesting in the way they act. We also don't know what the doctor's strategy is for treating this person. It could be that the new medication the doctor has prescribed to them has adverse side effects and is causing the person to act differently. It is best not to judge others. It is best that we be a source of positivity to them rather than a source of negativity.

Question 4: Do you know someone who passes judgment on people who take medication for anxiety or depression?

5A - Working With Our Doctor

Common uses of medication are those prescribed to help us process a sudden major life crisis. Medication can be tapered off once we have processed the crisis sufficiently. It is wise to work with our doctor when weaning off of medication.

Other mental health conditions require on-going medication treatment. These conditions are no different than taking insulin for diabetes or daily medication for a heart condition. No matter what kind of mental health challenge we have, it is best to consult our doctor for treatment options and work closely with them to help us attain optimal daily living.

5B - Stubbornness

Although most people don't pass judgment on those who struggle emotionally, they may pass judgment on a person who refuses to admit they have a problem. If there is evidence that we need treatment for a mental health condition, we should look into it. We shouldn't decline treatment. If we do, our condition escalates from being a problem with *weakness* to a problem with *stubbornness*. Being stubborn can be a character trait that works against our peace and happiness.

Question 5: Have people ever told you that you can be stubborn? Can you think of an instance when stubbornness impacted your life?

6A - "Admitting" in the Bible

King David & Bathsheba

In 2 Samuel Chapter 11 & 12, we read how King David had an affair with Bathsheba. He should have been out with his army fighting wars. Instead, from his palace, he happened to catch Bathsheba bathing one day, and he desired her and had her brought to him. Bathsheba became pregnant, and this caused a big problem for King David. He chose to cover up his sin by having Bathsheba's husband killed in battle so he could marry her.

6B - Delusion Set In

King David became deluded by his sin and he could no longer see himself as he was. God had to send David a prophet named Nathan, who, cunningly, revealed to David the terrible sin he had committed. This was a great blow to David's heart for he had walked very closely with God before this event.

6C - Honest Repentance

King David reached a point where he admitted he had done wrong. Psalm 51 is a powerful, heartfelt prayer of repentance to God to cleanse him of his sin and restore his relationship with God. God restored him.

King David chose to admit he was wrong and restoration came to his life.

Question 6: Have you ever made your life complicated by trying to cover up your mistakes?

7A - A Man Called Job (Pronounced "Jobe")

In the Book of Job, we read how a devout man of God, named Job, was tested in his faith. In a single day, Job lost his children, his servants, and his livestock! This was catastrophic for Job. He didn't know how to respond. Like most of us, he eventually began blaming God for his problems. It was at this point that God told Job in what areas he was going wrong. At once, Job repented, and thereafter, God began restoring all that Job had lost. In fact, Job received twice as much as he had before!

When Job found out that he was wrong, and he repented, his life began to improve.

Question 7: Have you ever apologized for mistakes you've made and had your life improve?

8A - The Prophet Jonah

Another story of repentance is in the Book of Jonah. This story illustrates God's amazing grace for his followers. In it, we read of a prophet, named Jonah, who was told by God to go to the city of Nineveh and tell them to repent of their sinful lifestyle. Jonah refused to obey God and began traveling in the opposite direction.

8B - Jonah's Disobedience Causes Problems

As Jonah was on a ship sailing away from Nineveh, a severe storm came up. The men were scared for their lives, and each man prayed to his own god to rescue them. While everyone else was terrified for their lives, Jonah was in the hull of the ship sleeping. The captain awakened him and said, "How can you sleep? Get up and pray to your God! Jonah refused. Then the crew cast lots, and the lot fell on Jonah. The crew asked Jonah, who are you? What have you done to cause this great storm? Jonah told them of his disobedience to God, and it scared them. Jonah told them to throw him overboard, and the storm would stop. So they threw Jonah overboard, and the storm stopped.

Question 8: Have innocent people ever suffered because of your wrong-doing?

9A - <u>Jonah is Rescued</u>

God had mercy on Jonah and sent a big fish to swallow him. Jonah stayed in the belly of the fish for 3 days and 3 nights. Finally, Jonah began to pray a prayer of repentance and God saved Jonah's life by causing the fish to vomit him onto dry land. After that, Jonah went to Nineveh and preached the message God wanted him to preach.

Jonah repented for disobeying God and did what he was supposed to do, and his life began to improve. Things also got better for the people in Nineveh, because everyone in the city repented and were spared from God's judgment.

9B - <u>God Is Eager To Forgive Us</u>

In 1 John Chapter 1, we see a well-known scripture on how eager God is to forgive us when we sin.

1 John 1:9 says, *"If we confess our sins, he is faithful and just to forgive us our sins, and to cleanse us from all unrighteousness."*

When we admit we are wrong and ask for God's forgiveness, He forgives us!

9C - <u>Honesty Is Needed</u>

For us to become healed emotionally, we need to become honest with ourselves and admit we have a problem. As we search for help, God's healing help will follow.

Question 9: God went to great lengths to show Jonah he was wrong. Has God ever gone to great lengths to show you something? Can you tell us about it?

10A - <u>Final Note</u>

Is realizing and admitting we have a problem in our emotions a life sentence of unhappiness? Not at all. We can begin to take time to learn how emotional healing works and see our emotional system heal. In fact, after we are well, we will become stronger than most people. We will also become a person who is able to support others who are going through life challenges.

* * * * * * *

TIP #4

Disarm the Shame

1A - As stated in Tip #3, emotional problems can sometimes carry a stigma. So for us to proceed smoothly in our recovery, we may need to disarm shame so it doesn't prevent us from reaching out for help.

We may be hearing a voice in our mind shouting, *"Don't tell the family secrets!"* But we shouldn't listen to that voice. That voice wants to keep us in bondage. Now is the time to tell what has happened to us. When we tell it to the right people, they will show us how to be set free from anxiety and depression.

Let's read some scriptures that show us that God wants us to live free of shame.

a) **Psalm 25:3** "Yea, let none that wait on thee be ashamed: let them be ashamed which transgress without cause."

b) **Psalm 31:1** "In thee, O LORD, do I put my trust; let me never be ashamed: deliver me in thy righteousness."

c) **Psalm 34:5** "They looked unto him, and were lightened: and their faces were not ashamed."

d) **Psalm 119:80** "Let my heart be sound in thy statutes; that I be not ashamed."

e) **Isaiah 54:4** "Fear not; for thou shalt not be ashamed: neither be thou confounded; for thou shalt not be put to shame: for thou shalt forget the shame of thy youth, and shalt not remember the reproach of thy widowhood any more."

f) **Isaiah 61:7** "For your shame ye shall have double; and for confusion they shall rejoice in their portion: therefore in their land they shall possess the double: everlasting joy shall be unto them."

g) **Joel 2:26** "And ye shall eat in plenty, and be satisfied, and praise the name of the LORD your God, that hath dealt wondrously with you: and my people shall never be ashamed."

h) **Romans 10:11** "For the scripture saith, Whosoever believeth on him shall not be ashamed."

i) **1 Peter 2:6** "Wherefore also it is contained in the scripture, Behold, I lay in Sion a chief corner stone, elect, precious: and he that believeth on him shall not be confounded."

1B - One Exception for Shame

The only time shame may occur is when the Holy Spirit is revealing to us that there is a sin in our life, for which, we need to repent. Even then, the shame should only be momentary until we pray a prayer of repentance.

1C - Reaching Out For Help

The thought of asking someone for help can sometimes scare us. Either our self-esteem is so low, or our pride is so great. We become afraid of appearing weak by asking for help. This can be a roadblock in our recovery.

Question 1: In general, do you find it difficult to ask for help? If so, can you tell us why?

2A - Step Out In Faith

Fear may try to prevent us from opening up to a few helpful people, but we know what God's antidote is for fear, it is **Faith**.

Faith Example No.1 - Jacob

Jacob had received the instruction from God to go back to his homeland, but he was scared of his brother Esau. (Previously, Jacob had done a shameful thing to Esau, he stole Esau's birthright.) However, Jacob continued traveling to his homeland anyway. He knew that he had heard from God to go back, so back he went. He was afraid, but he went back by faith, each step of the way. (Living by faith can sometimes be difficult.)

Genesis 32: 6-12 "And the messengers returned to Jacob, saying, We came to thy brother Esau, and also he cometh to meet thee, and four hundred men with him. ⁷ Then Jacob was greatly afraid and distressed: and he divided the people that was with him, and the flocks, and herds, and the camels, into two bands; ⁸ And said, If Esau come to the one company, and smite it, then the other company which is left shall escape. "

2B - ⁹And Jacob said, O God of my father Abraham, and God of my father Isaac, the LORD which saidst unto me, Return unto thy country, and to thy kindred, and I will deal well with thee: ¹⁰ I am not worthy of the least of all the mercies, and of all the truth, which thou hast shewed unto thy servant; for with my staff I passed over this Jordan; and now I am become two bands. ¹¹ Deliver me, I pray thee, from the hand of my brother, from the hand of Esau: for I fear him, lest he will come and smite me, and the mother with the children. ¹² And thou saidst, I will surely do thee good, and make thy seed as the sand of the sea, which cannot be numbered for multitude."

Thankfully, everything worked out between Jacob and Esau, since God had mellowed Esau's heart over the years.

2C - Faith Example No.2 - Moses

Forty years after Moses fled Egypt after killing a man, God told Moses to go back to Egypt and free His people from slavery. Over the years, Moses had lost all confidence in himself, to the point that he couldn't even speak well. He stuttered. (Sometimes, God waits until we are emptied of ourselves before He uses us.)

2D - Moses always knew he was born to set the Israelites free, but he tried to do it in his own strength and in his own time, and he failed. But this time he had a Word from God, *"bring forth my people the children of Israel out of Egypt..."*

Exodus 3:9-11 *(God speaking)* "Now therefore, behold, the cry of the children of Israel is come unto me: and I have also seen the oppression wherewith the Egyptians oppress them. ¹⁰ Come now therefore, and I will send thee unto Pharaoh, that thou mayest bring forth my people the children of Israel out of Egypt. ¹¹ And Moses said unto God, Who am I, that I should go unto Pharaoh, and that I should bring forth the children of Israel out of Egypt?"

Moses was very fearful, but that didn't stop God from using him. Moses had to walk by faith. He had to trust God each step of the way back to Egypt.

Question 2: Have you ever done a shameful thing like Jacob and Moses? Do you think these things are causing fear today?

3A - <u>Faith Example No.3 - Gideon</u>

The Israelites had been crying out to God for help for seven years. Finally, God told Gideon to lead an attack on the Midianite army. Gideon was just an ordinary Israelite and surprised to be chosen.

Judges 6:14-15 "And the LORD looked upon him, and said, Go in this thy might, and thou shalt save Israel from the hand of the Midianites: have not I sent thee? ¹⁵ And he said unto him, Oh my Lord, wherewith shall I save Israel? behold, my family is poor in Manasseh, and I am the least in my father's house."

3B - Gideon was so surprised and nervous about the battle that he requested a visible sign from God to prove that He wanted him to lead a battle. Twice Gideon asked for a sign, and twice God confirmed the sign. God was gracious toward Gideon; God knows those who are nervous, and He does His best to prepare them for their task. Gideon's mission was further challenged when God asked him to reduce the number of fighting men from 30,000 to 300! However, Gideon still won the battle. Gideon was not a confident fighter, but that didn't stop God from using him. Gideon had to walk by faith and trust God each step of the way.

Question 3: Have you ever had to do a difficult task and had it turn out well, as in the case of Jacob, Moses, and Gideon? Were you scared you might fail at first?

4A - In our recovery, we may not feel that our faith is strong enough for us to tell someone about our challenge. The good news is there are ways to increase our faith. We can start by identifying the truth.

4B - **<u>Truth 1</u> - We know we need help.** First off, it will help us if we truly believe we need help. We shouldn't minimize the seriousness of our condition. Here is a strategy that might help: We can ask ourselves this question: How would I view my problem if a friend approached me with the same problem? Would I suggest they go for help? If the answer is yes, then we should move forward in our plan to seek help.

4C - **<u>Truth 2</u> - We know God wants us well.** Indeed, God has given us this life for us to enjoy. We believe this when we look at the life of Jesus and see all the people He healed. To help convince our heart of this truth, we can read out loud the scriptures in Core Belief #6 - I Believe God Wants Me To Enjoy Good Health.

Question 4: Do you know anyone who God has healed?

5A - **Truth 3 - We know God educates people in all facets of life so they can help one another.** God has given gifts to men. He did it in the Old Testament days when he needed people to construct synagogues, palaces, and whole cities.

> **Exodus 35:35** "Them hath he filled with wisdom of heart, to work all manner of work, of the engraver, and of the cunning workman, and of the embroiderer, in blue, and in purple, in scarlet, and in fine linen, and of the weaver, even of them that do any work, and of those that devise cunning work."

5B - God also did it in the New Testament days, when he wanted His church to be educated and inspired.

> **1 Corinthians 12:4-10** "Now there are diversities of gifts, but the same Spirit. [5] And there are differences of administrations, but the same Lord. [6] And there are diversities of operations, but it is the same God which worketh all in all. [7] But the manifestation of the Spirit is given to every man to profit withal. [8] For to one is given by the Spirit the word of wisdom; to another the word of knowledge by the same Spirit;"

5C - "[9] To another faith by the same Spirit; to another the gifts of healing by the same Spirit; [10] To another the working of miracles; to another prophecy; to another discerning of spirits; to another divers kinds of tongues; to another the interpretation of tongues:"

Similarly, God has given knowledge to people about healing mental health problems. We need to search for such people in our community.

Question 5: Do you know anyone who has been gifted with a skill or spiritual gift?

6A - **Truth 4 - We know God wants us to live by faith.** As stated above, living by faith sometimes means we do things that we don't want to do. But there is no denying that God wants us to live by faith. In four places the Bible says, *"The just shall live by faith."* **Romans 1:17, Habakkuk 2:4, Galatians 3:11** and **Hebrews 10:38**. And in Hebrews 11:6, it says, *"Without faith it is impossible to please God."* Faith is critically important.

6B - **Truth 5 - We know God rewards those who step out in faith.** Throughout the Gospels, we read stories of how Jesus marveled at people's faith. (Faith is the currency of heaven. It is what moves the hand of God.)

6C - **Truth 6 - We know that professional people have high standards of confidentiality.** We can be confident that when we speak to a doctor, a nurse, a pastor or anyone who is a trained professional, will be held in strictest confidence. Confidentiality is also modeled by many recovery groups, including the Victory Tips Program.

6D - **Truth 7 - We know with God's help it *is* possible for us to ask for help.**

> **Matthew 19:26** "But Jesus beheld them, and said unto them, With men this is impossible; but with God all things are possible."

We may have surprised ourselves throughout our life by doing things we thought we could never do. Asking for help can be one of them.

By reading the above truths out loud, over and over, we can reach a point where we have the confidence to ask for help.

6E - <u>A Helpful Skill - Learn How To "Not Care."</u>

At first glance, this skill can sound counter-productive and even opposite of basic Christian tenets, but there is merit to it. If we are concerned with how people view us, it is possible to reach a point where we no longer care what people think about us. Let's read the following Bible verse.

Philippians 4:6 *"Be careful for nothing; but in everything by prayer and supplication with thanksgiving let your requests be made known unto God."*

The first part of the above verse, *"Be careful for nothing,"* can be reworded to say *"Don't care for anything."*

6F - Naturally, there are important things in life that we care deeply about, but for all the other aspects of life, we can reach a point where we say: *"I no longer care."* The more we say it, the more it can liberate us. When that happens, we enter a state of peace as mentioned in verse 7, below.

Philippians 4:7 *"And the peace of God, which passeth all understanding, shall keep your hearts and minds through Christ Jesus."*

6G - When we reach a point where we no longer care, we can access the peace of God. What kind of peace is it? Verse 7 says it is a peace that <u>passes all understanding</u>, a peace that is indescribable! That is great news for the person who is struggling with anxiety. With this understanding, consider having the mindset that you no longer care what people think about you.

Question 6: Have you ever reached a point where you no longer cared about something? How did it feel?

7A - <u>Practical Tips</u>

One way to help us step out of our "comfort zone" is to start saying positive affirmations to ourselves. This program has the "I Do Not Fear" Affirmation that can help with this. You can also write your own affirmations, such as:

a) "I no longer care what people think of me."

b) "I believe God is directing my steps to the right people."

c) "God's peace envelops me as I speak to people about my challenge."

Question 7: Have you ever used positive affirmations to help you have courage? If so, how did they work for you?

8A - Earlier, we talked about Jacob, Moses and Gideon living by faith. They had to do something they didn't want to do.

True, we may not *want* to let anyone know we are struggling, but we do something anyway, by faith. We go ahead and let someone know we need help. We realize God works through people, so we prayerfully choose people who we feel have some knowledge of the problem we have, or who may know people who can help us.

When we finally ask for help, our act of faith will put the wheels of heaven in motion; God will steer us to people who can help us resolve our anxiety and depression. Disarm the shame and go!

* * * * * * *

TIP #5

Form a Support Team

1A - In Tip #4 we learned about our need to ask for help. In Tip #5 we will learn what to look for in people who may be able to help us. We'll also learn that it is helpful to choose more than one or two people to help us at this critical time in our lives. The following Bible verses urge us to have many advisers.

a) **Proverbs 11:14** "Where no counsel is, the people fall: but in the multitude of counsellors there is safety."

b) **Proverbs 15:22** "Without counsel purposes are disappointed: but in the multitude of counsellors they are established."

c) **Proverbs 24:6** "For by wise counsel thou shalt make thy war: and in multitude of counsellors there is safety."

1B - Here is a verse about having helpers in our life.

Ecclesiastes 4:12 "And if one prevail against him, two shall withstand him; and a threefold cord is not quickly broken."

Question 1: What do you think of the idea of having a network of people in our lives to help us find peace and happiness?

2A - <u>What To Look For</u>

Not everyone can be a support-person in our lives. That is because most people cannot relate to feelings of severe anxiety and depression. Approaching certain people with our request for help can sometimes bring uneasiness to our relationship with them. Therefore, it is best to do a little research on the people we wish to enlist for our support team. Here are a few questions to ask ourselves about a candidate:

a) Do I respect them?

b) Do they have a calm demeanor?

c) Can they be trusted to keep my information confidential?

d) Do they have time to devote to speaking with me?

e) Have they been successful at overcoming difficulties in their own life?

f) Are they knowledgeable of God's Word, and are they living by God's Word?

Question 2: After reading the above questions, does anyone come to mind who you could approach to assist you in your recovery?

3A - If we are having difficulty identifying people to help us, here are some individuals to consider:

a) A chaplain.

b) A good friend.

c) A nurse or social worker.

d) A church home-group leader.

e) A loving and understanding family member.

f) A person leading or attending a recovery group.

g) A deacon, minister, or counselor at a church. (If you are a female, then the wife of a deacon, minister or counselor would be more appropriate.)

3B - <u>A Team and a Team Lead</u>

Out of the people we choose for our support team, we should select one person to oversee our recovery. We can call this person our Team Lead. We can call the others, Team Members.

It would be helpful if the Team Members could report to the Team Lead any contact they've had with us, and how their time with us went. The Team Lead should have everybody's contact information in order to delegate the necessary support we will need throughout our week. Should our Team Lead be unavailable when we call them, we need to call the Team Members to see who is available to help us at that time.

3C - <u>The Role of the Team Lead</u>

The ideal Team Lead should be somebody who is emotionally stable and has had some experience with emotional healing. A Team Lead will be somebody we can be accountable to each day. If our Team Lead feels we are drifting toward a negative frame of mind, they should alert the Team Members that help is needed.

Question 3: Which of your Team Members would be a good Team Lead to oversee your recovery?

4A - <u>Adjusting To Freedom</u>

Sometimes, as we get well, and have more freedom and happiness, our desire to do things increases. That is great. But sometimes what we feel we would like to do may not be in our best interest at that time. Freedom can be harmful if it isn't monitored and critiqued properly. It is best not to trust our own judgment in the beginning stages of our recovery. Instead, to get the opinions of those on our support team before we tackle any major projects.

Question 4: Have you ever had lots of freedom, but ended up making poor choices with that freedom?

5A - <u>An Important Benefit</u>

Team Leads and Team Members may not always have the answers to our questions, but they *can* provide us with a vital service – that of being a good listener. Knowing somebody cares enough to listen to us can be a great benefit in our recovery.

5B - <u>Gently Steering</u>

Another valuable trait of a Support Team is to know when to cut short our conversations if we start getting into a mode of inferiority, self-pity or anger. Doing so is most helpful when it is spoken to us with gentleness.

Question 5: Has someone you respected ever told you your attitude and words needed an adjustment? How did you respond?

6A - <u>Monitoring Our Diligence</u>

Good Team Members will be able to tell us if we begin losing our diligence in getting well. They should monitor our attendance at recovery meetings, joining conference calls, watching or listening to good teachings, reading books, reading affirmations, etc. If correction is needed and is given with gentleness, it will produce good results in our lives.

Question 6: Do you tend to make excuses for lax behavior?

7A - <u>"Team Leads" in the Bible</u>

The greatest Team Lead in the Bible is Jesus Christ. He taught 12 disciples for three years. He also influenced many others in that period. Jesus gives us many tips on how to live a happy, fruitful life. Thus, a good habit to form is to read a chapter a day in the Gospels – Matthew, Mark, Luke, or John.

7B - The following verses suggest that Jesus would be a good Team Lead.

a) **Matthew 11:29** (Jesus speaking) "Take my yoke upon you, and learn of me; for I am meek and lowly in heart: and ye shall find rest unto your souls."

b) **1 Peter 2:21** "For even hereunto were ye called: because Christ also suffered for us, leaving us an example, that ye should follow his steps:"

7C - <u>The Apostle Paul as a Team Lead</u>

Another great Team Lead in the Bible is the Apostle Paul. He wrote most of the New Testament. His teachings went far and wide showing Christians how to live a fruitful, victorious, Christian life. Paul challenges us to follow his lead. See the scriptures below.

a) **1 Corinthians 11:1** "Be ye followers of me, even as I also am of Christ."

b) **2 Thessalonians 3:7-9** "For yourselves know how ye ought to follow us: for we behaved not ourselves disorderly among you; [8] Neither did we eat any man's bread for nought; but wrought with labour and travail night and day, that we might not be chargeable to any of you: [9] Not because we have not power, but to make ourselves an ensample unto you to follow us."

c) **Philippians 4:9** "Those things, which ye have both learned, and received, and heard, and seen in me, do: and the God of peace shall be with you."

7D - <u>Elijah as a Team Lead</u>

A famous Team Lead in the Old Testament was Elijah. He had a close mentoring relationship with a man named Elisha. A record of how their relationship began is in 1 Kings 19. Below is verse 21.

1 Kings 19:21 *"And he returned back from him, and took a yoke of oxen, and slew them, and boiled their flesh with the instruments of the oxen, and gave unto the people, and they did eat. Then he arose, and went after Elijah, and ministered unto him."*

7E - When Elijah was about to leave the earth, he asked Elisha what he wanted. Elisha made a bold request of Elijah, and he got it!

2 Kings 2:9 *"And it came to pass, when they were gone over, that Elijah said unto Elisha, Ask what I shall do for thee, before I be taken away from thee. And Elisha said, I pray thee, let a double portion of thy spirit be upon me."*

Question 7: Have you ever asked someone to pray for you to receive the same, or greater, anointing upon your life, as is in their life?

8A - There are many people asking God to use them to help others. Our request for help can be the answer to their prayers. It can also be the first step to an amazing new life for us. So don't be shy. Form a support team!

* * * * * * *

TIP #6

Guard Your Thoughts

1A - Thoughts are powerful. Those of us who have trouble with our thinking can relate to the fact that when we let our thoughts go negative, we feel negative. That is going to change. God gives us tips on how to be an overcomer in life. This includes having the ability to think right thoughts!

Below is a profound scripture about our thinking:

Proverbs 23:7 "For as he thinketh in his heart, so is he:"

1B - This verse means our thinking reveals who we are.

Many of us think we are better than who we really are, and that hurts us. As long as we don't see the work that needs to be done in our hearts, we will never be motivated to change what we think and believe. From now on, may God help us see, clearly, who we are. And may we say from now on, *"I'm going to work with God to transform my life into the likeness of his Son, the Lord Jesus Christ. Jesus will be manifested in everything I think, say, and do."*

1C - The above Bible verse, Proverbs 23:7, tells us we are what we think about. Thus, we must be careful what we <u>believe</u> about ourselves, as this will affect what we <u>think</u> about ourselves.

In the above verse, the term, "heart", refers to our thinking. So we must "Keep" (or guard) our thoughts.

Question 1: Have you ever heard the term "Guard your thoughts?" What comes to mind about this?

2A - <u>What Influences Our Thinking?</u>

Our thinking, be it positive or negative, is the result of experiences we've had in our life. Some of these experiences were caused by our own choices, but many were caused by other people.

However, it isn't just our life experiences that affect us; it is also <u>how we *responded* to those experiences</u> that influences our thinking. We learn this in Tip #12 – Don't Judge.

Question 2: Can you tell us a negative experience in your life, and the way you thought about it after it happened? Do you still think that way about this event?

3A - Another Factor in Our Thinking

Sometimes Satan can influence our thoughts. **John 13:2** says, *"And supper being ended, the devil having now put into the heart of Judas Iscariot, Simon's son, to betray him;"* Here we see that Judas Iscariot was tempted to betray Jesus by the devil. Even though tempting thoughts come to us, we have a choice of whether we let them stay in our minds. Nobody forced Judas to betray Jesus. We know from scripture that Judas's role with the apostles was to oversee the finances, and yet he, himself, was a thief. (See John 12:6.)

3B - Watch Out For Our Weaknesses

In Matthew 26:15, we see that Judas had an inbred weakness for money. When he realized he could make money by handing Jesus over to the city officials, he began thinking about that. Those thoughts eventually lead to an action. In his mind, he probably knew he shouldn't do it, but his natural weakness for money may have overpowered his reasoning, and caused him to turn Jesus in.

Question 3: Can you remember a time when your natural weakness for something caused you to do something that you later regretted?

4A - Scripture Gives Us Clear Direction

We know that our experiences in life and the way we respond to those experiences can either set us up for success in life, or for failure. If the thoughts that come to us are negative, the scriptures tell us what we should do with them. In **2 Corinthians 10:5**, it says, *"Casting down imaginations, and every high thing that exalteth itself against the knowledge of God, and bringing into captivity every thought to the obedience of Christ;"*

4B - Casting down Imaginations

We need to judge our thoughts to see if they are positive or negative. If they are negative, we need to cast them out of our mind. The best way to keep out the bad thoughts is to have a steady flow of good thoughts going into our minds. We suggest people start memorizing God's Word. Once scripture is memorized, we can start saying the scriptures throughout our day and thus keep our minds thinking positive thoughts. Here are verses that support this principle:

a) **Psalm 119:11** "Thy word have I hid in mine heart, that I might not sin against thee."
b) **Proverbs 4:4** "He taught me also, and said unto me, Let thine heart retain my words: keep my commandments, and live."

Question 4: Can you think of a time when you casted down negative thoughts? How did it go?

5A - Distractions

Another way thoughts can come to us, is when they are put there by God. God wants to speak to us all day long if we let Him. So often we let our minds wander to problems in our life, or to the desire for wealth and material things and we fail to hear thoughts from the Holy Spirit. In **Romans 8:6**, it says, *"For to be carnally minded is death; but to be spiritually minded is life and peace."* When we begin to take control of our thoughts and keep them positive, they begin to reshape our beliefs, which will produce in us a mind of peace.

Question 5: What tends to distract you from thinking positive thoughts? You can say "Pass".

6A - Reprogramming

You may be saying, *"My mind is sometimes so wild, I can't control it."* That is a problem for some people. The good news is, our minds can be reprogrammed. Our mind is like a sophisticated computer. Our life's experiences, and judgments of those experiences can be "overwritten." We can enter new "data" into our mind and belief system that can prevent the negative thoughts from starting up.

6B - No matter how negative our thinking is, God gives us the ability to reprogram our thinking. Does that mean we forget the old thoughts were ever there? Not at all. Nor do we want that. The pain of our old way of thinking will one day be a great asset in our testimony of healing. Our story will captivate people and will give hope to those who are held down by anxiety and depression.

6C - The process of reprogramming can be time-consuming, but later on, when our new belief system has replaced our old belief system, we will have peace of mind. We will still have problems in our life, but the fear and inward struggle to conquer them, will be gone.

6D - Below is a key Bible verse that tells us to renew our minds. It also gives the benefits for doing so, when the job is complete.

Romans 12:2 "And be not conformed to this world: but be ye transformed by the renewing of your mind, that ye may prove what is that good, and acceptable, and perfect, will of God."

Question 6: Are you prepared to put in the time to renew your mind?

7A - God's Goal for Our Thinking

Below is another key scripture that deals with the area of our thinking. We would do well to memorize this verse and check ourselves, often, to see if we are practicing it.

Philippians 4:8 "Finally, brethren, whatsoever things are true, whatsoever things are honest, whatsoever things are just, whatsoever things are pure, whatsoever things are lovely, whatsoever things are of good report; if there be any virtue, and if there be any praise, think on these things."

7B - Use the Tools

The Victory Tips Program offers 6 Affirmations and 6 Core Beliefs that are great tools to use to reprogram our beliefs. Saying the ones that pertain to us, out loud, will speed us on to our desired goal of joy and peace.

We can go one step further and begin memorizing God's Word. This program offers computer files you can use to print scriptures onto card stock, will help you memorize the scriptures.

7C - God's Word is Powerful

Hebrews 4:12 "For the word of God is quick, and powerful, and sharper than any two edged sword, piercing even to the dividing asunder of soul and spirit, and of the joints and marrow, and is a discerner of the thoughts and intents of the heart."

Using God's Word is the best way to win in the battle for peace of mind.

Question 7: Have you ever experienced relief from negative feelings by speaking God's Word?

8A - <u>Stay Transparent</u>

As we journey toward peace and happiness, it is helpful to pray the following prayer regularly. Doing so will keep the channel open between ourselves and God. It will help us mature spiritually.

Psalm 139:23-24 "Search me, O God, and know my heart: try me, and know my thoughts: And see if there be any wicked way in me, and lead me in the way everlasting."

8B - <u>You Have God's Permission Not To Worry</u>

Read the words, below, that Jesus spoke to us. He wants us to rest in Him as we journey to happiness.

Matthew 6:25 "Take therefore no thought for the morrow: for the morrow shall take thought for the things of itself. Sufficient unto the day is the evil thereof."

Let's trust Jesus to lead us every step of the way. As we take time to assess our thoughts, Jesus will show us how to turn them around, and we will give Him all of the glory!

* * * * * * *

TIP #7

Speak Right Words

1A - Many people do not know that there is a link between the words we speak and the events that take place in our lives. The Bible has many scriptures that teach this truth. One of the better-known scriptures is in the account of the creation of the world. In **Genesis 1:3**, we read, *"Let there be light," and there was light."* After this God began to speak into existence, the earth, the water, the animals, and more. He did this by speaking words. We learn from this, that spoken words can have great power.

1B - <u>Jesus and Words</u>

Another well-known scripture on the power in words is **Mark 11:23**, when Jesus said: *"For verily I say unto you, That whosoever shall say unto this mountain, Be thou removed, and be thou cast into the sea; and shall not doubt in his heart, but shall believe that those things which he saith shall come to pass; he shall have whatsoever he saith."*

1C - <u>The Book of James and Words</u>

The Book of James also reveals the power of the tongue. **James 3:4-5** says, *"Behold also the ships, which though they be so great, and are driven of fierce winds, yet are they turned about with a very small helm, whithersoever the governor listeth. ⁵ Even so the tongue is a little member, and boasteth great things. Behold, how great a matter a little fire kindleth!"*

1D - Then verse 6 paints a very dramatic picture of the power of the tongue when it is allowed to speak negative words in a person's life. **James 3:6** says, *"And the tongue is a fire, a world of iniquity: so is the tongue among our members, that it defileth the whole body, and setteth on fire the course of nature; and it is set on fire of hell."*

1E - <u>More Evidence on the Power of Words</u>

There is more power in words than we may think. For instance **Proverbs 18:21** says, *"Death and life are in the power of the tongue: and they that love it shall eat the fruit thereof."* This statement teaches that we can speak life and health into our lives, or death and sickness. In **Mark 11:14**, Jesus spoke to the fig tree, and it died. He did this to illustrate to his disciples that there is power in our words. Here is the verse. *"And Jesus answered and said unto it (fig tree), No man eat fruit of thee hereafter for ever. And his disciples heard it."*

Question 1: Can you think back through your life and see how negative words spoken by you, or to you, have impacted your life in a negative way? If so, can you give us an example?

2A - <u>Out Of the Heart the Mouth Speaks</u>

From the verses below, we see that there is a connection between our thoughts and our words.

a) **Matthew 12:34** *"… for out of the abundance of the heart the mouth speaketh."*

b) **Matthew 12:35** *"A good man out of the good treasure of the heart bringeth forth good things: and an evil man out of the evil treasure bringeth forth evil things."*

2B - The Book of Proverbs also reveals the relation between our hearts and our words. In the verse below, we see how important it is to renew our minds, continually, to keep it thinking wise and proper thoughts. These thoughts will cause us to speak words that bring good results in our lives, and the lives of those around us.

Proverbs 16:23 says, *"The heart of the wise teacheth his mouth, and addeth learning to his lips."*

2C - This next verse reveals how important it is to guard our hearts, and why we should.

Proverbs 4:23 says, *"Keep thy heart with all diligence; for out of it are the issues of life."*

Our words come from our heart; thus our heart needs to be guarded and used only to think on good thoughts. For more on this, see Tip #6 – Guard Your Thoughts.

Question 2: Have you been speaking what is in your heart lately? If so, has it been positive or negative?

3A - <u>Careless Speaking</u>

In **Matthew 12:36** Jesus makes a startling statement. He says to us, *"But I say unto you, That every idle word that men shall speak, they shall give account thereof in the day of judgment."* These words of Jesus put new importance on our words.

Our words tend to be spoken so automatically that we barely take heed how we speak to each other. God is interested in people living a happy, peaceful life, but he knows that words that are carelessly spoken can cause strife, and this grieves God. Jesus follows the above verse in **Matthew 12:37** by saying, *"For by your words you will be justified, and by your words you will be condemned."* Let's begin to be watchful of the words we speak.

3B - <u>Our Words Can Defile Us</u>

A scripture in Matthew 15 talks about what defiles us. The Jews were so careful to wash their hands before eating and to obey all the other laws, but Jesus pointed out another way that a man can break God's laws. In **Matthew 15:11**, he says, *"Not that which goeth into the mouth defileth a man; but that which cometh out of the mouth, this defileth a man."* In essence, he said, *"Watch out what words come out of your mouth."*

3C - <u>God Gives Us a Tip</u>

The Book of Proverbs tells us we should keep our words correct. **Proverbs 5:1,2** reveals, *"My son, attend unto my wisdom, and bow thine ear to my understanding: ² That thou mayest regard discretion, and that thy lips may keep knowledge."* Therefore we need to read and meditate on God's truths so that our lips may speak what is right.

3D - <u>Speak Less</u>

Another way to control what comes out of our mouths is to speak fewer words. We talked about this in Tip #2 – Stop, and Be Still. Below are some scriptures that tell us to limit the number of words we speak.

a) **Proverbs 10:19** *"In the multitude of words there wanteth not sin: but he that refraineth his lips is wise."*

b) **Proverbs 17:27** "He that hath knowledge spareth his words: and a man of understanding is of an excellent spirit."

c) **Proverbs 17:28** "Even a fool, when he holdeth his peace, is counted wise: and he that shutteth his lips is esteemed a man of understanding."

d) **Ecclesiastes 5:2** *"Be not rash with thy mouth, and let not thine heart be hasty to utter any thing before God: for God is in heaven, and thou upon earth: therefore let thy words be few."*

Question 3: Do you know somebody who speaks so much that it gets them into trouble?

Question 4: Can you think of a person who is quiet, and comes across wise or self-controlled?

5A - <u>Comparing Foolish People with Wise People</u>

The Book of Proverbs makes a lot of comparisons between wise and foolish people. One of the trademarks of a foolish person is the content of their speech. Below are some scriptures about fools and the words they speak.

a) **Proverbs 13:20** *"He that walketh with wise men shall be wise: but a companion of fools shall be destroyed."*

b) **Proverbs 18:6** "A fool's lips enter into contention, and his mouth calleth for strokes."

c) **Proverbs 18:7** "A fool's mouth is his destruction, and his lips are the snare of his soul."

d) **Proverbs 18:8** "The words of a talebearer are as wounds, and they go down into the innermost parts of the belly."

e) **Ecclesiastes 10:12** "The words of a wise man's mouth are gracious; but the lips of a fool will swallow up himself."

Question 5: Do you know somebody who appears foolish and should change how they speak to others?

6A - <u>Warning To Teachers</u>

In the Book of James, God gives warning to people who want to be teachers of God's Word. **James 3:1** says, *"My brethren, be not many masters, knowing that we shall receive the greater condemnation."* Then in **James 3:13** it warns wise people to watch their actions. It says, *"Who is a wise man and endued with knowledge among you? let him shew out of a good conversation (lifestyle) his works with meekness of wisdom."*

Question 6: Can you think of a pastor or Bible teacher who should be more careful how they speak?

7A - <u>Words and Trouble</u>

Words can affect the amount of troubles we have in our lives. Below are descriptions of a person who speaks negatively.

- a) **Psalm 101:5** "Whoso privily slandereth his neighbour, him will I cut off: him that hath an high look and a proud heart will not I suffer."

- b) **Proverbs 10:8** "The wise in heart will receive commandments: but a prating fool shall fall."

- c) **Proverbs 11:11** " By the blessing of the upright the city is exalted: but it is overthrown by the mouth of the wicked."

- d) **Proverbs 12:6** "The words of the wicked are to lie in wait for blood: but the mouth of the upright shall deliver them."

- e) **Proverbs 12:13** "The wicked is snared by the transgression of his lips: but the just shall come out of trouble."

- f) **Proverbs 18:6** "A fool's lips enter into contention, and his mouth calleth for strokes."

- g) **Proverbs 18:8** "The words of a talebearer are as wounds, and they go down into the innermost parts of the belly."

- h) **Proverbs 19:5** "A false witness shall not be unpunished, and he that speaketh lies shall not escape."

- i) **Proverbs 21:23** "Whoso keepeth his mouth and his tongue keepeth his soul from troubles."

Question 7: Can you think of someone whose words may be hindering their success in life?

8A - <u>Words and Blessings</u>

Right words can produce good results in our lives. Below are the blessings for the person who speaks right words.

- a) **Proverbs 10:21** "The lips of the righteous feed many: but fools die for want of wisdom."

- b) **Proverbs 12:6** "The words of the wicked are to lie in wait for blood: but the mouth of the upright shall deliver them."

- c) **Proverbs 12:13** "The wicked is snared by the transgression of his lips: but the just shall come out of trouble."

- d) **Proverbs 12:25** "Heaviness in the heart of man maketh it stoop: but a good word maketh it glad."

- e) **Proverbs 13:2** "A man shall eat good by the fruit of his mouth: but the soul of the transgressors shall eat violence."

- f) **Proverbs 13:3** "He that keepeth his mouth keepeth his life: but he that openeth wide his lips shall have destruction."

g) **Proverbs 16:13** "Righteous lips are the delight of kings; and they love him that speaketh right."

h) **Proverbs 18:20** *"A man's belly shall be satisfied with the fruit of his mouth; and with the increase of his lips shall he be filled."*

i) **Proverbs 25:15** "By long forbearing is a prince persuaded, and a soft tongue breaketh the bone."

j) **Titus 2:7** "In all things shewing thyself a pattern of good works: in doctrine shewing uncorruptness, gravity, sincerity,"

8B - Words Affect Health

Our words can affect our health. In **Proverbs 12:18,** it is written, *"There is that speaketh like the piercings of a sword: but the tongue of the wise is health."*

Question 8: Have your words contributed to your health, either negatively or positively?

9A - Words and Prayer

One aspect of prayer is that we ask God for what we want. Following that, we can use our words to agree with His promises to us written in His Word. For example **Romans 4:17** *says* "… (God) *calleth those things which be not as though they were."* We can do the same.

Let's say we get a bad diagnosis from a doctor. The proper approach to this problem is to find Bible verses that reveal God's will for us to be well. Then, we pray and ask God for the healing we need, based on the verses we found.

9B - Next, we can begin to speak to the part of our body that is unwell, and we say, *"I have prayed, and I believe that God has healed my _____. I believe it is functioning normally. I believe it is healed in the name of Jesus, and I'm holding to my confession of healing no matter what symptoms come my way."*

After that, we can begin reading all of the scriptures on healing, even memorizing them so we can say them more often. In this way, we keep our faith strong as we *"call those things that are not, as though they were"* (**Romans 4:17**).

9C - More On How We Should Use Our Words

a) **Joshua 1:8** *"*This book of the law shall not depart out of thy mouth; but thou shalt meditate therein day and night, that thou mayest observe to do according to all that is written therein: for then thou shalt make thy way prosperous, and then thou shalt have good success."

b) **Ephesians 4:15** *"*But speaking the truth in love, may grow up into him in all things, which is the head, even Christ:"

c) **Ephesians 5:19** "Speaking to yourselves in psalms and hymns and spiritual songs, singing and making melody in your heart to the Lord;"

d) **Colossians 3:16** "Let the word of Christ dwell in you richly in all wisdom; teaching and admonishing one another in psalms and hymns and spiritual songs, singing with grace in your hearts to the Lord."

9D - Personalize the Word

Another way to use our words wisely is by speaking Bible-based affirmations out loud. For instance, **Romans 8:37** says, *"Nay, in all these things we are more than conquerors through him that loved us."* We can say to ourselves out loud, *"I am more than a conqueror through Christ!"* There are many verses in the Bible we can use in this way. See below for a few others. Also, see the Affirmations section of this program for others.

- a) **1 Corinthians 2:16** "...But we have the mind of Christ." We can say, *"I am intelligent, I can learn new things, I can remember things, and I can do all these things because I have the mind of Christ!"*

- b) **Philippians 4:13** "I can do all things through Christ which strengtheneth me." We can say, *"I can do all things that come my way. Indeed, I am well able!"*

- c) **Philippians 4:19** "But my God shall supply all your need according to his riches in glory by Christ Jesus." So we can say, *"My God meets all my needs in Christ Jesus!"*

9E - Speaking Rightly Pleases God

Proverbs 23:15-16 "My son, if thine heart be wise, my heart shall rejoice, even mine. ^{16} Yea, my reins shall rejoice, when thy lips speak right things."

9F - Confession and Salvation

The following verse reveals that our spoken words are used to help us become born again, **Romans 10:9** says, *"That if thou shalt confess with thy mouth the Lord Jesus, and shalt believe in thine heart that God hath raised him from the dead, thou shalt be saved."*

Jesus reveals another fact about our speech as it relates to our salvation. **Matthew 10:32-33** says, *"Whosoever therefore shall confess me before men, him will I confess also before my Father which is in heaven. ^{33} But whosoever shall deny me before men, him will I also deny before my Father which is in heaven."*

We need to develop our walk with God so finely that it becomes easy to speak to others about God and His wonderful plan of salvation.

Question 9: Have you made a decision to follow Jesus and to confess Him before others? If not, we can pause now and help you do that.

10A - Complaining

There are very destructive ways to use our words. Two of them are complaining and criticizing. Here is a scripture that cautions us to stay away from them.

Philippians 2:14 "Do all things without murmurings (grudging and complaining) and disputings:"

Question 10: How would you judge your level of complaining?

11A - Below is a scripture that says our communication should only be *"good to the use of edifying, that it may minister grace unto the hearers."*

Ephesians 4:29 "Let no corrupt communication proceed out of your mouth, but that which is good to the use of edifying, that it may minister grace unto the hearers."

11B - Below we see that we should never grudge other people.

James 5:9 "Grudge not one against another, brethren, lest ye be condemned: behold, the judge standeth before the door."

Question 11: Do you ever say unkind things about people?

12A - We should never grudgingly show people hospitality.

1 Peter 4:9 "Use hospitality one to another without grudging."

Below we see that we can arouse God's anger toward us when we complain.

a) **1 Corinthians 10:10** "Neither murmur ye, as some of them also murmured, and were destroyed of the destroyer."

b) **Exodus 16:8** "And Moses said, This shall be, when the LORD shall give you in the evening flesh to eat, and in the morning bread to the full; for that the LORD heareth your murmurings which ye murmur against him: and what are we? your murmurings are not against us, but against the LORD."

c) **Numbers 11:1** "And when the people complained, it displeased the LORD: and the LORD heard it; and his anger was kindled; and the fire of the LORD burnt among them, and consumed them that were in the uttermost parts of the camp."

12B - Below we see that even though Jesus knew He was going to die a horrible death, He did not complain.

a) **Isaiah 53:7** "He was oppressed, and he was afflicted, yet he opened not his mouth: he is brought as a lamb to the slaughter, and as a sheep before her shearers is dumb, so he openeth not his mouth."

b) **Matthew 27:13-14** "Then said Pilate unto him, Hearest thou not how many things they witness against thee? [14] And he answered him to never a word; insomuch that the governor marvelled greatly."

Let us be as noble as Jesus was in enduring the hardships of life. He is our great example.

Question 12: How often do you complain?

13A – <u>Lying</u>

Below we see how hurtful lying can be for us.

a) **Exodus 20:16** "Thou shalt not bear false witness against thy neighbour."

b) **Psalm 101:7** "He that worketh deceit shall not dwell within my house: he that telleth lies shall not tarry in my sight."

c) **Proverbs 6:16-19** "These six things doth the LORD hate: yea, seven are an abomination unto him: [17] A proud look, a lying tongue, and hands that shed innocent blood, [18] An heart that deviseth wicked imaginations, feet that be swift in running to mischief, [19] A false witness that speaketh lies, and he that soweth discord among brethren."

d) **Proverbs 12:19** " The lip of truth shall be established for ever: but a lying tongue is but for a moment."

e) **Proverbs 12:22** "Lying lips are abomination to the Lord: but they that deal truly are his delight."

f) **Proverbs 19:5** "A false witness shall not be unpunished, and speaketh lies shall not escape."

g) **Proverbs 19:9** "A false witness shall not be unpunished, and he that speaketh lies shall perish."

h) **Proverbs 24:28** "Be not a witness against thy neighbour without cause; and deceive with thy lips."

i) **Ephesians 4:25** "Wherefore putting away lying, speak every man truth with his neighbour: for we are members one of another."

j) **Colossians 3:9** "Lie not one to another, seeing that ye have put off the old man with his deeds;

k) **Revelation 21:8** "But the fearful, and unbelieving, and the abominable, and murderers, and whoremongers, and sorcerers, and idolaters, and all liars, shall have their part in the lake which burneth with fire and brimstone: which is the second death."

Question 13: How often do you lie?

14A - <u>Make A Decision</u>

Make a decision to speak what is right and uplifting to yourself and to all those you come in contact with. To help maintain your decision, read Affirmation #4, daily, "I Only Speak Right Words."

a) **Psalm 17:3** "Thou hast proved mine heart; thou hast visited me in the night; thou hast tried me, and shalt find nothing; I am purposed that my mouth shall not transgress."

b) **Proverbs 15:26** "The thoughts of the wicked are an abomination to the LORD: but the words of the pure are pleasant words."

c) **Ecclesiastes 5:6** "Suffer not thy mouth to cause thy flesh to sin; neither say thou before the angel, that it was an error: wherefore should God be angry at thy voice, and destroy the work of thine hands?"

d) **Ephesians 4:29** "Let no corrupt communication proceed out of your mouth, but that which is good to the use of edifying, that it may minister grace unto the hearers."

e) **Ephesians 5:4** "Neither filthiness, nor foolish talking, nor jesting, which are not convenient: but rather giving of thanks."

f) **Colossians 4:6** "Let your speech be always with grace, seasoned with salt, that ye may know how ye ought to answer every man."

g) **2 Timothy 2:16** "But shun profane and vain babblings: for they will increase unto more ungodliness."

<u>Conclusion</u>

There is good reason to examine the words we speak and to consciously make changes until our speech is pleasing to God.

* * * * * * *

TIP #8

Make Right Choices

1A - A railway switch is small, but is capable of sending a huge, heavy train in a completely different direction. Similarly, one small decision can send *our life* in a completely different direction; many times to heartache and loss. One way to prevent this, is found in the scripture below;

> **Proverbs 3:5,6** "Trust in the LORD with all thine heart; and lean not unto thine own understanding. ⁶ In all thy ways acknowledge him, and he shall direct thy paths."

It seems simple; ask God to come into our situation and guide us.

Question 1: Are you in the habit of asking God to guide you in all your endeavors?

2A - <u>Seek Assistance</u>

Heartaches begin when life gives us a problem in which we have little knowledge of how to solve it.

Whenever we come to a situation that requires more understanding than what we have, we need to get help. God doesn't want us to "think up" a way out of a problem with just our own limited understanding. More often than not, we will get ourselves into trouble by doing so.

2B - <u>Follow Children</u>

For the most part, children have no worries. All they have to do is, get good grades at school, do a little work around the house, and get along with other kids. They seldom worry about the future, and they rarely get upset over the past. Their focus is more or less on the present. Thus, their stress level is usually low, and their mood is generally good.

Question 2: Have you ever wished you were as happy and carefree as children?

3A - As far as basic needs such as food and shelter, most children don't worry about these, because their parents have faithfully met these needs, day in and day out; so they've developed a trust, or "faith," in their parents when it comes to these two vital needs. And their faith gives them peace.

Question 3: Did you grow up in a family that easily met your basic needs? If not, did you worry about how those needs would get met?

Question 4: Are you thankful for the needs that your parents *did* meet?

5A - If putting trust in parents works for children, why don't adults adopt the same trusting mentality toward their heavenly Father?

5B - <u>Children Easily "Unload."</u>

For the most part, children seldom get overwhelmed about trying to solve a problem on their own. They simply tell their parents what the problem is, and their parents tell them what to do about it. Children give the problem over to a more experienced person, and take the advice that is given to them. What a great way to live!

5C - The reason we adults don't do this can be that, over a period of time, we have developed the habit of keeping things to ourselves for reasons such as shame, fear, pride, or perhaps the challenge of solving it on our own. Any of these factors can lead us to not seeking help, and ultimately to failure and unhappiness.

5D - It's challenging; on one hand, God has gifted us with minds so we can think, dream, and figure things out; but on the other hand, if we do get an idea that we think is good, and follow through with it, it might fail, and we suffer loss. That is why life needs to be handled with care, and with prayer. So much can be at stake when we make poor choices. Again, let's read Proverbs 3:5,6.

> **Proverbs 3:5,6** "Trust in the LORD with all thine heart; and lean not unto thine own understanding. ⁶ In all thy ways acknowledge him, and he shall direct thy paths."

5E - <u>Another Scripture on Advice</u>

> **Proverbs 11:14** "Where no counsel is, the people fall: but in the multitude of counselors there is safety."

Question 5: Have you ever had a problem in which you sought advice from a number of people before acting on the issue? If so, how did it turn out?

6A - <u>There is Hope</u>

Does it mean our poor choices can be so hurtful that there is no way back to happiness and success? Thankfully, the answer is No. Consider this: The most compelling life stories are those of people who have suffered tremendous loss, but then have come back in triumph!

The very real hope of every person who has ever failed in life, is that they can rise and shine again. In so doing, they help themselves, and they become a beacon of hope to others.

Question 6: Can you think of a person whose life has been inspirational to you? If so, how low did they get, and how successful did they become later on?

7A - <u>Watch Out For "Small Thinking."</u>

If we have mental anguish over our poor choices, we need to understand that our losses can lead us to any number of new directions, many of which can lead us to success. God often works in mysterious ways. What we think is the end of the road, turns out to be a detour to something grand beyond our dreams. That's why we should not rely on just our own understanding, because it is so limiting.

So the question becomes: Are we bold enough to believe that God can bring good out of the bad, in our lives?

Question 7: Do you find yourself focusing on past problems, rather than finding out how they could lead you to a whole new direction?

8A - <u>A New Way to Handle Problems</u>

Our goal is to break free from constantly thinking about a problem, and begin to give our dilemmas to God and to others who have a greater understanding of the situation. That way we will stay at peace and will be better able to enjoy life. We shouldn't be like a person who gets an idea and immediately lunges into it on their own. When we get help with a problem, we will most likely save ourselves a lot of time, money and aggravation.

8B - <u>Bible Tip</u>

Reading a chapter a day from the Book of Proverbs is a good habit. There are 31 chapters in Proverbs, one chapter for each day of the month. It's packed with tips on how to live a happy, successful life.

<u>One More Reason to Make Right Choices</u>

One very important reason to make right choices is that our choices can often affect the lives of people around us, including our loved ones. The guilt of making a poor decision can be debilitating when we realize our decision has hurt other people; so be cautious and choose wisely.

8C - In addition, our sin can affect generations not yet born to us.

a) **Exodus 20:3-6** "Thou shalt not bow down thyself to them, nor serve them: for I the Lord thy God am a jealous God, visiting the iniquity of the fathers upon the children unto the third and fourth generation of them that hate me;"

b) **Exodus 34:6-7** "And the Lord passed by before him, and proclaimed, The Lord, The Lord God, merciful and gracious, longsuffering, and abundant in goodness and truth, ⁷ Keeping mercy for thousands, forgiving iniquity and transgression and sin, and that will by no means clear the guilty; visiting the iniquity of the fathers upon the children, and upon the children's children, unto the third and to the fourth generation."

c) **Jeremiah 32:18** "Thou showest lovingkindness unto thousands, and recompensest the iniquity of the fathers into the bosom of their children after them: the Great, the Mighty God, the LORD of hosts, is his name,"

Question 8: Can you think of people whose lives have been cursed because of their fore-fathers actions?

8C - <u>Final Note</u>

If we are careful to do everything we can to make right choices, and things still don't work out in our favor, we can take comfort in **Romans 8:28**, which says, *"And we know that all things work together for good to them that love God, to them who are the called according to his purpose."*

No matter what happens, when we put our trust in God, He can bring good out of any problem we face. Our life is in good hands when we give it to God!

* * * * * * *

TIP #9

Develop Your Faith

1A - At first glance faith seems like a vague, mystical concept, something that we could never truly understand or benefit from. However, the Bible says the opposite. The Bible even calls it a substance. In the 11th Chapter of the Book of Hebrews (the Faith Chapter), the Bible tells us what faith is. **Hebrews 11:1** says: *"Now faith is the substance of things hoped for, the evidence of things not seen."* In God's realm, faith is important. In fact, faith is the *"currency of heaven."* It is vital when looking to God for His help in our lives.

1B - So, the Bible calls faith a substance. It may not be something we can touch, but it is something we can see and hear. We see it in people's actions. And we can hear it in people's words.

<u>You Already Use Faith</u>

A simple example of using faith can be in the use of a chair. We see that it looks strong enough to hold our weight, and by the act of sitting on the chair, we show we have faith in it.

1C - <u>Faith is a Choice</u>

We can have strong faith, or we can have weak faith, the choice is ours. **Romans 10:17** says that *"faith cometh by hearing and hearing by the Word of God."* Faith comes by hearing God's Word. Thus, the more we saturate ourselves in the Bible, the stronger our faith becomes. Developing our faith takes time reading and speaking God's Word. But it starts with a choice, a burning desire to have strong faith.

Question 1: Have you ever met someone who had an unshakable faith in God? If so, have you ever wished you had that same kind of faith?

2A - <u>Faith Got Jesus's Attention</u>

Faith is a noun. But it is proven by our actions. On many occasions, Jesus told people that *"according to your faith you are healed."* What Jesus meant was, *"because you acted in a way that demonstrated your faith in me, I will respond to your action by giving you what you've asked for."* The following are some Bible stories that illustrate this point.

2B - The Centurion Soldier

In Matthew 8:5-13, Jesus offered to heal a soldier's servant by following him to his home to pray for his servant, but then the soldier made an amazing statement. In essence, he said, *"Jesus, you don't need to come to my house and do this personally. I believe you have enough spiritual power that if you simply speak a word, right here and now, my servant will be healed."* This comment amazed Jesus. Jesus told everyone present, *"Verily I say unto you, I have not found so great faith, no, not in Israel."* (**Matthew 8:10**) Jesus said to him, *"Go thy way; and as thou hast believed, so be it done unto thee."* (**vs. 13**) And it was! That is the power of strong faith.

2C - The Woman from Canaan

In Matthew 15:21-28, a desperate non-Jewish woman approached Jesus for the healing of her daughter who had been deeply bound by demon possession. Jesus replied to her that He wasn't sent to minister to Gentiles, just the Jews. But, in essence, the woman's response was, *"Yes, I know. But as you feed the ones you were sent to feed, some of the crumbs fall to the ground, and that is all I need, just a crumb."* That surprised Jesus. Again, he publicly taught the crowd based on what this woman said. Jesus esteemed her greatly for her faith, and spoke these words, *"O woman, great is thy faith: be it unto thee even as thou wilt."* (**Matthew 15:28**)

2D - The Woman with the Issue of Blood

In Mark 5:25-34 Jesus was on his way to cure a man's young daughter, when out of nowhere an older woman pushed her way through the crowd, with this in mind, *"If I can just touch Jesus's garment, I believe healing virtue will flow out of Him and into my sick body. I know he's busy so I won't bother him personally, I'll just sneak in and get what I need."* She finally did reach Jesus, and her healing happened <u>exactly</u> as she thought it would! A force of virtue instantly left Jesus and healed the sick woman. And it caused Jesus to ask, *"Who touched my clothes?"* (**Mark 5:30**) The woman came forward, and Jesus used her situation to teach countless millions a lesson on faith. Here it is: *If you can imagine it, you can have it*. It sounds remarkable, but it is true.

2E - We Have a Say

Mark 4:24 bears this out. Jesus cautioned us by saying, *"Take heed what ye hear: with what measure ye mete (measure it), it shall be measured to you: and unto you that hear shall more be given."*

Basically, He tells us to be careful how we hear things. The way we hear them, or imagine them, will be the way they work for us.

Based on what the woman, above, had seen of Jesus healing people, she concluded in her mind that her plan of simply touching Jesus's garment would heal her, and it did. In this way, we can have a say in how things turn out. Are we bold enough to ask and believe? That is the question.

2F - How Are You Hearing It?

When we read a passage of scripture like **Philippians 4:19**, which says, *"But my God shall supply all your need according to his riches in glory by Christ Jesus."*, do we think, *"How can God give me more money? I only make $500.00 a week on my job."* or do we think, *"Anything could happen, finances can come from many directions!* We need to think "outside the box." That is the earmark of a person who walks by faith. They refuse to limit God with their "small thinking."

Question 2: Have you ever trusted God to do something that could only have been done by a miracle?

3A - What's the Alternative?

The task of developing our faith will be time-consuming, but what is the alternative? The alternative is that we stay depressed, hopeless, and unmotivated.

The Bible challenges us to develop our faith.

a) **Hebrews 3:19** "So we see that they could not enter in because of unbelief."

b) **James 1:6-8** "But let him ask in faith, nothing wavering. For he that wavereth is like a wave of the sea driven with the wind and tossed. ⁷For let not that man think that he shall receive any thing of the Lord. ⁸A double minded man is unstable in all his ways."

Having weak faith makes life hard, and it can prevent us from receiving God's best for our lives.

Question 3: Have you ever met someone who had a goal in mind, but their lack of confidence made you think they would never reach their goal?

4A - Believing For Miracles

The risk of having weak faith should make us careful when choosing a home church. If our church never talks about how God still heals people today, and we get sick, our faith might not be built up enough to believe that God will heal us.

4B - As well, if our church never talks about how God still meets financial needs, and we need increased finances, our faith might not be built up enough to believe God will give us the finances we need. Our unbelief can prevent God from pouring into our lives the blessings He wants us to have.

There is nothing wrong with attending a church that doesn't teach the principles of faith; we just need to get Bible teaching from other sources, so our faith can keep growing.

Question 4: Has your lack of faith ever prevented you from going to God in confidence that He would help you?

5A - A Blank Check

God gave us His Word so we could saturate ourselves in it. By doing so, we can begin trusting Him for big things in our lives. If we don't need a miracle, we can believe God for miracles for other people.

In a sense, God has issued us a "blank check." We fill in "the amount" (what we are believing God for), and Jesus's death on the cross is what covers "the cost."

5B - Even if we don't receive everything we ask for, we are better off to ask big and receive *something,* than to have weak faith and receive nothing at all.

All of this takes faith, and developing mature faith takes time. It takes time in the reading and speaking of God's Word. There is no shortcut to developing strong faith.

5C - Actions Prove Faith

a) **Matthew 9:2** *"And, behold, they brought to him a man sick of the palsy, lying on a bed: and Jesus seeing their faith said unto the sick of the palsy; Son, be of good cheer; thy sins be forgiven thee."*

b) **Mark 2:5** *"When Jesus saw their faith, he said unto the sick of the palsy, Son, thy sins be forgiven thee."*

c) **Luke 5:20** *"And when he saw their faith, he said unto him, Man, thy sins are forgiven thee."*

5D - What Kind Of Signals Are You Sending?

Actions and words prove our faith. Thus, all through our day, we can be sending "faith signals" to heaven by our actions and words that show God we are trusting Him to act in our life.

Remember that people's *lack of faith* also got Jesus's attention, but, we don't want that. We want Him to stand continually amazed by our faith-affirming words and actions.

Question 5: Have you ever responded to a problem in a way that God would say was an act of faith?

6A - Forgiveness is Available

Does living the faith life mean we aren't going to make mistakes? Not at all. Everyone who begins the journey toward strong faith will make mistakes. When we make a mistake, we simply repent of it, receive our forgiveness by faith, and we move on.

6B - Repenting of sin means, we confess it to God, and make a decision not to do it again. If it is a habitual sin, we will need God's help, and likely the help of others to break the habit.

To get a greater understanding of God's willingness and grace to forgive our sins, read Core Belief #2 – "I Believe Christ's Crucifixion on the Cross Has Paid the Penalty For My Sin."

Question 6: Are you in the habit of confessing and repenting of your sins to God?

7A - We May Not Feel It

We may not always *feel* that God wants to help us, but we override those feelings by doing our actions by faith. That proves to God that we are doing our best to trust Him to help us. Some people complain to God that life isn't fair, but that doesn't win God's favor. He has stated in His Word that, *"The just shall live by faith.",* and that is what we will do. We will keep doing actions and speaking words that prove our faith. Faith is a lifestyle we can learn!

* * * * * * *

TIP #10

Respond Rather Than React

1A - If we were to describe the journey to emotional healing in a single sentence, it would be this: It is the process of learning how to *respond* to life's challenges, rather than *react* to them. We need to learn how to slow down our decision-making process when we get caught off guard. This Tip will help us do that.

1B - Natural reactions are great if they are coming from a healthy foundation, but if they are coming from a weak foundation, they can be crippling. If we give somebody struggling with anxiety and depression another situation to juggle in their lives, their natural reaction may be less than helpful. On the other hand, let's compare such a situation to an athlete who trains 4-6 hours daily so they can be their best on game day. Their natural reactions during the game will be practically perfect, and will help them achieve success in their sport.

1C - <u>Start Training!</u>

Just like an athlete who trains each day to improve their athletic abilities, we can also train in the area of our thinking to achieve a greater measure of personal well-being. This kind of training sharpens our ability to respond effectively to stressful situations, and will help us to stay peaceful so we can enjoy every aspect of our day.

Question 1: Do you know someone who trains diligently for any reason?

2A - <u>Who's Causing the Problem?</u>

Have you ever felt totally drained at the end of work days, for days on end? Life can be hard. And it can tempt us to believe that it is *our situation* or *person* in our life which is causing our unrest. However, the root problem is usually our improper response to the challenges in our life. That is great news because this means that it doesn't matter what the problem is in our lives, there are ways to respond to the problem that can take away the anxiety related to it. One of the programs slogans is: "There is a stress-cancelling response to every problem."

Question 2: Have you ever blamed other people or situations for your emotional unrest? Would you like to give us an example?

3A - Improper Responses – Bible Examples

King David and Bathsheba

In Tip #3, we looked at how King David sinned with Bathsheba, and how it led him astray in his life. David leaned on his own understanding, and it cost him the life of a very good soldier, Bathsheba's husband, Uriah. It also cost him the life of the child that was born to him and Bathsheba. It likely, also, caused David and Bathsheba sadness whenever they remembered their sin and the outcome of it. King David's natural reactions caused much grief and hardship.

3B - Jonah and the People of Nineveh

We also looked at the story of Jonah, how he did not like the people of Nineveh, and that he thought he could get away from doing his job. Jonah's incorrect reaction to his situation caused great loss of contents from the ship he was on, and it could have caused a great loss of life. His rebellion toward God, and his judgmentalism toward the Ninevites also cost him his peace and happiness. See below.

> 3C - **Jonah 3:10-4:3** "And God saw their works, that they turned from their evil way; and God repented of the evil, that he had said that he would do unto them; and he did it not. (Chapter 4) But it displeased Jonah exceedingly, and he was very angry. ² And he prayed unto the LORD, and said, I pray thee, O LORD, was not this my saying, when I was yet in my country? Therefore I fled before unto Tarshish: for I knew that thou art a gracious God, and merciful, slow to anger, and of great kindness, and repentest thee of the evil. ³ Therefore now, O LORD, take, I beseech thee, my life from me; for it is better for me to die than to live."

3D - Do The Job

Based on this story, it would have been easier for Jonah not to care who God sent him to, and simply do his job. Jonah had his own opinion of what he should do, and his natural reaction to not do his job got him into serious trouble.

Question 3: Can you think of a time at your job where your supervisor asked you to do a certain task, but you thought you knew better and did something else? If so, how did it turn out?

4A - Getting Too Entangled

Many times we fail to recognize the true origin of our problems. In some cases, we allow ourselves to get caught up in a battle that we could have avoided. The Bible cautions us on getting too wrapped up in the things of this life. The apostle Paul says it this way:

> **2 Timothy 2:4** "No man that warreth entangleth himself with the affairs of this life; that he may please him who hath chosen him to be a soldier."

4B - The True Origin of Problems

If the Christian life is a war, who are we fighting against? There is one main enemy to humanity, and that is Satan. The Bible says he tried to misuse his authority as the head angel to dethrone God in heaven (Isaiah 14). Because of this act of treason, God banished him from heaven to the earth, along with one-third of the angels.

For more information on the reality of Satan, read Core Belief #4 – I believe I have an Enemy, Satan.

4C - How Does Satan Operate?

Satan and demons (fallen angels) try to steer people away from God and the blessings He has for them through lies and misleading questions. If Satan can convince us that God doesn't love us, or if he can cause us to question that God is even in our life, then he can steal our peace of mind.

Question 4: Can you think of a time in your life when you felt that God didn't love you?

5A - Verses on Satan Using Lies

a) **John 8:44** *(Jesus speaking)* "Ye are of your father the devil, and the lusts of your father ye will do. He was a murderer from the beginning, and abode not in the truth, because there is no truth in him. When he speaketh a lie, he speaketh of his own: for he is a liar, and the father of it."

b) **2 Corinthians 11:3** "But I fear, lest by any means, as the serpent beguiled Eve through his subtilty, so your minds should be corrupted from the simplicity that is in Christ."

Below, is a verse showing how Satan uses questions;

Genesis 3:1 "Now the serpent was more subtle than any beast of the field which the LORD God had made. And he said unto the woman, Yea, hath God said, Ye shall not eat of every tree of the garden?"

Question 5: Knowing that Satan uses lies to upset our lives, what lies do you think he may be using to upset your peace of mind currently?

6A - Below are some common lies:

1) God doesn't love me.
2) I could never get married.
3) I could never forgive that person.
4) I could never be healed physically.
5) I could never be happy with my spouse.
6) Nobody would want to be my friend.
7) I need to have a spouse to be happy.
8) I could never be happy in my job.
9) I need money or things to be happy.
10) I'll never progress past this level of success.
11) I need to be loved and accepted to be happy.
12) I could never break free from my addiction.
13) I'll never have what it takes to be gainfully employed.
14) My worrying about problems shows that I am responsible.
15) My past is so bad; I'll never recover from my emotional wounds.
16) I could never be happy without this person. (e.g., A loved one who passes away)
17) I need to change my physical features to be happy and accepted. *(e.g., weight changes or cosmetic surgery.)*
18) I need to act a certain way to be happy and accepted. *(e.g., "I need to be the life of the party.)*

6B - The Thief

Satan is a liar, but he is also referred to as a <u>thief</u>, as described in the well-known scripture below.

John 10:10 *(Jesus speaking)* "The thief cometh not, but for to steal, and to kill, and to destroy: I am come that they might have life, and that they might have it more abundantly."

6C - Satan's Ultimate Goal

Satan will steal whatever he can; our health, our wealth, our possessions, but most of all, he wants to take our peace of mind. That's because our mind is the gateway to our life. He knows if he can steal our peace of mind, then he has a chance at stealing our life - through self-destruction. That is the ultimate "win" for Satan. He knows that nothing grieves the heart of God more than to have the person He gives the gift of life to, to throw it back in His face. Thankfully, we can stop Satan from stealing that from us, the way Jesus stopped him.

Question 6: Can you think of anything Satan has stolen from you?

7A - How Did Jesus Stop the Devil?

In this portion of scripture, we will watch Jesus in action as He uses a weapon, the Bible calls, the "Sword of the Spirit."

Matthew 4:1-11 "Then was Jesus led up of the Spirit into the wilderness to be tempted of the devil. ² And when he had fasted forty days and forty nights, he was afterward an hungred. ³ And when the tempter came to him, he said, If thou be the Son of God, command that these stones be made bread. ⁴ But he answered and said, It is written, Man shall not live by bread alone, but by every word that proceedeth out of the mouth of God."

7B - ⁵ Then the devil taketh him up into the holy city, and setteth him on a pinnacle of the temple, ⁶ And saith unto him, If thou be the Son of God, cast thyself down: for it is written, He shall give his angels charge concerning thee: and in their hands they shall bear thee up, lest at any time thou dash thy foot against a stone. ⁷ Jesus said unto him, It is written again, Thou shalt not tempt the Lord thy God. ⁸ Again, the devil taketh him up into an exceeding high mountain, and sheweth him all the kingdoms of the world, and the glory of them; ⁹ And saith unto him, All these things will I give thee, if thou wilt fall down and worship me. ¹⁰ Then saith Jesus unto him, Get thee hence, Satan: for it is written, Thou shalt worship the Lord thy God, and him only shalt thou serve. ¹¹ Then the devil leaveth him, and, behold, angels came and ministered unto him."

7C - Jesus knew God's Word, and He used it like a sharp sword to disarm the lies of Satan. The devil wanted to shorten the fast that Jesus was on, but Jesus said, *"It is written, man shall not live by bread alone, but by every word that proceedeth out of the mouth of God."*

Then, it appears the devil tried to make Jesus commit suicide, but Jesus said, *"It is written again, Thou shalt not tempt the Lord thy God."*

7D - Following that, the devil tried to get Jesus to worship him instead of the Father, but Jesus said, *"Get thee hence, Satan: for it is written, Thou shalt worship the Lord thy God, and him only shalt thou serve."*

7E - The great news is that we can do the same thing Jesus did. Jesus knew God's Word very well. If we apply ourselves, we, too, can learn God's Word.

Then, for example, if we get thoughts in our mind that our health is getting worse, or that God hasn't forgiven us, we can say, "No sir, Devil, it is written in **Psalm 103:3**, *"Who forgiveth all thine iniquities; who healeth all thy diseases;"*

7F - Or, if we get thoughts that God doesn't love us, we can say, "No sir, Devil, for it is written in **1 John 4:16** *"And we have known and believed the love that God hath to us. God is love; and he that dwelleth in love dwelleth in God, and God in him."*

7G - Or, if we get thoughts that God won't help us with our financial needs, we say, "No sir! For it is written in **Philippians 4:19** *"But my God shall supply all your need according to his riches in glory by Christ Jesus."*

7H - Use God's Weapons

By holding tightly to our core beliefs of who God says He is - our loving creator, we can keep ourselves at peace by trusting Him to keep His promises to us.

Just as Jesus used God's Word to defend Himself, God urges us to know and use His Word to defend ourselves.

As stated above, God has given His Word a specific name - the "Sword of the Spirit".

Ephesians 6:17 "And take the helmet of salvation, and the sword of the Spirit, which is the word of God:"

7J - The Sword of the Spirit is one of a number of items that God gives us, with which to fight our spiritual battles. Ephesians Chapter 6 lists them: the Belt of Truth, Breast Plate of Righteousness, Shoes of the Gospel of Peace, Shield of Faith, Helmet of Salvation, and the Sword of the Spirit. Become familiar with this gear and learn to use them every day as needed.

Question 7: Have you ever used God's Word to defend yourself from Satan's mental attacks?

8A - Not only is Satan called a liar and a thief; he is also referred to as a lion.

1 Peter 5:8 "Be sober, be vigilant; because your adversary the devil, as a roaring lion, walketh about, seeking whom he may devour:"

The devil is looking for an opening in our lives, that we give him, to gain entry into our affairs. When we walk closely with Jesus, He will show us ways to prevent Satan from upsetting situations in our lives.

Question 8: Is there an aspect of your life, presently, in which you feel Satan is causing you trouble?

9A - Cheerful In Problems

One of the unique and refreshing aspects of Christianity is the positive attitude we can have when facing challenges in our life. The following verses tell us that we can have good cheer in the midst of difficulties.

a) **John 16:33** "These things I have spoken unto you, that in me ye might have peace. In the world ye shall have tribulation: but be of good cheer; I have overcome the world."

b) **Romans 5:3,4** "And not only so, but we glory in tribulations also: knowing that tribulation worketh patience; And patience, experience; and experience, hope:"

c) **Colossians 1:11** "Strengthened with all might, according to his glorious power, unto all patience and longsuffering *(enduring injury or trouble)* with joyfulness;"

d) **James 1:2** "My brethren, count it all joy when you fall into divers temptations *(various trials)*;"

For more information on being cheerful in trials, read Tip #18 – Become an Optimist.

9B - Our Problems Don't Even Compare

Here we see that our present sufferings are not worth comparing to the glory that is waiting for us.

Romans 8:18 "For I reckon that the sufferings of this present time are not worthy to be compared with the glory which shall be revealed in us."

9C - View Problems Differently

To the Christian, problems can also be referred to as "blessings in disguise." That's because God has ways of taking problems and making them work out for our benefit.

Indeed, challenges don't have to get us anxious or depressed. However, this can only happen when we keep our spiritual focus on God and His Word. We don't want to be like Peter, in Matthew 14:23-32, when he was walking on the water with Jesus, he began to take his eyes off of Jesus and started looking at the wind and the waves, and he began to sink. Instead, we want to learn to keep our thoughts on God's Word, and on the promises He has for us.

9D - What's Our Job?

Our job as Christians is to <u>believe</u>. It is God's job to answer our prayers. The only way to truly believe, is to be hopeful, trusting and optimistic. Thankfully, we can learn how not to be disturbed by the challenges in our lives. We can learn to stay in control of our responses to our problems instead of reacting to them. We can learn to keep our peace of mind no matter what obstacles come our way!

Question 9: Can you tell us of a recent problem in your life and how you responded to it?

10A - Natural Reactions to Pain

A woman experienced prolonged labor while giving birth to her first child. Five hours, 10 hours, 15 hours; after 20 hours she began thinking of reasons why God was giving her such a difficult delivery. Her mind took her back through her life, and she started to remember all the times she hurt people, even in a small way. She became convinced that the reason she was in this difficult situation was because of the mistakes she had made. Others tried to tell her differently, but she couldn't see it. Fortunately, God helped her get through the delivery.

10B - Pain Can Be a Good Thing

A natural reaction to pain can be self-inspection. When pain makes us think about our past experiences, we can assess the circumstances to determine if we were guilty or not. If so, we can repent of it, and move on with our lives.

Pain, with its natural reaction of self-assessment, isn't a bad thing. It can cause us to do a thorough "house-cleaning" of our heart. After it is complete, we are ready to aim for new successes in our life!

Question 10: Has your pain ever caused you to do self-inspection?

11A - King David Arrives Home in Ziklag

In 1 Samuel 30, we read of the time when King David and his army came home to Ziklag, only to find that their city was burning, and their wives and children carried off by the Amalekite army. David and his men were overcome with terrible grief. They wept until they had no more strength to weep. The men even considered stoning David. David was greatly distressed. Then he asked God for advice. God's answer was: "Pursue and overtake." So they did, and they got their families back!

Question 11: After coming home from battle, and seeing their burnt and vacant city, could David have inquired of God <u>before</u> his distress set in, and thereby have avoided the emotional pain?

12A - Natural Reactions When Somebody Hurts Us

When somebody hurts us, the natural reaction is to want to hurt them back. But we should be careful when dealing with vengeance. Some people who have fought back have been injured, and even killed. Sometimes, the best thing to do is just forgive the person who hurt us and go on.

12B - When we refuse to forgive, we imprison ourselves. Thus, the act of forgiveness is more for the person who got hurt, rather than the person who injured us. It may *feel* like we cannot forgive the person, however, like love, forgiveness is an act of the will. *We can choose to forgive the person.* By doing so, we let God handle the person who hurt us, in His way and in His time. That is faith. We will know we truly have forgiven the person when we no longer obsess about the incident. If we are having difficulty forgiving someone, sometimes it is helpful to begin praying for the person, asking God to bless their life in every way.

> **Matthew 5:44** "But I say unto you, Love your enemies, bless them that curse you, do good to them that hate you, and pray for them which despitefully use you, and persecute you;"

Question 12: Is there someone in your life with whom you have vengeful thoughts? If so, what do you think about making a quality decision to forgive them?

13A - Natural Reaction When You Feel Depressed

Sometimes when we feel down, we make the mistake of trying hard not to *look* depressed. This can cause more anxiety because we are trying to be somebody we are not. Like the person who breaks their leg, a doctor will tell them not to put too much weight on it for a few weeks. The same goes for someone who is troubled emotionally. We shouldn't try too hard to look happy. Instead, we should become more of a spectator of life for a while until we heal up emotionally. In due time, our healing will come, and we will rejoice genuinely!

Question 13: Have you ever tried too hard to hide your emotional pain?

14A - <u>Avoid Isolation</u>

Another natural reaction when experiencing emotional pain can be to isolate ourselves from others. By keeping our problem a secret, we can rob ourselves of good people who can help us resolve our issue. It is best to go against our natural reaction and tell our doctor and loved ones how we are feeling. Then together, search for the help that is needed. For more on this, see Tip #5 – Form a Support Team.

Question 14: Have you ever withheld information from people who you knew could help solve your problem?

15A - <u>Natural Reaction When Life Gets Hard</u>

When life gets difficult, the natural reaction is to flee from a situation. We can get caught up in the mindset, *"The grass is greener on the other side."* If we feel compelled to move on, it is sometimes best to stay in a situation until we achieve victory in it. Then move on to something else. What we don't want, is to *"jump out of the frying pan and into the fire."* This will further complicate our problem.

Question 15: Have you ever tried to get out of a difficult situation by moving to something else, only to end up in worse circumstances?

16A - <u>Seeing Ourselves in Others</u>

Sometimes, when we begin seeing areas in our lives improve; we tend to see them in other people's lives as well. The temptation can be to tell others what their areas of weakness are. This can possibly hurt them, and can hurt us as well. It is best to be careful when sharing information related to someone else's recovery. Doing so with gentleness and humility will give us greater success in passing on the valuable truths we have learned.

The following verses give us tips on how to reach out to others.

a) **Matthew 7:5** "…first cast out the beam out of thine own eye; and then shalt thou see clearly to cast out the mote out of thy brother's eye."

b) **1 Corinthians 14:3** "But he that prophesieth speaketh unto men to edification, and exhortation, and comfort."

c) **Galatians 6:1** "…if a man be overtaken in a fault, ye which are spiritual, restore such an one in the spirit of meekness; considering thyself, lest thou also be tempted."

Question 16: Have you ever tried to help a person see a certain truth, but hurt yourself, and them, by doing so?

17A - <u>Natural Reaction When Healed from Fear</u>

Sometimes, when we get free from fear, we can become overly confident. Our new-found confidence can cause us to boldly do things that *may seem right to us*, but can lead us to more pain. We need to use our new found freedom wisely. Boldness should be tempered with wisdom. When recovering from fear, it is best to get feedback from others before making important decisions in our life.

Question 17: Have you ever been overly confident and tried to do something that eventually caused you pain?

18A - <u>Busyness</u>

Sometimes, when we become anxious, a natural reaction can be that we become overly busy. Our busyness can act as a distraction, preventing us from pursuing our healing, and thus prolonging our illness.

Question 18: Have you ever avoided facing problems in your life by getting overly busy?

19A - <u>Hurt by People at Church</u>

Because people make mistakes, the day may come when someone at our church hurts us. Our judgment toward someone at church can grow by causing us to pass judgment toward the church, and even God Himself. We shouldn't let the natural reaction to this hurt cause us to lose our church friendships, or our walk with God. It is best to resolve the hurt as soon as possible. We should be gracious and forgive. We should forgive people as if we ourselves made the mistake and would need forgiveness. For more on this, see Tip #21 – Collect "Grace Doors."

Question 19: Have you ever found yourself being judgmental toward a person, a church, a denomination, or even God Himself?

20A - With God's help we can learn how to <u>respond, rather than react</u> to the challenges of life.

* * * * * * *

Tip #11

Know Yourself

1A - Life has a way of leading us away from God's best for our lives. The problem is that change in our heart can happen so slowly that we aren't aware we are drifting away from God. What complicates this problem further is that we have inherent weaknesses that we may not be aware of, or not paying attention to. Not being aware of our weaknesses can be a serious problem. Our enemy, the devil, knows us better than we know ourselves, and he can use this knowledge against us. Let's take some time to identify our strengths and weaknesses, so we'll be ready for any challenge that comes our way.

1B - People in the Bible had weaknesses. God has given us their stories so we can learn from them.

Eve was too naïve when she was speaking with the serpent (Satan).

Genesis 3:1-6 "Now the serpent was more subtil than any beast of the field which the LORD God had made. And he said unto the woman, Yea, hath God said, Ye shall not eat of every tree of the garden? ² And the woman said unto the serpent, We may eat of the fruit of the trees of the garden: ³ But of the fruit of the tree which is in the midst of the garden, God hath said, Ye shall not eat of it, neither shall ye touch it, lest ye die. ⁴ And the serpent said unto the woman, Ye shall not surely die: ⁵ For God doth know that in the day ye eat thereof, then your eyes shall be opened, and ye shall be as gods, knowing good and evil. ⁶ And when the woman saw that the tree was good for food, and that it was pleasant to the eyes, and a tree to be desired to make one wise, she took of the fruit thereof, and did eat, and gave also unto her husband with her; and he did eat."

1C - Adam's weakness was his impulsiveness to take the fruit from Eve.

Question 1: Does anyone come to mind that is naïve like Eve, or impulsive like Adam?

2A - King Saul became jealous of young David.

1 Samuel 18:7-9 "The women sang as they played, and said, "Saul has killed his thousands, and David his ten thousands." ⁸ Then Saul became very angry. This saying did not please him. He said, "They have given David honor for ten thousands, but for me only thousands. Now what more can he have but to be king?" ⁹ And Saul was jealous and did not trust David from that day on."

Question 2: Can you think of anyone who gets jealous easily?

3A - King Solomon became addicted to women, and began marrying non-Jewish (Gentile) women.

When we start spending too much time with worldly people, it can reduce our love for God, and our service for Him. Solomon's story is very sad when you consider how he began his reign as king, with great humility and uprightness of heart toward God.

1 Kings 11:1-4 "But king Solomon loved many strange women, together with the daughter of Pharaoh, women of the Moabites, Ammonites, Edomites, Zidonians, and Hittites: ² Of the nations concerning which the LORD said unto the children of Israel, Ye shall not go in to them, neither shall they come in unto you: for surely they will turn away your heart after their gods: Solomon clave unto these in love. ³ And he had seven hundred wives, princesses, and three hundred concubines: and his wives turned away his heart. ⁴ For it came to pass, when Solomon was old, that his wives turned away his heart after other gods: and his heart was not perfect with the LORD his God, as was the heart of David his father."

Question 3: Do any Christians come to mind that spend too much time with non-Christian people?

4A - In Joshua Chapter 7, we read how the Israelite army suffered a devastating defeat. This caused Joshua to fall on his face before God to find out why they lost the battle. God said that there was sin in the camp. The camp was searched, and Achan confessed to stealing some of the booty from a previous battle. He suffered a terrible loss for doing so.

Joshua 7:24,25 "And Joshua, and all Israel with him, took Achan the son of Zerah, and the silver, and the garment, and the wedge of gold, and his sons, and his daughters, and his oxen, and his asses, and his sheep, and his tent, and all that he had: and they brought them unto the valley of Achor. ²⁵ And Joshua said, Why hast thou troubled us? the LORD shall trouble thee this day. And all Israel stoned him with stones, and burned them with fire, after they had stoned them with stones."

Question 4: Does anyone come to mind who likes nice things a little too much?

5A - One day King Nebuchadnezzar was in the middle of a prideful speech of how he built such a grand kingdom by his own might. Suddenly, God humbled him in a very dramatic way. For seven long years, King Nebechadnezzar lived like an ox in the field, grazing on grass.

Daniel 4:30-33 "The king spake, and said, Is not this great Babylon, that I have built for the house of the kingdom by the might of my power, and for the honour of my majesty? ³¹ While the word was in the king's mouth, there fell a voice from heaven, saying, O king Nebuchadnezzar, to thee it is spoken; The kingdom is departed from thee. ³² And they shall drive thee from men, and thy dwelling shall be with the beasts of the field: they shall make thee to eat grass as oxen, and seven times shall pass over thee, until thou know that the most High ruleth in the kingdom of men, and giveth it to whomsoever he will. ³³ The same hour was the thing fulfilled upon Nebuchadnezzar: and he was driven from men, and did eat grass as oxen, and his body was wet with the dew of heaven, till his hairs were grown like eagles' feathers, and his nails like birds' claws."

Question 5: Do you know anyone who is prideful? Did their pride cause them a downfall?

6A - Samson was one of the judges of Israel, and especially gifted by God to help liberate Israel from a forty year reign of the Philistines.

> **Judges 13:1-5** "And the children of Israel did evil again in the sight of the LORD; and the LORD delivered them into the hand of the Philistines forty years. ² And there was a certain man of Zorah, of the family of the Danites, whose name was Manoah; and his wife was barren, and bare not. ³ And the angel of the LORD appeared unto the woman, and said unto her, Behold now, thou art barren, and bearest not: but thou shalt conceive, and bear a son. ⁴ Now therefore beware, I pray thee, and drink not wine nor strong drink, and eat not any unclean thing: ⁵ For, lo, thou shalt conceive, and bear a son; and no razor shall come on his head: for the child shall be a Nazarite unto God from the womb: and he shall begin to deliver Israel out of the hand of the Philistines."

6B - Samson was born with the gift of strength. His strength was due to his long hair which had never been cut. But Samson had a weakness. He was careless about the secret of his power. After years of causing havoc for the Philistines, the Philistines convinced Samson's girlfriend, Delilah, to inquire of Samson the source of his great strength. Samson toyed with her for a while, giving her false sources. However, after Delilah's ongoing and tearful inquiries, Samson did the unthinkable; he told her the real source of his strength - his long hair. While sleeping that night, his hair was cut, and when he awoke, he was powerless to defend himself, and he became a slave of the Philistines.

> **Judges 16:17** "That he told her all his heart, and said unto her, There hath not come a razor upon mine head; for I have been a Nazarite unto God from my mother's womb: if I be shaven, then my strength will go from me, and I shall become weak, and be like any other man."

Question 6: Does anyone come to mind that treats their natural gift with casual disinterest, to a point where they allow Satan to play havoc in their lives?

7A - Now that we see how flawed Bible characters can be, it may be easier for us to confess our own areas of weakness.

Question 7: Do you know of any weaknesses in your life? Would you like to share any with the group?

8A - God sometimes uses other people to tell us what our weaknesses are. We would do well to take note of what people are telling us to see if there is any truth to what they are saying. We could also ask people who know us if they see any weaknesses in our lives.

Question 8: Has anyone ever talked to you about areas of weakness in your life, either in a serious, joking, or mean way? What was your reaction? What did you learn about yourself?

9A - Once we know our weaknesses, we can begin to work on improving those areas, so they become less of a handicap in our lives. A good strategy is to have accountability people in our lives, people we can confess our shortcomings to, and who can inspire us to be our best.

Question 9: Have you ever had an accountability person or group in your life? How did it help you?

10A - <u>Know Your Strengths</u>

God has given us strengths. He challenges us to find out our gifts.

Proverbs 25:2 "It is the glory of God to conceal a thing: but the honor of kings is to search out a matter."

Question 10: Has anyone ever told you, you were gifted in some way? How did you respond to it?

11A - Our gifts can bring us a measure of joy when we operate in them.

Question 11: In what ways have you been energized by your talents?

12A - Sometimes when we discover what our strengths are, we can become prideful. We can even use our gift for unjust gain. For instance, a salesperson that has a warm, caring personality can begin selling products that will benefit them more than the customer.

Question 12: Have you ever got a little prideful or careless after finding out what your gifts were? If so, can you tell us about it?

13A - Often, God uses our natural talents in the church.

Question 13: In what ways could you make use of your gifts in the church?

14A - Having an accurate understanding of our strengths and weaknesses can give us an edge in life. Becoming a life-long student of ourselves will help us to make right choices in our life, and will help us produce fruitful service for God, as well as happiness and peace for ourselves.

* * * * * * *

TIP #12

Don't Judge

1A - One major cause of anxiety and depression is the act of passing judgment on others. You might ask, *"Do I just turn a blind eye to anyone that does wrong to me?"* That depends on the situation. Every circumstance is different, and every person we come in contact with is different, thus requiring a particular response. Having a pastor or a support team in our life will give us people we can speak with, who can give us suggestions on how to best respond to a given situation.

1B - If it is an abusive situation we should first try to remove ourselves from the abuse. By doing so, we can better assess the hurtful action. We will then be better able to respond properly to it if it happens again. (To recognize abuse more readily, see the *"Types of Abuse"* section at the end of the book.)

1C - When someone abuses us it is natural to pass judgment on them. However, Jesus tells us not to judge others. Here are two such verses.

   a) **Matthew 7:1,2** (Jesus is speaking) "Do not judge, or you too will be judged. For in the same way you judge others, you will be judged, and with the measure you use, it will be measured to you."

   b) **Luke 6:37** "Judge not, and ye shall not be judged: condemn not, and ye shall not be condemned: forgive, and ye shall be forgiven:"

1D - When Jesus tells us not to judge, does that mean we can't judge the action? We know that judicial judges judge actions all the time. We also know that Jesus gives permission to judge people's actions when He says, *"Give not that which is holy unto the dogs, neither cast ye your pearls before swine,"* (Matthew 7:6) and *"Watch out for false prophets"* (Matthew 7:15-16). How do we determine who the dogs and pigs are, and the false prophets are if we not allowed to judge?

1E - When we share with people how sin is so damaging, how can we warn people who may be engaged in sinful actions such as *adultery, fornication, uncleanness, lasciviousness, idolatry, witchcraft, hatred, variance, emulations, wrath, strife, seditions, heresies, envyings, murders, drunkenness and revellings* (Galatians 5:19-21)? Won't listing these sins sound like we are passing judgment? It's a delicate issue.

1F - In John 7:24, Jesus tells us *"Judge not according to the appearance, but judge righteous judgment."* Examining the above references would make it appear it is permissible to judge a person's actions.

1G - For sure, we ought not judge the person. We ought not to judge them because we all have blind spots. Plus, it is only by God's grace that we aren't as mixed up as the person who wronged us.

Forms of Judging

Judgment Toward People

Often we get into the habit of passing judgment on others because we ourselves were judged in the past. Let's take some time to see in what ways others have judged us.

Question 1: Looking back at your youth, can you remember being judged by your parents? If yes, can you tell us why, and are they still passing judgment on you today?

Question 2: Did your parents pass judgment on others? If yes, can you tell us on whom?

Question 3: Can you remember being judged by kids at school? If yes, can you tell us why?

Question 4: Can you remember being judged by teachers or other adult leaders? If yes, can you tell us why?

5A - ### Judgment toward Institutions

Sometimes we face problems at school that cause us to pass judgment on schools.

Question 5: Looking back over your school years, can you remember passing judgment on your schools for any reason? If yes, can you tell us why?

6A - Sometimes we face problems on the job that cause us to pass judgment on companies that employ us.

Question 6: Can you remember passing judgment on companies or workers for any reason? If yes, can you tell us why?

7A - ### Judgment Toward Ideologies

Sometimes we are influenced by people who are prejudiced for one reason or another.

Question 7: Can you remember judging people who were different than you (race, ethnicity, religion, political persuasion, ideologies, etc.)? If yes, can you tell us why?

8A - ### Avoid this Kind of Judgment

One of the most damaging acts of judgment to our emotional health is that of judging ourselves. These kinds of judgments are characterized by critical, condemning, self-shaming, and other demeaning thoughts and feelings.

Question 8: Can you remember ever passing judgment on yourself? If yes, can you tell us why, and do you still pass judgment on yourself today?

10A - ### Judgment Scriptures

The scriptures are very clear on not passing judgment on other people. See the scriptures below.

a) **Luke 6:37** "Do not judge, and you will not be judged. Do not condemn, and you will not be condemned."

b) **James 2:3,4** "If you show special attention to the man wearing fine clothes and say, "Here's a good seat for you," but say to the poor man, "You stand there" or "Sit on the floor by my feet," have you not discriminated among yourselves and become judges with evil thoughts?"

c) **James 4:11,12** "Brothers, do not slander one another. Anyone who speaks against his brother or judges him speaks against the law and judges it. When you judge the law, you are not keeping it, but sitting in judgment on it. There is only one Lawgiver and Judge, the one who is able to save and destroy. But you—who are you to judge your neighbor?"

d) **1 Peter 2:23** "When they hurled insults at him (Jesus), he did not retaliate; when he suffered, he made no threats. Instead, he entrusted himself to him who judges justly."

10B - The Cure for Being Hurt When Being Judged

The way out of the pain of having been judged by others is through the act of forgiveness. Our natural reaction to those who have hurt us is to hurt them back, but that will only keep us in emotional distress. We must go against our natural reaction and consciously forgive the person who has hurt us. We do not have to *feel* like forgiving them. We forgive them not by our emotions, instead, as an act of our will, knowing it is the right thing to do. For more on this, see Tip #10 – Respond Rather Than React.

10C - One Important Reason to Forgive

After we have forgiven someone their hurtful action toward us, and the pain of it has gone, we will then have a story to share with others of how God has helped us through the act of forgiveness. That's why one of the slogans of the program is: *Don't focus on what you lost, focus on what you gained*. When we forgive someone who has hurt us, we gain a "platform" with which we can use to tell our story and inspire others to forgive, especially if what they are struggling with is a similar offense. Others will be helped by realizing they aren't the only ones who have suffered hurt, and they will be challenged to forgive their trespassers too.

Question 10: Do you have a trauma that God could use to help others with? Would you like to share that with us?

11A - A Helpful Skill to Learn

After recovering from the hurtful words spoken to us, we can ask God to help us to no longer care what people think of us. Faith in God will give us greater confidence. We will be better able to shrug off unkind words spoken to us or about us. We can be like Jesus when He spoke these words from the cross, *"Father, forgive them, for they know not what they do."* (Luke 23:34)

Question 11: Is there an area of your life in which you would like God to help you be more carefree?

12A - Learning to be non-judgmental will help us keep our peace of mind, and will help our personalities become more attractive, thus giving us greater happiness with those around us.

* * * * * * *

Tip #13

***

Be "Good Ground"

***

1A - Jesus tells us that the parable of the sower is a "stand-alone" parable. He asks, how will you know any parable if you don't know this one? Thus, it is good for us to read it, and glean everything we can from it. The title of this Tip comes from the soil types described in the parable. May God teach us something valuable as we read it.

1B - **Mark 4:3-20**

> "Hearken; Behold, there went out a sower to sow: ^{4} And it came to pass, as he sowed, some fell by the way side, and the fowls of the air came and devoured it up. ^{5} And some fell on stony ground, where it had not much earth; and immediately it sprang up, because it had no depth of earth: ^{6} But when the sun was up, it was scorched; and because it had no root, it withered away. ^{7} And some fell among thorns, and the thorns grew up, and choked it, and it yielded no fruit. ^{8} And other fell on good ground, and did yield fruit that sprang up and increased; and brought forth, some thirty, and some sixty, and some an hundred. ^{9} And he said unto them, He that hath ears to hear, let him hear. ^{10} And when he was alone, they that were about him with the twelve asked of him the parable."

1C - "^{11} And he said unto them, Unto you it is given to know the mystery of the kingdom of God: but unto them that are without, all these things are done in parables: ^{12} That seeing they may see, and not perceive; and hearing they may hear, and not understand; lest at any time they should be converted, and their sins should be forgiven them.^{13} And he said unto them, Know ye not this parable? and how then will ye know all parables? ^{14} The sower soweth the word. ^{15} And these are they by the way side, where the word is sown; but when they have heard, Satan cometh immediately, and taketh away the word that was sown in their hearts."

1D - "^{16} And these are they likewise which are sown on stony ground; who, when they have heard the word, immediately receive it with gladness; ^{17} And have no root in themselves, and so endure but for a time: afterward, when affliction or persecution ariseth for the word's sake, immediately they are offended. ^{18} And these are they which are sown among thorns; such as hear the word, ^{19} And the cares of this world, and the deceitfulness of riches, and the lusts of other things entering in, choke the word, and it becometh unfruitful. ^{20} And these are they which are sown on good ground; such as hear the word, and receive it, and bring forth fruit, some thirtyfold, some sixty, and some an hundred."

Question 1: What kind of ground are you when you hear God's Word taught?

a) **Hard Ground** - Do you dismiss it quickly?

b) **Stony Ground** – Are you interested in God's Word initially, but then let it slip away soon after?

c) **Thorny Ground** – Are you enthusiastic about God's Word, but easily allow the cares of life to limit you from getting closer to God and doing His work?

d) **Good Ground** – Are you really interested in God's Word and looking for every opportunity to read it and tell people the message of eternal life through Jesus?

* * * * * * *

TIP #14

Develop a Conqueror Mentality

1A - God wants each of us to be strong and able to handle any problem that comes our way. A good example of this is the young man David, who found out about a giant named, Goliath, who was making fun of the Israelite army. When the time came, David marched up in great boldness and he defeated the giant!

1B - Here is the account:

1 Samuel 17:20 – 51 "And David rose up early in the morning, and left the sheep with a keeper, and took, and went, as Jesse had commanded him; and he came to the trench, as the host was going forth to the fight, and shouted for the battle. [21] For Israel and the Philistines had put the battle in array, army against army. [22] And David left his carriage in the hand of the keeper of the carriage, and ran into the army, and came and saluted his brethren. [23] And as he talked with them, behold, there came up the champion, the Philistine of Gath, Goliath by name, out of the armies of the Philistines, and spake according to the same words: and David heard them."

1C - "[24] And all the men of Israel, when they saw the man, fled from him, and were sore afraid. [25] And the men of Israel said, Have ye seen this man that is come up? surely to defy Israel is he come up: and it shall be, that the man who killeth him, the king will enrich him with great riches, and will give him his daughter, and make his father's house free in Israel. [26] And David spake to the men that stood by him, saying, What shall be done to the man that killeth this Philistine, and taketh away the reproach from Israel? for who is this uncircumcised Philistine, that he should defy the armies of the living God? [27] And the people answered him after this manner, saying, So shall it be done to the man that killeth him."

1D - "[28] And Eliab his eldest brother heard when he spake unto the men; and Eliab's anger was kindled against David, and he said, Why camest thou down hither? and with whom hast thou left those few sheep in the wilderness? I know thy pride, and the naughtiness of thine heart; for thou art come down that thou mightest see the battle. [29] And David said, What have I now done? Is there not a cause? [30] And he turned from him toward another, and spake after the same manner: and the people answered him again after the former manner."

1E - "³¹ And when the words were heard which David spake, they rehearsed them before Saul: and he sent for him. ³² And David said to Saul, Let no man's heart fail because of him; thy servant will go and fight with this Philistine. ³³ And Saul said to David, Thou art not able to go against this Philistine to fight with him: for thou art but a youth, and he a man of war from his youth. "

1F - "³⁴ And David said unto Saul, Thy servant kept his father's sheep, and there came a lion, and a bear, and took a lamb out of the flock: ³⁵ And I went out after him, and smote him, and delivered it out of his mouth: and when he arose against me, I caught him by his beard, and smote him, and slew him. ³⁶ Thy servant slew both the lion and the bear: and this uncircumcised Philistine shall be as one of them, seeing he hath defied the armies of the living God. ³⁷ David said moreover, The LORD that delivered me out of the paw of the lion, and out of the paw of the bear, he will deliver me out of the hand of this Philistine. And Saul said unto David, Go, and the LORD be with thee."

1G - "³⁸ And Saul armed David with his armour, and he put an helmet of brass upon his head; also he armed him with a coat of mail. ³⁹ And David girded his sword upon his armour, and he assayed to go; for he had not proved it. And David said unto Saul, I cannot go with these; for I have not proved them. And David put them off him. ⁴⁰ And he took his staff in his hand, and chose him five smooth stones out of the brook, and put them in a shepherd's bag which he had, even in a scrip; and his sling was in his hand: and he drew near to the Philistine."

1H - "⁴¹ And the Philistine came on and drew near unto David; and the man that bare the shield went before him. ⁴² And when the Philistine looked about, and saw David, he disdained him: for he was but a youth, and ruddy, and of a fair countenance. ⁴³ And the Philistine said unto David, Am I a dog, that thou comest to me with staves? And the Philistine cursed David by his gods. ⁴⁴ And the Philistine said to David, Come to me, and I will give thy flesh unto the fowls of the air, and to the beasts of the field."

1J - "⁴⁵ Then said David to the Philistine, Thou comest to me with a sword, and with a spear, and with a shield: but I come to thee in the name of the LORD of hosts, the God of the armies of Israel, whom thou hast defied. ⁴⁶ This day will the LORD deliver thee into mine hand; and I will smite thee, and take thine head from thee; and I will give the carcases of the host of the Philistines this day unto the fowls of the air, and to the wild beasts of the earth; that all the earth may know that there is a God in Israel. ⁴⁷ And all this assembly shall know that the LORD saveth not with sword and spear: for the battle is the LORD's, and he will give you into our hands."

1K - "⁴⁸ And it came to pass, when the Philistine arose, and came, and drew nigh to meet David, that David hastened, and ran toward the army to meet the Philistine. ⁴⁹ And David put his hand in his bag, and took thence a stone, and slang it, and smote the Philistine in his forehead, that the stone sunk into his forehead; and he fell upon his face to the earth. ⁵⁰ So David prevailed over the Philistine with a sling and with a stone, and smote the Philistine, and slew him; but there was no sword in the hand of David."

1L - "⁵¹ Therefore David ran, and stood upon the Philistine, and took his sword, and drew it out of the sheath thereof, and slew him, and cut off his head therewith. And when the Philistines saw their champion was dead, they fled."

Question 1: What thoughts come to your mind after reading the story of David?

Question 2: In what area of your life do you need to develop a conqueror mentality?

3A - We, too, can have boldness like young David had. One way is by reading the following scriptures out loud over and over. By making it a priority in our lives to speak God's Word, we'll develop a connection with God that nothing else can. We can go one step further by memorizing the verses.

1) **Joshua 1:5** "There shall not any man be able to stand before thee all the days of thy life: as I was with Moses, so I will be with thee: I will not fail thee, nor forsake thee."

2) **2 Samuel 22:29-31** "For thou art my lamp, O LORD: and the LORD will lighten my darkness. ^{30} For by thee I have run through a troop: by my God have I leaped over a wall. ^{31} As for God, his way is perfect; the word of the LORD is tried: he is a buckler to all them that trust in him."

3) **2 Chronicles 16:9** "For the eyes of the LORD run to and fro throughout the whole earth, to shew himself strong in the behalf of them whose heart is perfect toward him. Herein thou hast done foolishly: therefore from henceforth thou shalt have wars."

4) **Psalm 18:32-40** "It is God that girdeth me with strength, and maketh my way perfect. ^{33} He maketh my feet like hinds' feet, and setteth me upon my high places. ^{34} He teacheth my hands to war, so that a bow of steel is broken by mine arms.^{35} Thou hast also given me the shield of thy salvation: and thy right hand hath holden me up, and thy gentleness hath made me great. ^{36} Thou hast enlarged my steps under me, that my feet did not slip. ^{37} I have pursued mine enemies, and overtaken them: neither did I turn again till they were consumed. ^{38} I have wounded them that they were not able to rise: they are fallen under my feet. ^{39} For thou hast girded me with strength unto the battle: thou hast subdued under me those that rose up against me. ^{40} Thou hast also given me the necks of mine enemies; that I might destroy them that hate me."

5) **Psalm 28:7** "The LORD is my strength and my shield; my heart trusted in him, and I am helped: therefore my heart greatly rejoiceth; and with my song will I praise him."

6) **Psalm 44:5-7** "Through thee will we push down our enemies: through thy name will we tread them under that rise up against us. ^{6} For I will not trust in my bow, neither shall my sword save me. ^{7} But thou hast saved us from our enemies, and hast put them to shame that hated us."

7) **Psalm 68:35** "O God, thou art terrible out of thy holy places: the God of Israel is he that giveth strength and power unto his people. Blessed be God."

8) **Psalm 138:3** "In the day when I cried thou answeredst me, and strengthenedst me with strength in my soul."

9) **Psalm 144:1,2** "Blessed be the LORD my strength which teacheth my hands to war, and my fingers to fight: ^{2} My goodness, and my fortress; my high tower, and my deliverer; my shield, and he in whom I trust; who subdueth my people under me."

10) **Proverbs 3:26** "For the LORD shall be thy confidence, and shall keep thy foot from being taken."

11) **Job 17:9** "The righteous also shall hold on his way, and he that hath clean hands shall be stronger and stronger."

12) **Isaiah 40:29** "He giveth power to the faint; and to them that have no might he increaseth strength."

13) **Isaiah 54:17** "No weapon that is formed against thee shall prosper; and every tongue that shall rise against thee in judgment thou shalt condemn. This is the heritage of the servants of the LORD, and their righteousness is of me, saith the LORD."

14) **Daniel 11:32** "And such as do wickedly against the covenant shall he corrupt by flatteries: but the people that do know their God shall be strong, and do exploits."

15) **Hosea 11:10** "They shall walk after the LORD: he shall roar like a lion: when he shall roar, then the children shall tremble from the west."

16) **Zechariah 4:6** "Then he answered and spake unto me, saying, This is the word of the LORD unto Zerubbabel, saying, Not by might, nor by power, but by my spirit, saith the LORD of hosts."

17) **Matthew 10:1** "And when He had called His twelve disciples to Him, He gave them power over unclean spirits, to cast them out, and to heal all kinds of sickness and all kinds of disease."

18) **Matthew 10:6-8** "But go rather to the lost sheep of the house of Israel. ^{7} And as ye go, preach, saying, The kingdom of heaven is at hand. ^{8} Heal the sick, cleanse the lepers, raise the dead, cast out devils: freely ye have received, freely give."

19) **Mark 6:7,13** "And he called unto him the twelve, and began to send them forth by two and two; and gave them power over unclean spirits;… And they cast out many devils, and anointed with oil many that were sick, and healed them."

20) **Mark 16:20** "And they went forth, and preached every where, the Lord working with them, and confirming the word with signs following. Amen."

21) **Luke 9:1** "Then he called his twelve disciples together, and gave them power and authority over all devils, and to cure diseases."

22) **Luke 10:19** "Behold, I give unto you power to tread on serpents and scorpions, and over all the power of the enemy: and nothing shall by any means hurt you."

23) **Acts 1:8** "But ye shall receive power, after that the Holy Ghost is come upon you: and ye shall be witnesses unto me both in Jerusalem, and in all Judaea, and in Samaria, and unto the uttermost part of the earth."

24) **Acts 2:43** "And fear came upon every soul: and many wonders and signs were done by the apostles."

25) **Acts 4:33** "And with great power gave the apostles witness of the resurrection of the Lord Jesus: and great grace was upon them all."

26) **Romans 15:19** "Through mighty signs and wonders, by the power of the Spirit of God; so that from Jerusalem, and round about unto Illyricum, I have fully preached the gospel of Christ."

27) **1 Corinthians 4:20** "For the kingdom of God is not in word, but in power."

28) **2 Corinthians 12:12** "Truly the signs of an apostle were wrought among you in all patience, in signs, and wonders, and mighty deeds."

29) **Philippians 4:13** "I can do all things through Christ which strengtheneth me."

30) **1 Thessalonians 1:5** "For our gospel came not unto you in word only, but also in power, and in the Holy Ghost, and in much assurance; as ye know what manner of men we were among you for your sake."

31) **Hebrews 2:4** "God also bearing them witness, both with signs and wonders, and with divers miracles, and gifts of the Holy Ghost, according to his own will?"

32) **1 John 2:20** "But ye have an unction from the Holy One, and ye know all things."

33) **1 John 2:27** "But the anointing which ye have received of him abideth in you, and ye need not that any man teach you: but as the same anointing teacheth you of all things, and is truth, and is no lie, and even as it hath taught you, ye shall abide in him."

Question 3: How do you feel after reading these verses out loud?

* * * * * *

TIP #15

Eliminate Wasted Thinking

1A - As we journey toward peace and happiness, we'll need to look at all the ways wasted thinking takes up room in our daily thoughts. In this Tip, we'll explore the various negative ways our mind can think. Then we'll look at ways to disarm these negative thought patterns when they come up.

1B - <u>Types of Wasted Thinking</u>

The following webpage describes 15 ways in which our thinking can be hindered. Please refer to psychcentral.com/lib/15-common-cognitive-distortions and read the introduction.

1C - <u>Filtering</u>

Please read the "Filtering" description at psychcentral.com/lib/15-common-cognitive-distortions.

1D - <u>"Filtering" in the Bible</u>

In 1Samuel 18, we see that even though the shepherd boy, David, killed a giant enemy of Israel, King Saul became angry because the boy became more famous than he.

1 Samuel 18:6-11 "came out of all cities of Israel, singing and dancing, to meet king Saul, with tabrets, with joy, and with instruments of musick. [7] And the women answered one another as they played, and said, Saul hath slain his thousands, and David his ten thousands. [8] And Saul was very wroth, and the saying displeased him; and he said, They have ascribed unto David ten thousands, and to me they have ascribed but thousands: and what can he have more but the kingdom?"

1E - "[9] And Saul eyed David from that day and forward. [10] And it came to pass on the morrow, that the evil spirit from God came upon Saul, and he prophesied in the midst of the house: and David played with his hand, as at other times: and there was a javelin in Saul's hand. [11] And Saul cast the javelin; for he said, I will smite David even to the wall with it. And David avoided out of his presence twice."

1F - <u>Saul Filtered Out the Positives</u>

David did become more famous than King Saul; however, David was not a threat to Saul's Kingdom. David was a young boy who fully loved God and the King. Saul had become David's father-in-law, so David was not a threat to King Saul; but Saul "filtered out" the positives. Saul's filtering caused him great stress in his mind, so much so that he needed David to play music to calm him down. It was a horrible existence for Saul; on one hand, he needed David to play for him, while on the other hand, he was furious with David's abilities and his fame.

1G - <u>Acknowledge Other People's Gifts</u>

Saul needed to accept David for who he was. David had developed a close relationship with God through the songs he was writing and singing while watching the sheep. He was likely meditating on what his Rabbi preached every Sabbath. He heard how Godly men should pray, praise and work, and he believed what he heard and practiced it. All of this helped transform David, a boy, into a "Giant" of a man, on the inside.

1H - <u>Saul Was Fear-Driven</u>

Saul needed to trust God that He would protect him. Instead, he let his fear of David stealing his throne, ruin his life. This burdened Saul with a lot of wasted thinking and emotional pain.

1J - <u>Conquering Filtering</u>

If we struggle with Filtering, it may be helpful to first see if fear is a root cause. If yes, then we would benefit from admitting we have a problem with fear. At this point, it would be helpful to find a couple of people we could contact when the fear begins causing us unrest. The next time our emotions are bothered, we could contact one of these people for support. See Tip #5 - Form A Support Team, for more on this. Meanwhile we could also read out loud, multiple times daily, the Affirmation #1 – I do Not Fear, as well as Core Belief #3 – I Believe God Wants Me to Live in Perfect Peace at All Times.

Noticing fear in our life, and responding to it effectively, will help us conquer Filtering.

Question 1: Can you think of an example of Filtered Thinking, or someone who has Filtered Thinking?

2A - <u>Polarized Thinking</u>

Please read the "Polarized Thinking" description at <u>psychcentral.com/lib/15-common-cognitive-distortions</u>.

2B - <u>"Polarized Thinking" In the Bible</u>

<u>The Apostles</u>

Here is a story of the disciples getting prideful with power.

Luke 9:51-55 "And it came to pass, when the time was come that he should be received up, he steadfastly set his face to go to Jerusalem, [52] And sent messengers before his face: and they went, and entered into a village of the Samaritans, to make ready for him. [53] And they did not receive him, because his face was as though he would go to Jerusalem. [54] And when his disciples James and John saw this, they said, Lord, wilt thou that we command fire to come down from heaven, and consume them, even as Elias did? [55] But he turned, and rebuked them, and said, Ye know not what manner of spirit ye are of."

2C - At this point, the disciples had become accustomed to being empowered by Jesus to heal people of diseases and the ability to cast out of evil spirits. It would appear they got carried away with that power and felt it was OK to kill these people because they were not welcoming Jesus and His disciples.

Question 2: Can you tell us a time when you got carried away with power?

3A - <u>Elijah and the Prophets of Baal</u>

Another example in the Bible of someone struggling with the effects of Polarized Thinking is the story of Elijah after he defeated the prophets of Baal.

> **1 Kings 19:13-14,18** "And it was so, when Elijah heard it, that he wrapped his face in his mantle, and went out, and stood in the entering in of the cave. And, behold, there came a voice unto him, and said, What doest thou here, Elijah? ¹⁴ And he said, I have been very jealous for the LORD God of hosts: because the children of Israel have forsaken thy covenant, thrown down thine altars, and slain thy prophets with the sword; and I, even I only, am left; and they seek my life, to take it away. ¹⁸ Yet I have left me seven thousand in Israel, all the knees which have not bowed unto Baal, and every mouth which hath not kissed him."

3B - <u>Elijah's Amazing Feat</u>

Elijah, indeed, had been busy for God, proving that the prophets of Baal (Satan) were no match for the living God. In one of the most dramatic events of a man of God, Elijah, single-handedly, humiliates and kills 450 false prophets.

3C - <u>Elijah's Depression</u>

Then remarkably, Elijah loses all faith in himself and in God, when he learned of Jezebel's anger toward him for killing all of her prophets. This unusual reaction from a mighty man of God could've occurred because he was physically exhausted after the events of the previous days. After Jezebel's threat to kill Elijah, Elijah ran for his life until he finally stopped twenty-four hours later. He then begged God to kill him.

3D - <u>Elijah's Pride</u>

After resting a couple of days, Elijah went on a 40-day journey in the wilderness. Then God spoke to him. And we find out that Elijah was full of pride as he described to God all he had been doing the previous days for God. He also thought he was the only one left who served God. God had to let him know He still had 7,000 priests who hadn't bowed the knee to Baal.

3E - <u>Tip for God's Workers</u>

All of our godly activity is good, but when it begins to make us think we are better than the next person, we need to step back and renew our humility, and remember that we are nothing without God's help in our lives.

3F - <u>Conquering Polarized Thinking</u>

If we struggle with Polarized Thinking, we could benefit from stepping back and praying about situations before reacting to them. We could benefit from reading Tip #12 – Don't Judge, Tip #25 – Collect Grace Doors, and Tip #20 – Practice Humility, as well as reading, multiple times daily, Affirmation #3 – I Flow in Harmony and Love.

Question 3: Can you tell us a time where you were experiencing some major victories in your life and how those victories drained you physically, or distorted your thinking?

Question 4: Can you think of someone who struggles with Polarized Thinking (black or white thinking)?

5A - <u>Over-Generalization</u>

Please read the "Over-Generalization" description at psychcentral.com/lib/15-common-cognitive-distortions.

5B - <u>Conquering Over-Generalization</u>

Here is an example of Over-Generalization and some possible tips to conquer it:

Let's imagine someone is preparing to learn how to drive a car, and they watch a show on television about a new driver who gets into an accident during their first time behind the wheel. The viewer might now be fearful of learning how to drive a car. To conquer that fear, they might want to check the statistics of how many people get into car accidents during their first time driving. The odds are very low. They could also begin to meditate on the truth that God wants His people to live by faith, and not by fear. They could help themselves by reading out loud, multiple times daily, Affirmation #1 – I Do Not Fear. Finally, they could get into the car, in a safe area, and boldly start learning how to drive a car. It might be difficult, but it can be done.

Question 5: Can you think of someone who struggles with Over-Generalization?

6A - <u>Jumping to Conclusions</u>

Please read the Jumping to Conclusions description at psychcentral.com/lib/15-common-cognitive-distortions.

6B - An example of someone who struggles with Jumping to Conclusions could be if we started a new friendship, and that person suddenly stops texting us and refuses to answer our calls. We could negatively assume that we have offended the other person. Later, we find out that the person had lost their cell phone, which prevented them from texting us or calling us back. Meanwhile, we would have wasted time feeling badly, and needlessly trying to figure out how we offended this person.

6C - <u>Jumping To Conclusions in the Bible</u>

In Joshua Chapter 22, the Israelites were ready to go to war with the Tribes of Reuben, Gad, and Manasseh, because they wrongly assumed that the altar they built was a sign that they were rebelling against God. Here is God's advice:

Proverbs 25:8 "Go not forth hastily to strive, lest thou know not what to do in the end thereof, when thy neighbour hath put thee to shame."

Good advice.

6D - <u>Conquering Jumping To Conclusions</u>

If we struggle with Jumping To Conclusions, we could first consider Slogan #28 - Sleep On It. Sometimes, time has a way of resolving problems.

We could also take time to reflect on the idea that we don't have to care what people think about us. If people leave our circle of friendship, there could be a good reason for it, and we don't need to know the reason; we can leave that in God's hands. We could benefit from saying, multiple times daily, Affirmation #3 – I Flow in Harmony and Love.

Question 6: Can you think of someone who wastes time jumping to conclusions?

7A - Catastrophizing

Please read the Catastrophizing description at psychcentral.com/lib/15-common-cognitive-distortions.

7B - Catastrophizing in the Bible

In Numbers Chapter 13, God told Moses to send twelve leaders of Israel, to spy out the land that God wanted the Children of Israel to own and to live in. Ten of the twelve men came back fearful, and gave bad reports.

> **Numbers 13:30-33** "We be not able to go up against the people; for they are stronger than we. [32] And they brought up an evil report of the land which they had searched unto the children of Israel, saying, The land, through which we have gone to search it, is a land that eateth up the inhabitants thereof; and all the people that we saw in it are men of a great stature. [33] And there we saw the giants, the sons of Anak, which come of the giants: and we were in our own sight as grasshoppers, and so we were in their sight."

7C - The result of having so many fearful leaders was that Israel had to wander in the wilderness 40 years! God wanted all the fearful and disobedient people to die off before helping them move into their new homeland. There can be dire consequences to being fearful!

7D - Conquering Catastrophizing

If we struggle with the habit of thinking that catastrophes are always coming our way, we need God's help to calm down. We need to realize that God is well able to prevent bad things from happening, and if He doesn't, we need to have faith that He can bring good out of any negative situation (See Romans 8:28 below). A good place to start in conquering Catastrophizing is by reading out loud, multiple times daily, Affirmation #1 – I Do Not Fear, and Tip #9 – Develop Your Faith.

> **Romans 8:28** "And we know that all things work together for good to them that love God, to them who are the called according to his purpose."

Question 7: Can you think of someone who wastes time thinking that disasters are coming their way?

8A - Personalization

Please read the Personalization description at psychcentral.com/lib/15-common-cognitive-distortions.

8B - Conquering Personalization

If we struggle with Personalization, it is helpful to realize that life does not revolve around us. We can learn to step back from a situation and not get emotionally involved in everything that goes on around us. We could also learn that it's OK to be more of an observer of life, and not feel guilty for doing so. In addition, we could realize that whatever happens to us or others around us is completely fixable by God. We can learn to give everything to God and let Him direct the events of people's lives as He sees fit, and we can learn to be OK with that. We could benefit from reading all six Affirmations multiple times daily.

Question 8: Can you think of someone who wastes time thinking and talking about a mysterious link between their lives and other people's lives (Personalization)?

9A - Control Fallacies

Please read the Control Fallacies description at psychcentral.com/lib/15-common-cognitive-distortions.

9B - Conquering Control Fallacies

If we struggle with Control Fallacies, we could realize we don't have to be controlled by other people. In the example used on the webpage, the person could have slowed down and done a better job instead of rushing through it. We could also realize that other people's happiness is not our responsibility. Reading the Affirmations, multiple times daily, would be helpful in conquering this condition, as well.

Question 9: Can you think of someone who wastes time thinking they don't measure up, or that other people's happiness is dependent on them?

10A - Types of Wasted Thinking – Fallacy of Fairness

Please read the Fallacy of Fairness description at psychcentral.com/lib/15-common-cognitive-distortions.

10B - Conquering Fallacy of Fairness

If we struggle with Fallacy of Fairness we could realize that life simply isn't fair, and that it is helpful to accept what is handed to us, and make the best of it. We could also consider that we don't need everyone around us to agree with our point of view. It can also be helpful to realize that we only have a limited understanding; and that there are many things we can learn from others. If we struggle with this, we can help ourselves by considering that we sometimes win people to our way of thinking, and sometimes we don't, and to be OK with that. We could benefit from saying, multiple times daily, Affirmation #3 – I Flow in Harmony and Love.

Question 10: Can you think of someone who wastes time thinking and talking about how unfair life is?

11A - Blaming

Please read the Blaming description at psychcentral.com/lib/15-common-cognitive-distortions.

11B - Blaming in the Bible

Below we see how Adam blamed Eve, and Eve blamed the serpent for deceiving her. Blaming got in the way of them taking responsibility for their actions.

a) **Genesis 3:11,12** "And he said, Who told thee that thou wast naked? Hast thou eaten of the tree, whereof I commanded thee that thou shouldest not eat? [12] And the man said, The woman whom thou gavest to be with me, she gave me of the tree, and I did eat."

b) **Genesis 3:13** "And the LORD God said unto the woman, What is this that thou hast done? And the woman said, The serpent beguiled me, and I did eat."

11C - Conquering Blaming

If we struggle with blaming, we could benefit by realizing that it is normal to make mistakes. We are fallible creatures. That's why we need God to help us live our lives. We could also realize that when we do make mistakes, it is good to quickly admit where we went wrong. Doing so, can give us greater respect from others when they see we are willing to accept responsibility for our mistakes. We can learn to embrace our humanity, and the grace that we need when we make mistakes. To conquer Blaming, it can be helpful to read out loud, multiple times daily, Affirmation #1 - I Do Not Fear, and Affirmation #3 - I Flow in Harmony and Love.

11D - Here are some scriptures on being quick to admit guilt.

a) **Leviticus 5:5** "And it shall be, when he shall be guilty in one of these things, that he shall confess that he hath sinned in that thing:"

b) **2 Samuel 24:10** "And David's heart smote him after that he had numbered the people. And David said unto the LORD, I have sinned greatly in that I have done: and now, I beseech thee, O LORD, take away the iniquity of thy servant; for I have done very foolishly."

Question 11: Can you think of someone who wastes time blaming others for their mistakes and their unhappiness?

12A - <u>Shoulds</u>

Please read the Shoulds description at psychcentral.com/lib/15-common-cognitive-distortions.

12B - <u>Conquering Shoulds</u>

If we struggle with Shoulds, we could benefit from realizing that God wants us to relax. God does have guidelines for us, but one of His main directives is for us not to fret. This includes, not worrying, or judging people who do not keep our list of rules. It's great that we have high expectations for ourselves and others, but we should first model such standards in our own lives. Our actions can speak *for* us. If we feel compelled to share our expectations with others, we could do it in love, gentleness, and humility. This will give us better results. We would benefit from saying, multiple times daily, Affirmation #3 – I Flow in Harmony and Love.

Question 12: Can you think of someone who wastes time being prideful about what they do, or judgmental about what other people do?

13A - <u>Emotional Reasoning</u>

Please read the Emotional Reasoning description at psychcentral.com/lib/15-common-cognitive-distortions.

13B - <u>Conquering Emotional Reasoning</u>

If we struggle with Emotional Reasoning, we could realize that feelings a fickle. They are subject to change depending on various factors, usually by our fears! Therefore we could first benefit from reading Tip #9 – Develop Your Faith, and reading, multiple times daily, Affirmation #1 – I Do Not Fear. We would also benefit from meditating on **2 Corinthians 5:7** *"We walk by faith not by sight."* A person who walks by faith doesn't pay too much attention to how things look or how they feel, they base what they want, upon God's willingness to answer prayer, and they hold on, in patience, until they receive what they've asked for. If we don't like how things feel, we change our situation, or ourselves, using our faith.

Question 13: Can you think of someone who wastes time being misdirected by feelings?

14A - <u>Fallacy of Change</u>

Please read the Fallacy of Change description at psychcentral.com/lib/15-common-cognitive-distortions.

14B - Conquering Fallacy of Change

If we struggle with Fallacy of Change, we could benefit from realizing that we can be perfectly happy even if circumstances or people around us don't change for the better. We could give people around us the grace to learn in their own time, and in their own way. We could also benefit from saying, multiple times daily, Affirmation #3 - I Flow in Harmony and Love, as well as saying Core Belief #3 – I Believe God Wants Me to Live in Perfect Peace.

Question 14: Can you think of someone who wastes time thinking of ways to make people change?

15A - Global Labeling

Please read the Global Labeling description at psychcentral.com/lib/15-common-cognitive-distortions.

15B - Conquering Global Labeling

If we struggle with Global Labeling, we could benefit from realizing we don't have to try so hard to sound impressive or make a point. We can relax and not judge. That way we can enjoy our lives, and make it enjoyable for others. We could also benefit by saying, multiple times daily, Affirmation #3 - I Flow in Harmony and Love.

Question 15: Can you think of someone who wastes time coming up with damaging comparisons and judgments – Global Labeling?

16A - Always Being Right

Please read the Always Being Right description at psychcentral.com/lib/15-common-cognitive-distortions.

16B - Conquering Always Being Right

If we struggle with always having to be right, we would benefit from realizing that as humans we all make mistakes occasionally, and thus it isn't worth getting upset over. We just have to keep trying to do our best without getting stressed out about it. We could also benefit from saying, multiple times daily, Affirmation #3 - I Flow in Harmony and Love, as well as Affirmation #1 - I Do Not Fear.

Question 16: Can you think of someone who wastes time trying to always be right?

17A - Heaven's Reward Fallacy

Please read the Heaven's Reward Fallacy description at psychcentral.com/lib/15-common-cognitive-distortions.

17B - Conquering Heaven's Reward Fallacy

If we struggle with Heaven's Reward Fallacy, we can benefit from remembering that the greatest person we could make sacrifices for is God, and that we can't "out-give" God. Eventually, He will reward us. We can ask God to help us keep our eyes on Him, and do all things for God, rather than having our eyes on others and doing things for them.

Question 17: Can you think of someone who wastes time expecting approval from people and working overly hard to get it?

18A - <u>Other Kinds of Wasted Thinking</u>

<u>Appearance</u>

A lot of advertising is focused around people's looks. It is natural to want to present ourselves in the best way possible; and it can also be enjoyable. The problem comes in when we obsess about our looks. Any thinking that goes beyond basic, everyday grooming could be wasted thinking. Questions we can ask ourselves can include: Do I dislike anything about my looks? Do I spend time thinking about how to change the features of my looks? Is my value as a person dependent on my looks? Am I focused on these features because I feel people will like me more if I change them? If we answer yes to any of these questions, we might want to work on resolving this issue in our lives.

18B - <u>The Unimportance of Appearance in the Bible</u>

The following are Bible verses that teach that, in God's eyes, a person's looks is unimportant. Notice what attribute *is* important, is having a loving heart.

a) **1 Samuel 16:7** "But the LORD said unto Samuel, Look not on his countenance, or on the height of his stature; because I have refused him: for the LORD seeth not as man seeth; for man looketh on the outward appearance, but the LORD looketh on the heart."

b) **Proverbs 31:30** "Favour is deceitful, and beauty is vain: but a woman that feareth the LORD, she shall be praised."

c) **1 Peter 3:3,4** "Whose adorning let it not be that outward adorning of plaiting the hair, and of wearing of gold, or of putting on of apparel; ⁴But let it be the hidden man of the heart, in that which is not corruptible, even the ornament of a meek and quiet spirit, which is in the sight of God of great price."

18C – Below, are scriptures about our immense value, just the way we are.

a) **Psalm 139:13,14** "For thou hast possessed my reins: thou hast covered me in my mother's womb. ¹⁴I will praise thee; for I am fearfully and wonderfully made: marvellous are thy works; and that my soul knoweth right well."

b) **Isaiah 43:4** "Since thou wast precious in my sight, thou hast been honourable, and I have loved thee: therefore will I give men for thee, and people for thy life."

c) **Luke 12:7** "But even the very hairs of your head are all numbered. Fear not therefore: ye are of more value than many sparrows."

Question 18: Can you think of someone who wastes time thinking about how to improve their looks?

19A - <u>Income Ability</u>

Sometimes we dislike ourselves because we feel we don't earn enough money. It's natural to want to earn enough money to meet all of our financial needs. The problem comes in when we obsess about how to make more and more money. Some questions to ask ourselves might be: Is my value as a person dependent on my income? Do I dislike myself because I cannot earn enough money? Would the extra money I earn be spent on things I don't need? If we answered yes to any of these questions, we might want to work on resolving this issue in our lives. Here are some Bible verses to consider.

a) **Luke 3:14** "And the soldiers likewise demanded of him, saying, And what shall we do? And he said unto them, Do violence to no man, neither accuse any falsely; and be content with your wages."

b) **1 Timothy 6:6** "But godliness with contentment is great gain."

c) **2 Timothy 2:4** "No man that warreth entangleth himself with the affairs of this life; that he may please him who hath chosen him to be a soldier."

Question 19: Can you think of someone who wastes time thinking of ways to earn more money?

20A - <u>Our Spouse</u>

Sometimes we waste time being upset at our spouse. We don't realize we have the ability to help our spouse become a great person. We also may not realize we have the power to love our spouse in spite of past conflicts we've had with them, as well as, in spite of existing weaknesses they might have. Some questions to ask ourselves might be: Do I spend time being angry with my spouse? Do I spend time looking at other people and wish they were my spouse? Do I think I am too good for my spouse? If we answered yes to any of these questions, we might want to work on resolving this issue in your life.

Question 20: Can you think of someone who wastes time being judgmental toward their spouse?

21A - <u>Addiction</u>

Sometimes we develop addictions that cause us to waste time thinking about how to get our next fix. Addictions can be conquered. The Victory Tips Program can help in conquering an addiction. We have a short Tip on conquering an addiction, #23. Our daily telephone support calls can also help in conquering an addiction.

Question 21: Can you think of someone who wastes time thinking about how and when to get their next fix?

22A - The bottom line is that God wants us to live with peace of mind. We should never settle for a mind that is tossed to and fro with the cares of life. We can learn how to tame our mind and live in peace.

* * * * * * *

Tip #16

Develop a Disciplined Lifestyle

1A - The essence of discipline is denying ourselves things of low value to gain something of greater value. Few great things in life are accomplished without discipline. Every athlete will tell you it took discipline of diet, exercise and practice to become good at what they do. Every successful business person will tell you it took long hours and hard work to get to where they got in the business world. Discipline is a key ingredient to living a successful life.

Question 1: Can you think of a person who is successful and disciplined? If so, can you tell us in what way they are disciplined?

2A - <u>Bible Verses on Being Disciplined and Self-Controlled</u>

a) **Galatians 5:22-23** "But the fruit of the Spirit is love, joy, peace, longsuffering, gentleness, goodness, faith, Meekness, temperance (self-control): against such there is no law."

b) **1 Thessalonians 5:6** "Therefore let us not sleep, as do others; but let us watch and be sober."

c) **Titus 1:8** *(a bishop)* But a lover of hospitality, a lover of good men, sober, just, holy, temperate;"

d) **1 Peter 1:13** "Wherefore gird up the loins of your mind, be sober, and hope to the end for the grace that is to be brought unto you at the revelation of Jesus Christ;"

e) **1 Peter 5:8** "Be sober, be vigilant; because your adversary the devil, as a roaring lion, walketh about, seeking whom he may devour:"

Question 2: Can you recall anyone in your life who taught you to be disciplined? If so, what did they say to you?

3A - Following, are instructions Paul gave to Titus on how Christians should live. Much of it relates to being disciplined.

<u>Discipline Tips for Older Men</u>

Titus 2:2 "That the aged men be sober, grave, temperate, sound in faith, in charity, in patience."

3B - Discipline Tips for Older and Younger Women

Titus 2:3-5 "The aged women likewise, that they be in behaviour as becometh holiness, not false accusers, not given to much wine, teachers of good things; ⁴That they may teach the young women to be sober, to love their husbands, to love their children, ⁵To be discreet, chaste, keepers at home, good, obedient to their own husbands, that the word of God be not blasphemed."

3C - Discipline Tips for Young Men

Titus 2:6-8 "Young men likewise exhort to be sober minded. ⁷In all things shewing thyself a pattern of good works: in doctrine shewing uncorruptness, gravity, sincerity, ⁸sound speech, that cannot be condemned; that he that is of the contrary part may be ashamed, having no evil thing to say of you."

3D - Discipline Tips for Employees

a) **Titus 2:9** "Teach slaves to be subject to their masters in everything, to try to please them, not to talk back to them, but to show that they can be fully trusted, so that they will make the teaching about God our saviour attractive."

b) **Ephesians 6:5-8** "Servants, be obedient to them that are your masters according to the flesh, with fear and trembling, in singleness of your heart, as unto Christ; ⁶Not with eyeservice, as menpleasers; but as the servants of Christ, doing the will of God from the heart; ⁷With good will doing service, as to the Lord, and not to men: ⁸Knowing that whatsoever good thing any man doeth, the same shall he receive of the Lord, whether he be bond or free."

3E - Discipline and Children

Another aspect of life requiring discipline is in the area of raising children. The following verses talk about the need to "punish" (discipline) our children when they do wrong, demonstrating that true love must sometimes be tough.

a) **Proverbs 13:24** "He that spareth his rod hateth his son: but he that loveth him chasteneth him betimes."

b) **Proverbs 19:18** "Chasten thy son while there is hope, and let not thy soul spare for his crying."

c) **Proverbs 23:13** "Withhold not correction from the child: for if thou beatest him with the rod, he shall not die."

d) **Proverbs 29:17** "Correct thy son, and he shall give thee rest; yea, he shall give delight unto thy soul."

Question 3: Can you think of anyone's children who would benefit from better discipline? If so, how are they trying to discipline their children presently?

4A - Discipline and Diet

a) **Proverbs 23:21** "For the drunkard and the glutton shall come to poverty: and drowsiness shall clothe a man with rags."

b) **Philippians 3:19** "Whose end is destruction, whose God is their belly, and whose glory is in their shame, who mind earthly things."

Question 4: Can you think of someone who would benefit from being disciplined in the area of diet?

5A - Discipline and Exercise

With factories becoming more automated and people spending more time online, the general population is reducing the amount of physical activity they do. Yet, the human body was made to do manual labor, to be physically fit. Physical work and exercise, develops muscles, accelerates the heart, and clears the mind. Not prioritizing physical activity can place a person at risk of premature death, due to high blood pressure, heart disease, obesity, and other silent killers. It also puts a person at risk of injury, due to occasional over-exertion.

Below, are some scriptures about maintaining our physical bodies.

a) **Proverbs 24:5** "A wise man is strong; yea, a man of knowledge increaseth strength."

b) **Proverbs 31:17** "She girdeth her loins with strength, and strengtheneth her arms."

c) **Isaiah 40:31** "But they that wait upon the Lord shall renew their strength; they shall mount up with wings as eagles; they shall run, and not be weary; and they shall walk, and not faint."

d) **Romans 12:1** "I beseech you therefore, brethren, by the mercies of God, that ye present your bodies a living sacrifice, holy, acceptable unto God, which is your reasonable service."

e) **1 Corinthians 6:19,20** "What? know ye not that your body is the temple of the Holy Ghost which is in you, which ye have of God, and ye are not your own? ^{20} For ye are bought with a price: therefore glorify God in your body, and in your spirit, which are God's."

f) **1 Corinthians 9:27** "But I keep under my body, and bring it into subjection: lest that by any means, when I have preached to others, I myself should be a castaway."

g) **1 Corinthians 10:31** "Whether therefore ye eat, or drink, or whatsoever ye do, do all to the glory of God."

Question 5: Can you think of someone who would benefit from an exercise program?

6A - Jesus Chose Disciples

When Jesus walked the earth, He chose for Himself, twelve disciples. The word "disciple" is the root word, for the word "discipline."

6B - An Analogy of Discipline in Nature

A nicely landscaped yard got that way because someone took the time to get rid of weeds, trim the bushes, plant beautiful flowers, and so on. All of this took time and hard work, but in the end it makes for a beautiful yard. So too with mental well-being; it can take effort to identify and uproot wrong beliefs and replace them with proper, life-giving beliefs. But in due time, a happy, peaceful life will emerge and be a joy for the person, and for those around them.

Question 6: In what way can you see yourself improving your self-discipline?

* * * * * * *

Tip #17

Develop a Lifestyle of Holiness

According as he hath chosen us in him before the foundation of the world, that we should be holy and without blame before him in love: Ephesians 1:4

1A - The central theme of the Bible is to show us how to have a relationship with God and the forgiveness we need through our Lord Jesus Christ. In the Old Testament, we read about God's high standards for daily living. They were so high that no one was able to achieve it. People sinned. The only thing that could pay the penalty for sin was blood. Thus, in the Old Testament God instructed His people to sacrifice animals once a year to pay for the sins of the people.

1B - Then a better sacrifice came, the Lord Jesus Christ. Two thousand years ago, the blood of a sinless man, Jesus Christ, was spilled, to pay the penalty for the sin of all of humanity. It was a horrendous day - but a monumental day, the day Jesus allowed Himself to be nailed to a cross. Because of Jesus, we can trade our sin nature for a new nature. Thank God for Jesus!

1C - Why did Jesus have to die? Why did animals have to die? Because of sin.

If sin is so terrible that it cost the lives of numerous animals, and the life of a perfect human being - Jesus Christ, shouldn't we be living holy lives? Absolutely.

The problem is that living holy lives rarely comes up in people's minds. Most people end up living half-hearted, semi-holy lives. This kind of lifestyle can become a hindrance to our happiness.

1D - We should understand, however, that our motive for living a holy life is not so that we can *buy* ourselves a place in heaven after we die. The Bible says that our best works are like filthy rags in God's sight (See Isaiah 64:6 below). Our good works could never be good enough to save our souls. We need the sacrifice of Jesus to cleanse our souls of sin.

Isaiah 64:6 "But we are all as an unclean thing, and all our righteousnesses are as filthy rags; and we all do fade as a leaf; and our iniquities, like the wind, have taken us away."

1E - Our holy living is a bi-product of living a life connected with God.

God is very gracious. He has an end goal for us to achieve, as far as holy living is concerned; however, He also extends grace to those who are just starting their Christian walk, and have difficulties in their behavior. God understands the challenges that people have to work through before they develop a life of holiness. Thus, for most people change happens gradually.

1F - Our reason for living a holy life is to honor God for saving our souls, and to be an example to others.

Also, a holy life helps us to share the good news of Jesus's sacrifice more effectively.

Do you care what God cares about? God cares about people, people who need to hear the Gospel of Jesus Christ. Thus, He needs faithful people willing to let Him live His life through them. It is an amazing experience. Are you one of these people? Then, consider developing a lifestyle of holiness.

Question 1: Have you ever considered the importance of living a holy life?

2A - At this point, it is important to outline what a Christian should do if they sin. Eventually, we will all miss the mark in trying to live a God-honoring life. When this happens, we need to come to God in humility, and confess our sin, and ask Him to forgive us, based on the sacrifice Jesus made, for us, on the cross. See the verse below.

1 John 1:9 "If we confess our sins, he is faithful and just to forgive us our sins, and to cleanse us from all unrighteousness."

By faith, we receive our forgiveness, and we go on. We should also take steps, to prevent us from falling into that same sin again. Otherwise, it becomes a habit or an addiction. With the right support and direction, we can learn to overcome our negative behaviors. (See Tip #23 – Conquer The Addiction, for more on this.)

Question 2: Have you developed the habit of going straight to God for His forgiveness, and for His help in the weak areas of your life?

3A - Below are some verses about God's ultimate goal for us relating to holy living.

a) **2 Timothy 1:9** "Who hath saved us, and called us with an holy calling, not according to our works, but according to his own purpose and grace, which was given us in Christ Jesus before the world began,"

b) **2 Timothy 2:19** "Nevertheless the foundation of God standeth sure, having this seal, The Lord knoweth them that are his. And, let every one that nameth the name of Christ depart from iniquity."

c) **Titus 1:7-8** "For a bishop must be blameless, as the steward of God; not selfwilled, not soon angry, not given to wine, no striker, not given to filthy lucre; But a lover of hospitality, a lover of good men, sober, just, holy, temperate (self-controlled);"

d) **Titus 2:12** "Teaching us that, denying ungodliness and worldly lusts, we should live soberly, righteously, and godly, in this present world;"

e) **James 1:19,20** "Wherefore, my beloved brethren, let every man be swift to hear, slow to speak, slow to wrath: [20] For the wrath of man worketh not the righteousness of God."

f) **James 1:21** "Wherefore lay apart all filthiness and superfluity of naughtiness, and receive with meekness the engrafted word, which is able to save your souls."

g) **1 Peter 2:11** "Dearly beloved, I beseech you as strangers and pilgrims, abstain from fleshly lusts, which war against the soul;"

h) **2 Peter 3:11** "Seeing then that all these things shall be dissolved, what manner of persons ought ye to be in all holy conversation and godliness,"

Question 3: Is God asking for too much of His people, to live upright lives?

4A - <u>Verses Relating to Purity</u>

a) **1 Tim 5:1-2** "Rebuke not an elder, but intreat him as a father; and the younger men as brethren; The elder women as mothers; the younger as sisters, with all purity."

b) **1 Tim 5:20,22** "Them that sin rebuke before all, that others also may fear. ^{22} Lay hands suddenly on no man, neither be partaker of other men's sins: keep thyself pure."

c) **1 Peter 1:22** "Seeing ye have purified your souls in obeying the truth through the Spirit unto unfeigned love of the brethren, see that ye love one another with a pure heart fervently:"

Question 4: Do you think you might like the challenge of trying to live a pure life?

5A - <u>Knowledge Can Help Us Stay Pure</u>

Proverbs 2:11 "Discretion shall preserve thee, understanding shall keep thee:"

<u>The Bible Talks About Our "Old Self" and Our "New Self"</u>

a) **Galatians 5:24** "And they that are Christ's have crucified the flesh with the affections and lusts."

b) **Colossians 3:9-10** "Lie not one to another, seeing that ye have put off the old man with his deeds; ^{10} And have put on the new man, which is renewed in knowledge after the image of him that created him:"

c) **1 Peter 1:14-16** "As obedient children, not fashioning yourselves according to the former lusts in your ignorance: ^{15} But as he which hath called you is holy, so be ye holy in all manner of conversation; ^{16} Because it is written, Be ye holy; for I am holy."

d) **2 Timothy 2:21** "If a man therefore purge himself from these, he shall be a vessel unto honour, sanctified, and meet for the master's use, and prepared unto every good work."

5B - <u>Verses on the Lusts of the Flesh</u>

a) **Romans 13:14** "But put ye on the Lord Jesus Christ, and make not provision for the flesh, to fulfil the lusts thereof."

b) **Galatians 5:16** "This I say then, Walk in the Spirit, and ye shall not fulfil the lust of the flesh."

5C - <u>Verses on Sexual Purity</u>

a) **Proverbs 5:20** "And why wilt thou, my son, be ravished with a strange woman, and embrace the bosom of a stranger?"

b) **Ephesians 5:3** "But fornication, and all uncleanness, or covetousness, let it not be once named among you, as becometh saints;"

c) **Colossians 5:5,6** "Mortify therefore your members which are upon the earth; fornication, uncleanness, inordinate affection, evil concupiscence, and covetousness, which is idolatry: ⁶ For which things' sake the wrath of God cometh on the children of disobedience:"

d) **1 Thessalonians 4:3-7** "For this is the will of God, even your sanctification, that ye should abstain from fornication: ⁴ That every one of you should know how to possess his vessel in sanctification and honour; ⁵ Not in the lust of concupiscence, even as the Gentiles which know not God: ⁶ That no man go beyond and defraud his brother in any matter: because that the Lord is the avenger of all such, as we also have forewarned you and testified. ⁷ For God hath not called us unto uncleanness, but unto holiness."

Question 5: Do you know someone who has a problem with sexual purity?

6A - <u>Shame is Associated with Sin</u>

Ephesians 5:12 "For it is a shame even to speak of those things which are done of them in secret."

Question 6: Have you experienced shame with some of the things you've done?

7A - <u>Holy Living Includes Holy Speaking</u> (For more on this, see Tip #7 – Speak Right Words)

a) **Ephesians 5:4** "Nor should there be obscenity, foolish talk or coarse joking, which are out of place, but rather thanksgiving."

b) **James 1:26** "If any man among you seem to be religious, and bridleth not his tongue, but deceiveth his own heart, this man's religion is vain."

c) **1 Peter 3:10-11** "For he that will love life, and see good days, let him refrain his tongue from evil, and his lips that they speak no guile: ¹¹ Let him eschew evil, and do good; let him seek peace, and ensue it."

Question 7: Do you know anyone whose speech needs to be improved?

8A - <u>Reckless Living Can Prevent Us From Getting To Heaven</u>

a) **Ephesians 5:5-7** "For this ye know, that no whoremonger, nor unclean person, nor covetous man, who is an idolater, hath any inheritance in the kingdom of Christ and of God. ⁶ Let no man deceive you with vain words: for because of these things cometh the wrath of God upon the children of disobedience. ⁷ Be not ye therefore partakers with them."

b) **Hebrews 12:14** "Follow peace with all men, and holiness, without which no man shall see the Lord:"

Question 8: Is spending eternity with God in heaven something you want, and worth living holy for?

9A - <u>We are a Light With Holy Lives</u>

Ephesians 5:8-10 "For ye were sometimes darkness, but now are ye light in the Lord: walk as children of light: [9] (For the fruit of the Spirit is in all goodness and righteousness and truth;) [10] Proving what is acceptable unto the Lord."

9B - We should keep our minds on good things.

Colossians 3: 1-3 "If ye then be risen with Christ, seek those things which are above, where Christ sitteth on the right hand of God. [2] Set your affection on things above, not on things on the earth. [3] For ye are dead, and your life is hid with Christ in God."

Question 9: What are good ways to help keep our minds on good things?

10A - <u>Develop these Traits</u>

a) **Colossians 3:12** "Put on therefore, as the elect of God, holy and beloved, bowels of mercies, kindness, humbleness of mind, meekness, longsuffering;"

b) **1 Timothy 2:15** "Notwithstanding she shall be saved in childbearing, if they continue in faith and charity and holiness with sobriety."

c) **2 Timothy 2:22** "Flee also youthful lusts: but follow righteousness, faith, charity, peace, with them that call on the Lord out of a pure heart."

d) **Titus 2:2** "That the aged men be sober, grave, temperate, sound in faith, in charity, in patience."

e) **Titus 2:3-5** "The aged women likewise, that they be in behaviour as becometh holiness, not false accusers, not given to much wine, teachers of good things; [4] That they may teach the young women to be sober, to love their husbands, to love their children, [5] To be discreet, chaste, keepers at home, good, obedient to their own husbands, that the word of God be not blasphemed."

f) **Titus 2:6-8** "Young men likewise exhort to be sober minded. [7] In all things shewing thyself a pattern of good works: in doctrine shewing uncorruptness, gravity, sincerity, [8] Sound speech, that cannot be condemned; that he that is of the contrary part may be ashamed, having no evil thing to say of you."

g) **2 Peter 1:5-9** "And beside this, giving all diligence, add to your faith virtue; and to virtue knowledge; [6] And to knowledge temperance; and to temperance patience; and to patience godliness; [7] And to godliness brotherly kindness; and to brotherly kindness charity. [8] For if these things be in you, and abound, they make you that ye shall neither be barren nor unfruitful in the knowledge of our Lord Jesus Christ. [9] But he that lacketh these things is blind, and cannot see afar off, and hath forgotten that he was purged from his old sins."

Question 10: Which of these traits seem appealing to you? How would you develop them?

Tip #16 – Develop a Lifestyle of Holiness

11A - <u>Live a Life Worthy of God</u>

- a) **Colossians 1:10** "That ye might walk worthy of the Lord unto all pleasing, being fruitful in every good work, and increasing in the knowledge of God;"

- b) **1 Thessalonians 2:11,12** "As ye know how we exhorted and comforted and charged every one of you, as a father doth his children, [12] That ye would walk worthy of God, who hath called you unto his kingdom and glory."

- c) **2 Thessalonians 1:5** "Which is a manifest token of the righteous judgment of God, that ye may be counted worthy of the kingdom of God, for which ye also suffer:"

- d) **2 Thessalonians 1:11** "Wherefore also we pray always for you, that our **God** would count you **worthy** of this calling, and fulfil all the good pleasure of his goodness, and the work of faith with power:"

11B - <u>Live Blameless Lives</u>

- a) **Proverbs 20:7** "The just man walketh in his integrity: his children are blessed after him."

- b) **1 Thessalonians 3:13** "To the end he may stablish your hearts unblameable in holiness before God, even our Father, at the coming of our Lord Jesus Christ with all his saints."

- c) **1 Thessalonians 5:21-23** "Prove all things; hold fast that which is good. [22] Abstain from all appearance of evil. [23] And the very God of peace sanctify you wholly; and I pray God your whole spirit and soul and body be preserved blameless unto the coming of our Lord Jesus Christ."

- d) **2 Peter 3:14** "Wherefore, beloved, seeing that ye look for such things, be diligent that ye may be found of him in peace, without spot, and blameless."

Question 11: Striving for a blameless life can seem like a daunting task. How do you feel about this?

12A - <u>Our Good Life is a Testimony to Others</u>

- a) **2 Corinthians 9:13** "Whiles by the experiment of this ministration they glorify God for your professed subjection unto the gospel of Christ, and for your liberal distribution unto them, and unto all men;"

- b) **1 Peter 2:12** "But these, as natural brute beasts, made to be taken and destroyed, speak evil of the things that they understand not; and shall utterly perish in their own corruption;"

12B - An effective way to attain and maintain holy living is by memorizing scripture, then speaking it to ourselves throughout our day. Contact us for computer files that can be used to print Bible verse cards to help with this.

* * * * * * *

Tip #18

Become an Optimist

1A - Can you think of someone who is always optimistic? Is that a good way to be? In this Tip, we will learn how optimism relates to the Christian life. The definition of **optimism** in the Merriam-Webster dictionary is: *"The tendency to be hopeful and to emphasize or think of the good part in a situation rather than the bad part, or the feeling that in the future good things are more likely to happen than bad things:"*

Question 1: In general, what is your level of optimism?

2A - Below, are some quotes on optimism.

a) "Optimism is the faith that leads to achievement. Nothing can be done without hope and confidence." – Helen Keller

b) "One of the things I learned the hard way was that it doesn't pay to get discouraged. Keeping busy and making optimism a way of life can restore your faith in yourself." – Lucille Ball

c) "Be fanatically positive and militantly optimistic. If something is not to your liking, change your liking." – Rick Steves

d) "A healthy attitude is contagious but don't wait to catch it from others. Be a carrier." – Author Unknown

Question 2: What thoughts come to your mind after reading the above quotes on optimism?

3A - The Book of Galatians give an overview of the character traits of people who follow Christ. Some burst with optimism, others not so readily at first glance. Let's see how they relate.

Galatians 5:22,23 "But the fruit of the Spirit is love, joy, peace, longsuffering, gentleness, goodness, faith, [23] Meekness, temperance: against such there is no law."

3B - **Love** – An optimistic person loves people. No matter what the person has done, they still love them. They believe that person will improve when they are treated with love, so they step out in faith to love them. They may not *trust* them immediately, but they show good faith by associating with them and offering them unconditional love.

3C - **Joy** – An optimistic person has joy. They believe the best is yet to come. They have confidence in God's blessings upon their life, and they have confidence in themselves that they can do all things through Christ. They have seen how circumstances and people have turned around because of their joy, so they continually operate in joy. Circumstances may challenge their joy but they swerve around them and keep right on going.

Question 3: How does your optimism show forth in love and joy?

4A - **Peace** – An optimistic person has peace. They believe God has everything in control. They know God blesses those who live righteous lives, and they have peace knowing that there is no sin blocking them from God's flow of blessings. If they do sin, they know they can quickly repent of it, and, once again, live in a state of peace and favor in God's kingdom. Their optimism gives them peace!

4B - **Longsuffering** (Patience) – An optimistic person is patient. They believe in God's ability to help them do everything at the right time. They are busy, but at the same time they are at rest on the inside, trusting God. If things slow them down, they don't get flustered, they look at it as an opportunity to learn from the hindrance, or to help someone in need at that moment. Their optimism gives them peace as they wait.

4C - **Gentleness** – An optimistic person is gentle. They know the valuable truth Jesus taught, *"And as ye would that men should do to you, do ye also to them likewise."* (**Luke 6:31**) They know that people respond better to gentleness than to aggression, so they model gentleness. Gentleness is a hallmark of maturity, and it keeps the social atmosphere happier.

Question 4: How does your optimism show forth in peace, patience, and gentleness?

5A - **Goodness** – Two definitions of good or goodness is 'honorable' and 'favorable.' Optimism can feed both of these attributes for the optimistic person. Optimism attracts honor and favor. Optimists "raise the bar" of what is possible and causes people to see challenges in a different light, giving the optimist increased honor and favor. This helps spur growth and advancement. Optimists feed their spirit with God's Word, which saturates them with goodness. This sets them apart from others.

5B - **Faith** – An optimistic person naturally operates in an atmosphere of faith. Their positive disposition draws blessings toward them. Now, give a natural optimist teaching on biblical faith, and you have a person who is unstoppable. They know that big problems are no match for them and God, and they boldly embrace challenges until their desired goal is achieved. The optimist, with faith, stands in a league of their own.

Question 5: How does your optimism show forth in goodness and faith?

6A - **Meekness** – The Merriam-Webster dictionary defines meekness as: *"enduring injury with patience and without resentment."* An optimistic person knows there is value in suffering and does not shy away from it. They know that some of humanities greatest feats have come from great suffering. To the optimist, not a second of God's grace is lost in the midst of life's challenges. They endure with patience for as long as it takes, and always without resentment.

6B - **Temperance** (Self-control) – An optimistic person has good self-control. They know it is wise to forego a small pleasure now to reap a great blessing in the future. They know how easy it is for someone to <u>react</u> to a problem and further complicate their problems. An optimist's self-control protects them. They respond rather than react. Self-control is their best investment for a bright future, and they guard it well.

Question 6: How does your optimism show forth in meekness and temperance?

7A - <u>Optimism in the Bible</u>

<u>Taking the Promised Land</u>

In Tip #15 – Eliminate Wasted Thinking, we saw how ten of the twelve Israelite leaders said they could not beat the giants in a war to take the Promised Land that God had given them (Numbers Chapter 13). The other two, Joshua and Caleb, said, they were well able to beat the giants. Below, is Caleb's appeal to go in and take the land.

> **Numbers 11:30** "And Caleb stilled the people before Moses, and said, Let us go up at once, and possess it; for we are well able to overcome it."

7B - Joshua and Caleb were optimistic, the others were pessimistic. Because the pessimistic people persuaded the others to hold back, all of Israel had to wander in the wilderness for 40 years until the pessimistic people all died. Associating with well-meaning, pessimistic people can bring problems in our lives.

Question 7: Can you think of pessimistic people in your life who are negatively affecting you? What do you think of reducing your contact with them?

8A - <u>The Optimism of David</u>

In Tip #14 – Develop a Conqueror Mentality, we talked about the shepherd boy, David, finding out about the giant, Goliath, how he was taunting the Israelite army. David became bold and spoke the following words.

> **1 Samuel 17:43-47** "And the Philistine said unto David, Am I a dog, that thou comest to me with staves (wooden staff)? And the Philistine cursed David by his gods. [44] And the Philistine said to David, Come to me, and I will give thy flesh unto the fowls of the air, and to the beasts of the field."

8B - [45] Then said David to the Philistine, Thou comest to me with a sword, and with a spear, and with a shield: but I come to thee in the name of the LORD of hosts, the God of the armies of Israel, whom thou hast defied. [46] This day will the LORD deliver thee into mine hand; and I will smite thee, and take thine head from thee; and I will give the carcases of the host of the Philistines this day unto the fowls of the air, and to the wild beasts of the earth; that all the earth may know that there is a God in Israel. [47] And all this assembly shall know that the LORD saveth not with sword and spear: for the battle is the LORD's, and he will give you into our hands."

8C - Sure enough, David killed Goliath, and everyone was amazed at his feat of power, as well as his faith in God. David was optimistic; everyone else was pessimistic. David's optimism attracted God's power in his life and helped him defeat Goliath.

Question 8: Can you think of a "giant" in your life that God is waiting to help you conquer?

9A - <u>Healing the Lame Man</u>

In Acts Chapter 3, scripture records the story of the apostle Peter healing the lame man at the temple.

Acts 3:1-9 "Now Peter and John went up together into the temple at the hour of prayer, being the ninth hour. ² And a certain man lame from his mother's womb was carried, whom they laid daily at the gate of the temple which is called Beautiful, to ask alms of them that entered into the temple; ³ Who seeing Peter and John about to go into the temple asked an alms."

9B - ⁴ And Peter, fastening his eyes upon him with John, said, Look on us. ⁵ And he gave heed unto them, expecting to receive something of them. ⁶ Then Peter said, Silver and gold have I none; but such as I have give I thee: In the name of Jesus Christ of Nazareth rise up and walk. ⁷ And he took him by the right hand, and lifted him up: and immediately his feet and ankle bones received strength. ⁸ And he leaping up stood, and walked, and entered with them into the temple, walking, and leaping, and praising God.⁹ And all the people saw him walking and praising God:"

9C - Peter was boldly optimistic that God would heal the paralytic man.

Peter and John had received extraordinary power from God to start the Christian church. The miracles were evidence that God was with the apostle's, to prove that their message about Jesus Christ was true.

Question 9: Is there a ministry that God wants you to start, for which you need His help?

10A - In Acts Chapter 16, we see how praising God caused Paul and Silas to be freed from prison.

Acts 16:18-26 "And this did she many days. But Paul, being grieved, turned and said to the spirit, I command thee in the name of Jesus Christ to come out of her. And he came out the same hour. ¹⁹ And when her masters saw that the hope of their gains was gone, they caught Paul and Silas, and drew them into the marketplace unto the rulers, ²⁰ And brought them to the magistrates, saying, These men, being Jews, do exceedingly trouble our city, ²¹ And teach customs, which are not lawful for us to receive, neither to observe, being Romans."

10B - ²² And the multitude rose up together against them: and the magistrates rent off their clothes, and commanded to beat them. ²³ And when they had laid many stripes upon them, they cast them into prison, charging the jailor to keep them safely: ²⁴ Who, having received such a charge, thrust them into the inner prison, and made their feet fast in the stocks. ²⁵ And at midnight Paul and Silas prayed, and sang praises unto God: and the prisoners heard them. ²⁶ And suddenly there was a great earthquake, so that the foundations of the prison were shaken: and immediately all the doors were opened, and every one's bands were loosed."

10C - Paul and Silas chose to be optimistic and praised God while they suffered for His name, and God miraculously freed them from prison.

Question 10: Is there a problem in your life in which God wants you to be optimistic and praise Him in?

11A - <u>Ways to Become an Optimist</u>

<u>Speak Your Way to Optimism</u>

The Bible says in **Romans 4:17** *"(As it is written, I have made thee a father of many nations,) before him whom he believed, even God, who quickeneth the dead, <u>and calleth those things which be not as though they were</u>."*

11B - This principle of speaking things into existence, shows us that when we pray for something, we can help it along by speaking faith-affirming words that depict the item we want, has already come into existence. That's what God does – He speaks things into existence. So, we can start saying:

- a) My life is great.
- b) My job is great.
- c) My spouse is great.
- d) My church is great.
- e) My pastor is great.
- f) My apt (or house) is great.
- g) My school is great.
- h) My teachers are great.
- i) My parents are great.
- j) My siblings are great.
- k) My neighbors are great.
- l) My vehicle is great.
- m) My job search is great.
- n) My city has great employers.
- o) My public transportation is great.

11C - All of these statements can be true when we compare them with other people's experience.

Our words can have a significant influence on our beliefs. Our beliefs are important because they influence our automatic thinking. With positive beliefs, our minds automatically think positive. For more on this principle, read Tip #7 - Speak Right Words.

Question 11: Do you speak positive words to improve optimism in your life?

12A - <u>Be Thankful</u>

Another way to maintain optimism is by being thankful.

For example, when we consider everything we do with the help of modern appliances, we can be thankful for each appliance. Below are a few verses on being thankful. For more information on gratitude, read Tip #25 – Be Thankful.

- a) **Psalm 107:1** "O give thanks unto the LORD, for [he is] good: for his mercy [endureth] for ever."
- b) **Ephesians 5:20** "Giving thanks always for all things unto God and the Father in the name of our Lord Jesus Christ;"
- c) **Colossians 3:15** "And let the peace of God rule in your hearts, to the which also ye are called in one body; and be ye thankful."
- d) **1 Thessalonians 5:18** "In every thing give thanks: for this is the will of God in Christ Jesus concerning you."

Question 12: What are you in the habit of being thankful for?

13A - <u>Make Friends with Optimists</u>

The Bible has a lot to say about the people we associate with. Below are some verses about relationships.

a) **Proverbs 1:10** "My son, if sinners entice thee, consent thou not."

b) **Proverbs 13:20** "He that walketh with wise [men] shall be wise: but a companion of fools shall be destroyed."

c) **Proverbs 14:7** "Go from the presence of a foolish man, when thou perceivest not [in him] the lips of knowledge."

d) **Proverbs 22:24-25** "Make no friendship with an angry man; and with a furious man thou shalt not go: ^{25} Lest thou learn his ways, and get a snare to thy soul."

e) **1 Corinthians 15:33** "Be not deceived: evil communications corrupt good manners."

Question 13: Can you think of any optimistic people you could get to know more?

Question 14: What do you think of making optimism something to strive for in your life?

* * * * * *

TIP #19

Eliminate Anger

1A - Anger is a definite hindrance to happiness. Many of us have triggers that bring on our anger. It is helpful to take time to assess the root causes of our anger and learn how to disarm it.

In a June 29, 2017 article in Time Magazine entitled, "The Rage Flu - Why All This Anger is Contagious and Making Us Sick, Dr. Gary Slutkin, founder of Cure Violence, and a faculty member of the University of Illinois at Chicago is quoted as saying *"Violence and violent speech meet the criteria of disease... Like a virus, violence makes more of itself. Rage begets more rage. And it spreads because we humans are wired to follow our peers."*

1B - The author of the magazine article, Susanna Schrobsdorff, adds that *"...if extreme speech becomes acceptable in one realm, it's likely to spread to overlapping realms – from the dinner table, to social feeds, to a political demonstration. ...And for the more vulnerable, those who are mentally unstable or disenfranchised, this sickness can lead to actual violence directed at the person or institution that symbolizes their disappointment."* Ms. Schrobsdorff also quotes Dr. Slutkin as saying *"Undesirable social norms are becoming more prevalent."*

1C - <u>Anger and Anxiety</u>

Something to note is that there can be a link between anxiety and anger. If we've never learned how to calm ourselves down, and problems come up, they can trigger an anger response in us. When we see that our anger can "freeze" those around us, we can use it to influence others to do what we want - whenever we want. However, our anger can stop us from developing emotionally.

Question 1: What tends to trigger your anger?

2A - Jesus was very much against anger.

Matthew 5-22 "But I say unto you, That whosoever is angry with his brother without a cause shall be in danger of the judgment: and whosoever shall say to his brother, Raca, shall be in danger of the council: but whosoever shall say, Thou fool, shall be in danger of hell fire."

2A - Anger is so destructive that the Bible advises us to get rid of it before bedtime.

Ephesians 4:26 "Be ye angry, and sin not: let not the sun go down upon your wrath:"

Question 2: Do you make it a habit to forgive everyone before sunset?

3A - The Bible implies that there is a link between anger and the devil. Right after the above verse, it says, "Neither give place to the devil." (**Ephesians 4:27**)

3B - The following verses link anger to evil.

a) **Psalms 37:8** "Cease from anger, and forsake wrath: fret not thyself in any wise to do evil."

b) **Ephesians 4:31** "Let all bitterness, and wrath, and anger, and clamour, and evil speaking, be put away from you, with all malice:"

3C - The following scripture shows how anger in King Saul's life brought about torment from an evil spirit.

1 Samuel 18:9-11 "And Saul eyed David from that day and forward. [10] And it came to pass on the morrow, that the evil spirit from God came upon Saul, and he prophesied in the midst of the house: and David played with his hand, as at other times: and there was a javelin in Saul's hand. [11] And Saul cast the javelin; for he said, I will smite David even to the wall with it. And David avoided out of his presence twice."

Question 3: Have you ever witnessed anger that made you see a connection between anger and the devil?

4A - Four Synonyms

Ephesians 4:31 "Let all bitterness, and wrath, and anger, and clamour, and evil speaking, be put away from you, with all malice:"

The above verse gives us four synonyms for the word anger: bitterness, wrath, clamor, and malice.

Question 4: Is there anything in your life that you are bitter about?

5A - The Bible verse below gives us a unique verb for what to do with anger.

Psalms 37:8 "Cease from anger, and forsake wrath: fret not thyself in any wise to do evil."

The meanings of the word "forsake" are 1) to quit or leave entirely; abandon; desert; and, 2) to give up or renounce (a habit, way of life, etc.).

Question 5: Can you see yourself forsaking (abandoning) anger? Can you see yourself renouncing anger, and committing to living a whole new life free of anger?

6A - The same verse links anger with fretting and worrying.

Psalms 37:8 "Cease from anger, and forsake wrath: fret not thyself in any wise to do evil."

Question 6: Do you have any worries that contribute to you getting angry?

7A - Ephesians 4:31 *(above)*, gives us another adjective for the word anger: Malice. It is defined as the desire to inflict injury, harm, or suffering on another, either because of a hostile impulse or deep-seated meanness.

Question 7: Have you ever wanted to inflict pain on someone?

8A - Here is another scripture on synonyms for anger and to not be associated with it.

Colossians 3:8 "But now ye also put off all these; anger, wrath, malice, blasphemy, filthy communication out of your mouth."

8B - The Bible tells us that anger is something that fools have a problem with.

Ecclesiastes 7:9 "Be not hasty in thy spirit to be angry: for anger resteth in the bosom of fools."

Question 8: Has anyone told you that you were foolish? If so, was it in connection with anger?

9A - On the contrary, people who are slow to wrath are looked upon as wise, with great understanding.

Proverbs 14:29 "He that is slow to wrath is of great understanding: but he that is hasty of spirit exalteth folly."

Question 9: Do people tell you that you are wise?

10A - The following verse gives two tips on how to avoid anger.

James 1:19-20 "Wherefore, my beloved brethren, let every man be <u>swift to hear</u>, <u>slow to speak</u>, slow to wrath:"

Question 10: When conflict arises, do you give people adequate time to state their case?

11A - A hot-tempered person attracts conflict.

Proverbs 15:18 "A wrathful man stirreth up strife: but he that is slow to anger appeaseth strife."

Soft speech can remove anger in a situation.

Proverbs 15:1 "A soft answer turneth away wrath: but grievous words stir up anger."

Question 11: Do you make it a point to soften your speech when anger is building up in you or those around you?

12A - <u>A Wise Man Watches How He Responds</u>

There is a saying that says, "Choose your battles wisely." In the following scripture, we see the benefits of backing off from tense situations.

Proverbs 19:11 "The discretion of a man deferreth his anger; and it is his glory to pass over a transgression."

Here we see that a wise man can defer his anger. That means wise people can tell when it isn't a good time to discuss a problem with someone, so they put it off for a while. A wise person will sometimes even pass over someone's mistake, giving the other person grace.

Question 12: Can you see yourself not reacting to a problem, and even letting a matter go?

13A - The following verse states that anger is not from God.

James 1:20 "For the wrath of man worketh not the righteousness of God."

13B - <u>This Can Cause Anger</u>

Many times anger occurs because we are passing judgment on people. The Bible has much to say about not passing judgment on people. The way we judge others will be the way God judges us.

a) **Matthew 7:1,2** (Jesus is speaking) "Do not judge, or you too will be judged. For in the same way you judge others, you will be judged, and with the measure you use, it will be measured to you."

b) **Luke 6:37** – "Judge not, and ye shall not be judged: condemn not, and ye shall not be condemned: forgive, and ye shall be forgiven:"

Refer to Tip #12 – Don't Judge, for more information on not passing judgment.

Question 13: Would you like God to judge you the way you judge others?

14A - Knowing how to prevent anger has great value.

Proverbs 16:32 "He that is slow to anger is better than the mighty; and he that ruleth his spirit than he that taketh a city."

Question 14: Are you happy with the way you disarm anger in your life?

15A - Anger can hinder us from making friends with emotionally healthy people.

Proverbs 22:24-25 "Make no friendship with an angry man; and with a furious man thou shalt not go: [25] Lest thou learn his ways, and get a snare to thy soul."

Question 15: Do you know of angry people who could benefit from making friends with healthier individuals?

Are you up for the challenge of learning how to disarm anger in your life? To help you do this, consider giving people a dollar for every time they see you angry. It will be a good investment in your life!

* * * * * *

TIP #20

Practice Humility

1A - Learning to be humble is one of the most attractive attributes we can develop. The word "humble" is defined as having, or showing, a modest or low estimate of one's importance.

We don't have to *be* lower in importance; rather we give others the privilege of being higher than us.

Jesus taught the paradox, to become great, one must become humble.

a) **Matthew 18:4** "Whosoever therefore shall humble himself as this little child, the same is greatest in the kingdom of heaven."

b) **Matthew 23:12** "And whosoever shall exalt himself shall be abased; and he that shall humble himself shall be exalted."

1B - Jesus taught us humility by displaying it in a number of ways.

First, He was born in a humble place, a barn.

Luke 2:16 "And they came with haste, and found Mary, and Joseph, and the babe lying in a manger."

1C - Second, He was humble toward His parents.

Luke 2:51 "And he went down with them, and came to Nazareth, and was subject unto them: but his mother kept all these sayings in her heart."

1D - Third, Jesus never had a house.

Luke 9:58 "And Jesus said unto him, Foxes have holes, and birds of the air have nests; but the Son of man hath not where to lay his head."

1E - Fourth, Jesus spent His teaching days as a servant.

a) **Matthew 20:28** "Even as the Son of man came not to be ministered unto, but to minister, and to give his life a ransom for many."

b) **Luke 22:27** "For whether is greater, he that sitteth at meat, or he that serveth? is not he that sitteth at meat? but I am among you as he that serveth."

c) **Philippians 2:7** "But made himself of no reputation, and took upon him the form of a servant, and was made in the likeness of men:"

d) **Philippians 2:8** "And being found in fashion as a man, he humbled himself, and became obedient unto death, even the death of the cross."

1F - Jesus was not self-willed.

John 6:38 "For I came down from heaven, not to do mine own will, but the will of him that sent me."

1G - The apostle Paul told us to be humble.

Colossians 3:12 "Put on, therefore, as the elect of God, holy and beloved, bowels of mercies, kindness, humbleness of mind, meekness, longsuffering;"

1H - The writer of Proverbs spoke highly of humility.

a) **Proverbs 15:33** "The fear of the LORD is the instruction of wisdom; and before honour is humility."

b) **Proverbs 18:12** "Before destruction the heart of man is haughty, and before honour is humility."

Question 1: Can you think of someone who portrays humility?

Question 2: How would you rate your level of humility?

3A - We can see a greater importance of humility when we understand how negative the opposite is - pride.

a) **Proverbs 8:13** "The fear of the LORD is to hate evil: pride, and arrogancy, and the evil way, and the froward mouth, do I hate."

b) **Proverbs 16:5** "Every one that is proud in heart is an abomination to the LORD: though hand join in hand, he shall not be unpunished."

c) **Proverbs 16:18** "Pride goeth before destruction, and an haughty spirit before a fall."

3B - Humility is a very attractive character trait, and can be displayed with very little effort. Notice the easy-going sense we feel in the following quote from Jesus.

Matthew 11:29, 30 "Take my yoke upon you, and learn of me; for I am meek and lowly in heart: and ye shall find rest unto your souls. For my yoke is easy, and my burden is light."

Question 3: Can you think of anyone who is humble, and would you agree that their demeanor feels effortless?

4A - When we don't humble ourselves, sometimes God will humble us, through life events.

Deuteronomy 8:2 "And thou shalt remember all the way which the LORD thy God led thee these forty years in the wilderness, to humble thee, and to prove thee, to know what was in thine heart, whether thou wouldest keep his commandments, or no."

4B - Our humility can cause God to lift us out of evil.

- a) **1 Kings 21:29** "Seest thou how Ahab humbleth himself before me? because he humbleth himself before me, I will not bring the evil in his days: but in his son's days will I bring the evil upon his house."

- b) **2 Chronicles 7:14** "If my people, which are called by my name, shall humble themselves, and pray, and seek my face, and turn from their wicked ways; then will I hear from heaven, and will forgive their sin, and will heal their land."

- c) **2 Chronicles 12:7** "And when the LORD saw that they humbled themselves, the word of the LORD came to Shemaiah, saying, They have humbled themselves; therefore I will not destroy them, but I will grant them some deliverance; and my wrath shall not be poured out upon Jerusalem by the hand of Shishak."

- d) **2 Chronicles 12:12** "And when he humbled himself, the wrath of the LORD turned from him, that he would not destroy him altogether: and also in Judah things went well."

- e) **2 Chronicles 32:26** "Notwithstanding Hezekiah humbled himself for the pride of his heart, both he and the inhabitants of Jerusalem, so that the wrath of the LORD came not upon them in the days of Hezekiah."

Question 4: Can you think of a time that God was humbling you?

5A - Sometimes we need to show humility.

- a) **2 Kings 22:19** "Because thine heart was tender, and thou hast humbled thyself before the LORD, when thou heardest what I spake against this place, and against the inhabitants thereof, that they should become a desolation and a curse, and hast rent thy clothes, and wept before me; I also have heard thee, saith the LORD."

- b) **Psalms 35:13** "But as for me, when they were sick, my clothing was sackcloth: I humbled my soul with fasting; and my prayer returned into mine own bosom."

Question 5: Have you ever done something to show your humility toward God?

6A - God will hear the prayers of the humble.

- a) **2 Kings 22:19** "Because thine heart was tender, and thou hast humbled thyself before the LORD, when thou heardest what I spake against this place, and against the inhabitants thereof, that they should become a desolation and a curse, and hast rent thy clothes, and wept before me; I also have heard thee, saith the LORD."

- b) **2 Chronicles 34:27** "Because thine heart was tender, and thou didst humble thyself before God, when thou heardest his words against this place, and against the inhabitants thereof, and humbledst thyself before me, and didst rend thy clothes, and weep before me; I have even heard thee also, saith the LORD."

6B - God's rescuing power can come to the humble person.

> **Job 22:29** "When men are cast down, then thou shalt say, There is lifting up; and he shall save the humble person."

6C - Do this when you are in trouble with people.

> **Proverbs 6:3** "Do this now, my son, and deliver thyself, when thou art come into the hand of thy friend; go, humble thyself, and make sure thy friend."

6D - God will dwell with you when you are humble.

> **Isaiah 57:15** "For thus saith the high and lofty One that inhabiteth eternity, whose name is Holy; I dwell in the high and holy place, with him also that is of a contrite and humble spirit, to revive the spirit of the humble, and to revive the heart of the contrite ones."

6E - The humble person can become the greatest person.

   a) **Proverbs 29:23** "A man's pride shall bring him low: but honour shall uphold the humble in spirit."

   b) **Luke 14:11** "For whosoever exalteth himself shall be abased; and he that humbleth himself shall be exalted."

   c) **Luke 18:14** "I tell you, this man went down to his house justified rather than the other: for every one that exalteth himself shall be abased; and he that humbleth himself shall be exalted."

   d) **James 4:10** "Humble yourselves in the sight of the Lord, and he shall lift you up."

   e) **1 Peter 5:6** "Humble yourselves therefore under the mighty hand of God, that he may exalt you in due time:"

Question 6: What are some ways you can be humble?

* * * * * *

Tip #21

Collect "Grace Doors"

1A - It was Thanksgiving weekend, and a gentleman was waiting his turn to drive out of a grocery store parking lot. To his left, he saw an older woman backing out of her parking spot heading straight for his driver's door. It looked like she wasn't going to stop, so the man honked his horn, but her car kept going and hit his door. The two drivers got out of their vehicles to assess the damage, and to exchange driver's licenses and insurance information. The gentleman could smell alcohol on the breath of the other driver.

1B - About an hour later, the gentleman called the woman driver and told her, "I've decided not to pursue the insurance claim on the dented door. I am a handy person, so repairing the door is not a big deal for me. Plus, I know one day I'm going to make a mistake and will need grace, so I am "paying it forward" by giving you grace for the dented door. I hope you have a nice Thanksgiving weekend."

1C - The woman was speechless. Her husband had to come on the phone to finish the call. The gentleman explained to the husband what he had just told his wife. The husband said his wife was speechless and thanked the man very much for the call.

1D - This example shows what we mean by the term "Grace Door," a situation in which we give someone grace for a mistake they have made.

Question 1: Have you ever given someone grace like this? If so, can you tell us about it?

2A - The truth is, we all make mistakes, and it's only a matter of time before we make our next mistake. Thus, it's good to be prepared for them. One way to be prepared is to have "Grace Doors" in our "account." That means having a number of past instances where we have given grace to people for the mistakes they made that affected us.

2B - The Bible says that we reap what we sow. If we have given grace to others, we *ourselves* can expect to receive grace when *we* make a mistake. See the following scriptures about us reaping what we sow.

   a) **2 Corinthians 9:6** "But this I say, He which soweth sparingly shall reap also sparingly; and he which soweth bountifully shall reap also bountifully."

b) **Galatians 6:7** "Be not deceived; God is not mocked: for whatsoever a man soweth, that shall he also reap."

Question 2: Can you think of a time when you reaped what you sowed? Are you in a situation now in which you could give grace to someone?

3A - <u>Grace Was God's Idea</u>

Below are stories of grace in the Bible.

Noah was a righteous man living in a world of sinners. At the time, God wanted to destroy the human race and start again. Noah was the only righteous man living. Noah's history of right living caused him to find grace with God.

Genesis 6:8,9 "But Noah found grace in the eyes of the LORD. ⁹ These are the generations of Noah: Noah was a just man and perfect in his generations, and Noah walked with God."

3B - <u>Lot</u>

Another example of God giving grace to someone is the story of Lot and his family. They lived in the cities of Sodom and Gomorrah. These cities had become so filled with sin that many people were suffering because of it. God decided He had no choice but to destroy the cities.

In contrast, God gave grace to Lot and his family who lived there, by allowing them to escape before His fierce anger wiped out the cities.

Genesis 19:19 "Behold now, thy servant hath found grace in thy sight, and thou hast magnified thy mercy, which thou hast shewed unto me in saving my life;"

3C - <u>Jacob</u>

God gave Jacob twelve sons. His eleventh son was named Joseph; Joseph became Jacob's favorite son. Thus, the other brothers didn't like Joseph. One day they sold him to slave traders and then told Jacob a lion killed Joseph. Jacob was heart-broken. Joseph went through some ups and downs in a foreign country, but in the end he became a top leader in Egypt. When a famine gripped the area, Jacob and his family traveled to the one area with food – Egypt. There Jacob was reacquainted with his lost son Joseph – such grace from God! God also gave grace to Jacob by keeping him and his family alive during a famine.

Genesis 46:30 "And Israel said unto Joseph, Now let me die, since I have seen thy face, because thou art yet alive."

3D - <u>God's Grace Toward Us</u>

The most notable example of grace is when God, our Father, sent His only begotten son, Jesus, to pay the penalty for our sin, by dying on a cross. We deserved death because of our sin, but Jesus willingly died in our place. That is profound grace.

Romans 5:8 says, "But God commendeth his love toward us, in that, while we were yet sinners, Christ died for us."

Only a sinless man could pay the penalty of our sin, and that was Jesus.

3E - <u>Our Grace toward Others</u>

    Just as God gave us grace through Jesus, God expects us to give grace to others.

  a) **Matthew 6:12** "And forgive us our debts, as we forgive our debtors."

  b) **Ephesians 4:32** "And be ye kind one to another, tenderhearted, forgiving one another, even as God for Christ's sake hath forgiven you."

  c) **Colossians 3:13** "Forbearing one another, and forgiving one another, if any man have a quarrel against any: even as Christ forgave you, so also do ye."

    If it is within our power to forgive someone, we should forgive them.

3F - However, it is good to keep in mind that we sometimes hurt people by letting them *off the hook* too easily. They could start feeling entitled to our forgiveness, thus abuse our good nature. Each case is different; so we need to pray for wisdom that God will help us know when to use "tough love," and when to freely forgive. For the most part, live a lifestyle of grace, and you will be given grace yourself.

                          * * * * * * *

TIP #22

Volunteer

1A - When our day-to-day life becomes a constant struggle, it can be tempting to just stay home and do nothing. However, great blessings await us if we will move out of our comfort zone and help make a difference in other people's lives. A great way to do this is through volunteering. Real benefits can be had, even if we only volunteer for an hour a week.

1B - It can be surprising how God uses our volunteering to direct us to new people who can enrich our lives. He can also use our past experiences to help us to do a good job in a volunteer position. Volunteering has a way of expanding our vision to new ideas we could never have come up with otherwise. Here's how volunteering can help us.

a) Volunteering can help take our mind off whatever is bothering us.

b) Volunteering helps us network with others.

c) Volunteering can lead to promotions.

d) Volunteering can advance our career.

e) Volunteering can help us live a more active lifestyle.

f) Volunteering can add a sense of fun and excitement to our lives.

Question 1: Can you tell us in what ways you've volunteered in the past? If so, how did it help you?

2A - <u>A Good Distraction</u>

Volunteering can help distract us from thinking negatively. This is a huge benefit for people who struggle with anxiety or depression. Choosing a volunteer position that entails meeting new people and learning new skills helps this further.

Question 2: Can you tell us about the people you've met and things you've learned while volunteering?

3A - <u>Networking for Employment</u>

Volunteering can help us network with others. People who watch us volunteer may know an employer who is looking to hire for a paid position.

3B - <u>Promotion</u>

Doing a good job as a volunteer prepares us for greater responsibility in the future. The Bible says, if we are faithful in little, God can entrust us with greater.

a) **Matthew 25:23** "His lord said unto him, Well done, good and faithful servant; thou hast been faithful over a few things, I will make thee ruler over many things: enter thou into the joy of thy lord."

b) **Luke 16:10** "He that is faithful in that which is least is faithful also in much: and he that is unjust in the least is unjust also in much."

So get ready for promotion!

3C - <u>Above the Rest</u>

More than ever employers are looking to give back to their communities. Thus, some of them look for people who like to volunteer. If our resume shows volunteer work, it can put us ahead of other candidates who haven't volunteered.

Question 3: Has volunteering helped you meet key people or led to a promotion in your career?

4A - <u>More Active</u>

For someone who struggles with depression, a volunteer position that requires physical activity can help them feel more productive, improve their physical health, and improve their sleep.

Question 4: Have you ever had a physically active volunteer position? If so, how did it help you?

5A - <u>Fun</u>

Some volunteer positions require us to do activities with people. Some of these activities can lead to some great fun, making the exercise beneficial for both the volunteer and the people being helped.

Question 5: Have you ever had enjoyable times volunteering?

6A - <u>Volunteering (Serving) in the Bible</u>

There are a lot of Bible verses on being of service to others.

a) **Proverbs 11:25** "The liberal soul shall be made fat: and he that watereth shall be watered also himself."

b) **Matthew 20:26** "But it shall not be so among you: but whosoever will be great among you, let him be your minister;"

c) **Mark 9:35** "And he sat down, and called the twelve, and saith unto them, If any man desire to be first, the same shall be last of all, and servant of all."

d) **Mark 10:42-44** "But Jesus called them to him, and saith unto them, Ye know that they which are accounted to rule over the Gentiles exercise lordship over them; and their great ones exercise authority upon them. But so shall it not be among you: but whosoever will be great among you, shall be your minister: [44] And whosoever of you will be the chiefest, shall be servant of all."

e) **Mark 10:45** "For even the Son of man came not to be ministered unto, but to minister, and to give his life a ransom for many."

f) **John 12:26** "If any man serve me, let him follow me; and where I am, there shall also my servant be: if any man serve me, him will my Father honour."

g) **Galatians 5:13** "For, brethren, ye have been called unto liberty; only use not liberty for an occasion to the flesh, but by love serve one another."

h) **1 Corinthians 4:1-2** "Let a man so account of us, as of the ministers of Christ, and stewards of the mysteries of God. [2] Moreover it is required in stewards, that a man be found faithful."

i) **Ephesians 2:10** "For we are his workmanship, created in Christ Jesus unto good works, which God hath before ordained that we should walk in them."

j) **Philippians 2:5-7** "Let this mind be in you, which was also in Christ Jesus: [6] Who, being in the form of God, thought it not robbery to be equal with God: [7] But made himself of no reputation, and took upon him the form of a servant, and was made in the likeness of men:"

6B - A Key Place to Volunteer

A great place to volunteer is at church. Here are some reasons why.

a) We get to know some of the nicest people around.

b) We work together to achieve a common goal.

c) We get a sense of purpose.

d) We can be used of God to inspire someone who may be struggling.

e) We position ourselves to meet God in a very special way – serving in His house.

f) We encourage our pastor and the leadership team by volunteering.

g) We become good role models to those around us.

6C - The Nicest People

Many older people have been church members for a long time and have developed into strong, cheerful Christians. Their love for God, for their church, and for the community is attractive. Serving at church puts us into direct contact with these amazing people, and it positions us to be blessed by their Christ-filled lives. This blessing is especially helpful when we are recovering from an emotional wound.

Also, these fine Christian people become great candidates for the role of support team members in our life. See more on this in Tip #5 – Form a Support Team.

Question 6: Have you made some quality friendships at a local church? If so, can you tell us about them?

7A - <u>Achieving a Common Goal</u>

A popular saying is, "Teamwork makes the dream work." This can apply to church life. Every church member has unique, God-given strengths, and when church members are operating in their gifts together, the results can be remarkable.

7B - <u>Teamwork in the Bible</u>

Below is a profound story that perfectly demonstrates the power of unity.

Genesis 11:1-8 "And the whole earth was of one language, and of one speech. ² And it came to pass, as they journeyed from the east, that they found a plain in the land of Shinar; and they dwelt there. ³ And they said one to another, Go to, let us make brick, and burn them thoroughly. And they had brick for stone, and slime had they for morter. ⁴ And they said, Go to, let us build us a city and a tower, whose top may reach unto heaven; and let us make us a name, lest we be scattered abroad upon the face of the whole earth. ⁵ And the LORD came down to see the city and the tower, which the children of men builded."

7C - "⁶ And the LORD said, Behold, the people is one, and they have all one language; and this they begin to do: and now nothing will be restrained from them, which they have imagined to do. ⁷ Go to, let us go down, and there confound their language, that they may not understand one another's speech. ⁸ So the LORD scattered them abroad from thence upon the face of all the earth: and they left off to build the city."

7D - These people had discovered the power of unity. But because the goal was something that displeased God, God decided to confuse their languages and scatter them all over the earth. Indeed, there is great power in teamwork.

Question 7: Have you ever helped out on a big project at church? If so, how did it feel?

8A - <u>Sense of Purpose</u>

One of the easiest ways to breathe new life into a depressed person is by helping them choose an inspirational goal. This also applies to churches. A good church leader can help a church maintain vibrancy by choosing great goals for the church to reach for.

8B - <u>Volunteering at Church</u>

A church should take time to help members see the importance of the various jobs that need to be done for the church, and they should gladly take time to explain thoroughly the tasks at hand. As well, the leaders should take time to see that the job was done properly, and if needed, lovingly offer helpful tips on how to improve the job next time. They should also express appreciation for all that has been done. All of this validates the church members and gives them a sense of importance for their contribution to the church.

Question 8: Have you ever felt a sense of purpose for the tasks you have taken on at your church?

Question 9: Have you ever been sincerely thanked for your contribution at your church? How did it feel?

10A - <u>Inspire Someone</u>

When we take time to help at church, we can meet new people. Some of these people may be struggling. Even people who look as if everything is going well could be good at hiding their pain. God has a way of letting us know who these hurting people are, so we can befriend them and inspire them.

Question 10: Has God ever helped you meet people at church who needed a friend?

11A - <u>Meeting God in a Very Special Way</u>

In essence, the body of believers is God's home. His holiness and love should be evident in a local church. When it is, this draws God's presence. Whenever we walk into a church, or volunteer at a church, we should have a sense of optimism that in some way we will meet with God and receive an impartation of His power and grace in our life. When you go to church, be expectant! That is faith!

Here is a Bible story of a miracle that happened at a local church.

11B - **Acts 3:1-8** "Now Peter and John went up together into the temple at the hour of prayer, being the ninth hour. ² And a certain man lame from his mother's womb was carried, whom they laid daily at the gate of the temple which is called Beautiful, to ask alms of them that entered into the temple; ³ Who seeing Peter and John about to go into the temple asked an alms. ⁴ And Peter, fastening his eyes upon him with John, said, Look on us. ⁵

11C - And he gave heed unto them, expecting to receive something of them. ⁶ Then Peter said, Silver and gold have I none; but such as I have give I thee: In the name of Jesus Christ of Nazareth rise up and walk. ⁷ And he took him by the right hand, and lifted him up: and immediately his feet and ankle bones received strength. ⁸ And he leaping up stood, and walked, and entered with them into the temple, walking, and leaping, and praising God."

Question 11: Do you go to church with a sense of optimism that God is going to reveal Himself to you?

12A - <u>Encourage Your Pastor</u>

Being a pastor or an elder in a local church can be a difficult job. Volunteering our time to help the church can mean so much to a pastor and others in leadership. It can help energize them to be all that God needs them to be, at that church.

Question 12: Have you ever taken time to show appreciation to your pastor and the church staff?

13A - <u>Beware of Complaining at Church</u>

It is important when we serve at our church that we do not fall into the habit of complaining about the church or its members. Gossip in a church can be extremely harmful. We should be ready to take someone aside to explain this truth to them if we see they are bothered by a church-related problem. We should even consider helping the person resolve the issue at hand. For more on this, go to Tip #7 – Speak Right Words, and Tip #12 – Don't Judge. Below are some scriptures that caution us to avoid complaining.

a) **Ephesians 4:29** "Let no corrupt communication proceed out of your mouth, but that which is good to the use of edifying, that it may minister grace unto the hearers."

b) **Philippians 2:14** "Do all things without murmurings and disputings:"

c) **James 5:9** "Grudge not one against another, brethren, lest ye be condemned: behold, the judge standeth before the door."

Question 13: Have you ever helped a person resolve an issue they had about the church?

14A - Become a Role Model

Churches, in general, and growing churches especially, need good role models for people it be inspired by, and to follow. Here are two scriptures on being a good example.

a) **Matthew 5:16** "Let your light so shine before men, that they may see your good works, and glorify your Father which is in heaven."

b) **1 Timothy 4:12** "Let no man despise thy youth; but be thou an example of the believers, in word, in conversation, in charity, in spirit, in faith, in purity."

Question 14: Have you ever been inspired by someone at your church? What was it about them that caught your attention?

15A - In the verse below, Jesus tells us that the harvest is plenteous but the laborers are few. Therefore, churches often need more volunteers.

Matthew 9:37-38 "Then saith he unto his disciples, The harvest truly is plenteous, but the labourers are few; 38 Pray ye therefore the Lord of the harvest, that he will send forth labourers into his harvest."

New people will be attracted to the church when they see members doing their best to share the gospel message, either one-to-one, or by volunteering in larger evangelistic projects.

15B - Jesus gave us the Great Commission, to go out and make disciples of all men and women, teaching them all that Jesus taught us. Some churches are taking this very seriously, and are developing movie-producing skills in order to create impressive, full-length movies. These movies present the gospel in ways that everyday people can relate to. Whatever methods our church uses to promote the gospel, it will require people to be committed to the tasks, people willing to be good role models where they are.

Question 15: Has your church talked about big ways in which to spread the gospel of Jesus Christ?

16A - Volunteering is definitely a helpful strategy to improve your mood and aim your life in the direction of success.

* * * * * * *

TIP #23

Conquer the Addiction

1A - Addictions are fast becoming a major problem in our communities, with some areas reaching crisis levels. Therefore the church should be ready to meet the needs of people caught in a cycle of defeat due to addictions.

1B - Any activity we feel compelled to do regularly, to feel better, could be an addiction. We shouldn't be fooled by the low statistics of a behavior. If we need something to dull emotional pain, we should assess the root cause of this urge to see if it is an addiction. Some of the more common addictions are over-eating, alcohol, drugs, pornography, sex, shopping, gambling, video gaming, television, and work. Sadly, addictions are even prevalent in the church. We need God to help us in this regard.

Below are some scriptures related to addiction.

a) **Deuteronomy 21:20** "And they shall say unto the elders of his city, This our son is stubborn and rebellious, he will not obey our voice; he is a glutton, and a drunkard."

b) **Proverbs 23:21** "For the drunkard and the glutton shall come to poverty: and drowsiness shall clothe a man with rags."

c) **Matthew 11:19** "The Son of man came eating and drinking, and they say, Behold a man gluttonous, and a winebibber, a friend of publicans and sinners. But wisdom is justified of her children."

d) **Luke 7:34** "The Son of man is come eating and drinking; and ye say, Behold a gluttonous man, and a winebibber, a friend of publicans and sinners!"

Question 1: What addictions do people, you know, struggle with today?

2A - Reasons to Break an Addiction

Financial Loss

One significant loss that can come from addictions is financial. Life *without* an addiction can be difficult enough when it comes to managing our money; add an addiction and our financial stability is further weakened.

The Bible advises us to stay clear of debt.

a) **Deuteronomy 15:6** "For the Lord thy God blesseth thee, as he promised thee: and thou shalt lend unto many nations, but thou shalt not borrow; and thou shalt reign over many nations, but they shall not reign over thee."

b) **Proverbs 22:7** "The rich ruleth over the poor, and the borrower is servant to the lender."

c) **Luke 14:28** "For which of you, intending to build a tower, sitteth not down first, and counteth the cost, whether he have sufficient to finish it?"

d) **Romans 13:8** "Owe no man anything, but to love one another: for he that loveth another hath fulfilled the law."

Question 2: Can you think of anyone who is in debt because of an addiction?

3A - <u>Loss of Relationships</u>

Many families have been torn apart because of a loved one who is entrenched in an addiction. Although there are many support groups in almost every community, there are still people who are not getting the help they need to break free of their addiction.

Question 3: Can you think of anyone who is going through great stress because of a loved one caught in an addiction?

4A - <u>Loss of Time</u>

Another loss, is the loss of time that we spend engrossed in our addiction. The family of a famous lead singer of a 1970s music group reported that the singers dying words were, "So much wasted time..." Wasted time can be something we *all* could assess in our lives, more so, for those with addiction.

4B - Below we see the Bible cautions us to beware of wasting time.

a) **Psalms 90:12** "So teach us to number our days, that we may apply our hearts unto wisdom."

b) **Ephesians 5:16** "Redeeming the time, because the days are evil."

c) **Colossians 4:5** "Walk in wisdom toward them that are without, redeeming the time."

Question 4: Can you think of anyone who wastes time because of an addiction?

5A - <u>Loss of Public Services</u>

Another consequence of addictions is the toll it takes on police services, first responders, and hospital staff. It isn't just the cost of their time; it is also the emotional toll it takes on these public service providers while doing their jobs. They see people at their worst, and it can cause them to develop PTSD (Post Traumatic Stress Disorder), a debilitating mental illness that can lead to suicide.

Question 5: Can you think of anyone who is in public service and has to provide care for those with addictions? How does their job affect them?

6A - <u>Toll on Children</u>

Nobody wants to see children get hurt, but this can happen because of addictions. Children don't know how to mentally process something like an angry parent or sibling who is fighting an addiction. The frightening experiences children are exposed to can have a profound, negative effect on them for the rest of their lives. Further, an addiction can be inherited by the child, and thus become a generational problem within families.

Question 6: Can you think of any children who have been traumatized because of addiction?

7A - <u>Toll on Industry</u>

A notable council on drug addiction states that drug abuse alone costs employers $80 billion a year. High employee turnover rates, lower quality of work, workplace theft, absenteeism, accidents, and sick time, all play a part in reducing profitability for corporations. Losses corporately can mean fewer finances going to community endeavors.

Question 7: Can you think of anyone who works in human resources, or owns a company, and deals with employees who have addictions? What do they say about helping employees with addictions?

8A - <u>Breaking the Addiction</u>

Addictions can be challenging to break. There needs to be a sincere desire to quit the addiction. From a Christian standpoint, we could see the addiction as sin. We must reach a point where we are so turned off by our *sin,* that we want to do something about it.

8B - Jesus said, if you want to follow Him, you have to deny yourself. People with addictions find it difficult to deny themselves. See scriptures below.

- a) **Mark 8:34** "And when he had called the people unto him with his disciples also, he said unto them, Whosoever will come after me, let him deny himself, and take up his cross, and follow me."
- b) **Luke 9:23 & Matthew 16:24** "And he said to them all, If any man will come after me, let him deny himself, and take up his cross daily, and follow me."

Question 8: In what way do you deny yourself?

9A - The Bible says that one of the fruits of the Spirit is self-control.

Galatians 5:22-23 "But the fruit of the Spirit is love, joy, peace, longsuffering, gentleness, goodness, faith, [23] Meekness, temperance (self-control): against such there is no law."

Most addicts will admit nonetheless that they have very little self-control.

Question 9: How would you rate your level of self-control?

10A - Below are some steps we can take that can help us break an addiction.

<u>Step 1 - Ask Ourselves "Why Do We Do It?"</u>

Often there is a mental health condition causing us to have an addiction. Many people need relief from symptoms of guilt, anxiety, or depression. Once we resolve the mental health issue, our addiction will be easier to beat.

Question 10: Do you know anyone who has pinpointed the root cause of why they have an addiction?

11A - <u>Step 2 - Think Rationally About the Addiction</u>

Many people don't think rationally about their addiction. They tell themselves it isn't as bad as it is. They minimize the significance of the addiction and its effect on their life.

Question 11: Do you know anyone who minimizes the effects of their addiction?

12A - <u>Step 3 - Pray</u>

It is helpful to ask God for His assistance in breaking our addiction. Some people testify that God miraculously healed them of their addiction instantaneously. Since this is possible, we, too, can aim our faith toward God to give us a complete and instant healing from our addiction. It may seem too large a task to ask, but we remind ourselves that God takes great pleasure in people who are bold enough to ask Him for big things. (For more on this read Tip #9 – Develop Your Faith.)

12B - When we pray a prayer of this nature, it is helpful to couple our prayer with action. We might want to write out our prayer and the date we prayed it, as a memorial to ourselves and to God that we have invited Him into this great need we have, and that we are expecting Him to give us this healing.

12C - We could also ask the elders of our church to anoint us with oil and pray a prayer of healing. The Bible instructs us to do this for those who need healing in their physical bodies, but it can also be used for breaking an addiction.

>**James 5:14** "Is any sick among you? let him call for the elders of the church; and let them pray over him, anointing him with oil in the name of the Lord:"

12D - Another way to couple our prayer with action is by disposing of any of the addictive substance we may still have in our possession.

Another way to couple our prayer with action is by giving a donation. We aren't *buying* our healing; giving a donation is just another way to show God we are serious about our request and that we are willing to sacrifice for it. If our finances are low, we can volunteer our time to help someone.

12E - <u>Our Prayer</u>

The actual prayer that we pray doesn't have to be long or perfect. It can be as simple as, *"God, I believe Jesus died for my sins, and for the healing of my body. My body (or mind) needs to be set free from this addiction. Please heal me, so I am no longer controlled by this substance (or action). I ask this in Jesus's name."*

12F - We could then call someone from our church and tell them what we have just prayed and done, and ask them to help us keep our commitment to God, to never go back to the addiction.

Whether our healing is instant or gradual, below are some practical steps we can take to help ourselves stay free of our addiction.

Question 12: Do you know anyone who God has set free from addiction?

13A - Step 3 - Replace Bad Habits with Good Habits

The Victory Tips Program suggests that we take up memorizing Bible verses. We can become so busy learning new verses that we distract ourselves from the thoughts of the addiction. This also is a great way to get closer to God.

Question 13: Do you know anyone who successfully replaced bad habits with good habits?

14A - Step 4 - Identify Trigger Times

There can be times during our day when we are more prone to give in to our addiction, such as break times, meal times, evenings, pay-days, holidays, etc. We can prepare for these times by having other activities to do in place of the negative habit; perhaps something healthy like focused breathing, an exercise routine, a relaxation routine, prayer or Bible study.

Question 14: Can you suggest activities to do in place of addictive behaviors?

15A - Step 5 - Limit Access to the Substance

One way to cut off access to our substance is by not carrying cash. Not having money can prevent us from purchasing our drug of choice. If we have an online addiction, we could consider removing the computer from our home.

We could also avoid going near places we used to go to for our "fix."

As well, we could also break off friendships with those who have addictions, and make friends with people who don't have addictions. A church can be a great place to meet people without addictions.

Question 15: Can you think of other ways a person might cut off access to their drug of choice?

16A - Step 6 - Be Accountable to People

It can be helpful to find people we can call every day, to let them know how we're doing. If we have the person's permission, we don't have to feel bad if we need to contact them multiple times a day. It can be helpful to find several people in our lives to call, in case one isn't available when we need to speak with them. Surrounding ourselves with people who care about us, and who never feel we have contacted them too much, is very helpful. We shouldn't let shame prevent us from getting the help we need. We may need a lot of support at present, but we should realize that someday we can be the support person for someone else in need. For more on this topic see Tip #5 – Form a Support Team.

Question 16: If you have an addiction, can you think of people who may be helpful in providing accountability for you? How might you find others?

17A - Step 7 – Learn About the Addiction

Knowledge is power. We can do research online, or we can get books, CDs, or DVDs, at the library.

We could also find good recovery groups and start attending meetings regularly. We can also learn much by speaking with people who have conquered a similar addiction.

Question 17: Do you know of good resources to help people with addictions?

18A - <u>Step 8 – Reward Yourself</u>

We can be our own best friend by rewarding ourselves when we make even the slightest progress in our attempts to conquer our addiction.

Question 18: What are good ways you reward yourself?

19A - With God's help we can become overcomers in every way of or lives, including conquering addictions. We can begin to see ourselves as a conqueror. For more on this concept see Tip #14 – Develop a Conqueror Mentality. For more practical help in breaking an addiction, contact us.

* * * * * *

TIP #24

Have a Vision for Your Life

1A - God has created us for a purpose. The Bible says He laid out the purpose for our lives before we were even born. **Ephesians 2:10** says, *"For we are his workmanship, created in Christ Jesus unto good works, which God hath before ordained that we should walk in them."*

Our life's purpose will eventually begin manifesting at some point in our life. We call this birthing stage of a mission, a vision. It is a captivating, irresistible sense of something we must do. It can come suddenly, or it can happen slowly, over days, weeks, and months. The following scripture gives us a sense of the importance of a vision.

Proverbs 29:18 "Where there is no vision, the people perish: but he that keepeth the law, happy is he."

Question 1: Have you ever had a vision or a sense of what you were supposed to do?

2A - <u>Begin with a Prayer</u>

Life can have a way of *"knocking the wind out of us."* The challenges of life can sometimes seem impossible to conquer, and we are tempted to adopt a defeatist attitude. But just because one door of opportunity closes on us, doesn't mean new doors can't open. If a dream we've been holding on to falls apart, we can ask God for a new purpose for our life, and He will give it to us. Here is a well known Bible verse on getting guidance. We can use it to help steer us to our next vision, or goal, in life.

Proverbs 3:5-6 "Trust in the LORD with all thine heart; and lean not unto thine own understanding. ⁶ In all thy ways acknowledge him, and he shall direct thy paths."

Question 2: Have you ever felt like you couldn't go any further? If so, would you like to share with us what happened?

3A - <u>Become Unstoppable!</u>

It may surprise us what new directions God has for us. When they come, they will infuse us with a new zest for life. The following are some people in the Bible who had a vision for their life, and it caused them to become unstoppable.

a) Noah had a vision of building a large boat for God. Doing so took him a very long time (120 years), but he didn't give up. It gave him purpose, and it saved him and his family! (Genesis 6 & 7)

b) Moses had a vision of setting the Israelites free from the Egyptians. After God met him at a burning bush, He sent Moses to complete the mission. Doing so was stressful, but he kept at it until the Israelites were free. (Exodus 3)

c) Joseph had a vision of his family bowing down to him. Life became very difficult for him but he kept living for God, and God eventually made him Prime Minister of Egypt! Amazingly, his family did bow down before him! (Genesis 37)

d) Paul had a vision of preaching the gospel for Jesus all over the world. No matter how hard it was, he kept at it, and eventually, God used his preaching and his letters to reach millions of people for Christ. His letters make up most of the New Testament!

Question 3: Have you ever received new direction for your life? If so, how did it make you feel?

4A - <u>Beware of Some Visions</u>

The peculiar thing about a vision is that it can either be a positive, life-giving goal, or it can be a negative, hurtful purpose. An example of a negative vision is in the life of Haman, a vizier under King Ahasuerus of Persia, who lived around 465 B.C. Haman took offense to Mordecai, a Jew, for not bowing down to him when he went by.

Esther 3:6 "And he thought scorn to lay hands on Mordecai alone; for they had shewed him the people of Mordecai: wherefore Haman sought to destroy all the Jews that were throughout the whole kingdom of Ahasuerus, even the people of Mordecai."

4B - Haman built a set of gallows 50 feet high, and a 75 foot high sharpened, impaling pole, with which to impale Mordecai. These were eventually used to impale Haman, himself. Haman's vision cost him his life.

Question 4: Have you ever had an irresistible sense of what you were supposed to do, but had it hurt you?

5A - <u>Check Your Vision</u>

So we've prayed for direction. We've gotten an answer. It feels good. What do we do next? We can check our vision by asking ourselves the following questions. Answers to these questions can help determine the value of the new goal we have in mind.

a) What does God's Word say about this new vision?

b) What do my church friends say about this new direction?

c) What do respected church leaders think of the idea?

6B - <u>Heavenly Value</u>

In evaluating a vision, something to consider is the spiritual value of the work we would like to do. The following verses tell us our works will one day, "be burned," to see if there is any spiritual value in them.

1 Corinthians 3:13-15 "Every man's work shall be made manifest: for the day shall declare it, because it shall be revealed by fire; and the fire shall try every man's work of what sort it is. ¹⁴ If any man's work abide which he hath built thereupon, he shall receive a reward. ¹⁵ If any man's work shall be burned, he shall suffer loss: but he himself shall be saved; yet so as by fire."

Question 5: Have you ever told others about your vision? If so, how did they respond?

6A - Once the concept of the vision is affirmed, take time to write it out in more detail. The following verse tells us to write out our vision.

Habakkuk 2:2-3 "And the LORD answered me, and said, Write the vision, and make it plain upon tables, that he may run that readeth it. ³ For the vision is yet for an appointed time, but at the end it shall speak, and not lie: though it tarry, wait for it; because it will surely come, it will not tarry."

Most visions can only be accomplished with help from others. Writing out the vision gives new people a way of understanding what the vision is and how to help bring it into reality.

Question 6: Have you ever had a yearning desire to do something in which you took time to write it out?

7A - <u>Getting Help</u>

Next, we'll want to create a plan of how to bring this vision to reality. It is a good idea to contact people who have some skill in the kind of work that the vision requires. The Bible says a lot about getting good counsel.

   a) **Proverbs 12:15** "The way of a fool is right in his own eyes: but he that hearkeneth unto counsel is wise."

   b) **Proverbs 15:22** "Without counsel purposes are disappointed: but in the multitude of counsellors they are established."

   c) **Proverbs 24:6** "For by wise counsel thou shalt make thy war: and in multitude of counsellors there is safety."

7B - At this point, it's important to be careful who we share our vision with. Some "would-be" helpers might only see reasons why our vision could never come to pass. This can cause doubt in our mind and discourage us from going any further with the goal.

Question 7: Have you ever contacted someone for advice about a vision you had? How did they respond?

8A - <u>Set Goals</u>

It's important to start setting goals so we can track our progress. This will also help us accomplish tasks in a shorter time frame. Our counselors can help us with this. The following scriptures challenge us to work hard at completing our God-given tasks.

   a) **2 Chronicles 15:7** "Be ye strong therefore, and let not your hands be weak: for your work shall be rewarded."

   b) **Proverbs 21:5** "The thoughts of the diligent tend only to plenteousness; but of every one that is hasty only to want."

c) **Philippians 3:14** "I press toward the mark for the prize of the high calling of God in Christ Jesus."

8B - <u>Stay in Prayer</u>

It is helpful to stay close to God in prayer throughout our work so we can detect any adjustments we may need to make along the way.

As an example, after Jesus was born, Joseph received a change of course from an angel in a dream.

Matthew 2:13 "And when they were departed, behold the angel of the Lord appeareth to Joseph in a dream, saying, Arise, and take the young child and his mother, and flee into Egypt, and be thou there until I bring thee word: for Herod will seek the young child to destroy him."

8C - We should stay in prayer, so we don't waste time doing something we weren't supposed to do.

Psalm 127:1 "Except the LORD build the house, they labour in vain that build it: except the LORD keep the city, the watchman waketh but in vain."

Enjoy the excitement of creating something new! God is the "Great Creator," so we'll be in good company when we include God in our project!

* * * * * *

TIP #25

Be Thankful

1A - Another helpful attribute to develop in our lives is that of being thankful. Scientific research shows that thankfulness boosts the immune system and increases blood supply, both of which contribute to improved physical and emotional health. Research also shows that it enhances alertness, enthusiasm, energy, and sleep improvements. All of these benefits contribute to less stress, anxiety, and depression.

The Bible refers to thanksgiving many times. Below are some of the key verses for gratitude.

Question 1: How would you rate your level of thankfulness?

2A - Below is a verse that tells us to be thankful for all things. Does the Apostle Paul mean for us to be thank for bad things that happen to us, as well? Good question.

Ephesians 5:20 "Giving thanks always for all things unto God and the Father in the name of our Lord Jesus Christ;"

Below is a verse that tells us to be thankful "in" all things. This is something we can definitely do, if not the above.

1 Thessalonians 5:18 "In everything give thanks: for this is the will of God in Christ Jesus concerning you."

Question 2: Can you think of a time when you were thankful "for" or "in" a negative event in your life?

3A - <u>A Good Reason To Be Thankful – God's Mercy</u>

The Bible doesn't just say "give thanks," sometimes it says "O give thanks."

a) **Psalms 106:1** "Praise ye the LORD. O give thanks unto the LORD; for he is good: for his mercy endureth for ever."

b) **Psalms 118:1** "O give thanks unto the LORD; for he is good: because his mercy endureth for ever."

That means His mercy is so good; it implies, "Look! See how great it is!"

Question 3: How highly do you value God's mercy in your life? Can you tell us a time He showed great mercy to you?

4A - <u>Thankful In Times of Loss</u>

Life can also include times of loss. And while these losses can try to derail our lives, we can help offset the loss by, remembering, and, being thankful for, the times *before* the loss. Such as a loved one passing away or becoming ill. We can remember the good times before the loss of our loved one.

Or in the case of an automobile becoming too expensive to repair, we can throw a party for the years of service that we *did* get out of it.

Question 4: Has your life ever been derailed by a loss, but you found something to be thankful for in spite of it?

5A - A loss can be a difficult time in our lives. It is the perfect time to prove Christ's words that He spoke to the Apostle Paul, in **2 Corinthians 12:9**, *"My grace is sufficient for thee: for my strength is made perfect in weakness."* We can find hidden strength in Christ.

Question 5: Have you ever found unexpected grace to get through a hard time in your life?

6A - The verse below talks about the things we do and say, how we should do it all in the name of the Lord Jesus, and with thanksgiving to God.

Colossians 3:17 "And whatsoever ye do in word or deed, do all in the name of the Lord Jesus, giving thanks to God and the Father by him."

6B - The scripture below tells us to present our requests to God with thanksgiving.

Philippians 4:6 "Be careful for nothing; but in everything by prayer and supplication with thanksgiving let your requests be made known unto God."

Here are other verses on thanksgiving.

a) **Colossians 2:6,7** "As ye have therefore received Christ Jesus the Lord, so walk ye in him: [7] Rooted and built up in him, and stablished in the faith, as ye have been taught, abounding therein with thanksgiving.

b) **Colossians 3:15** "And let the peace of God rule in your hearts, to the which also ye are called in one body; and be ye thankful."

c) **Colossians 4:2** "Continue in prayer, and watch in the same with thanksgiving;"

Question 6: Are you in the habit of starting your prayer requests with thanksgiving?

7A - The following scripture tells us to enter His presence with thanksgiving.

Psalms 100:4 "Enter into his gates with thanksgiving, and into his courts with praise: be thankful unto him, and bless his name."

7B - The following are other scriptures on being thankful.

a) **1 Chronicles 16:34** "O give thanks unto the LORD; for he is good; for his mercy endureth for ever."

b) **Nehemiah 12:46** "For in the days of David and Asaph of old there were chief of the singers, and songs of praise and thanksgiving unto God."

c) **Psalm 26:7** "That I may publish with the voice of thanksgiving, and tell of all thy wondrous works."

d) **Psalm 50:14** "Offer unto God thanksgiving; and pay thy vows unto the most High:"

e) **Psalm 69:30** "I will praise the name of God with a song, and will magnify him with thanksgiving."

f) **Psalm 95:2** "Let us come before his presence with thanksgiving, and make a joyful noise unto him with psalms."

g) **Psalm 107:22** "Let us come before his presence with thanksgiving, and make a joyful noise unto him with psalms."

h) **Psalm 116:17** "I will offer to thee the sacrifice of thanksgiving, and will call upon the name of the Lord."

i) **Psalm 147:7** "Sing unto the Lord with thanksgiving; sing praise upon the harp unto our God:"

j) **Amos 4:5** "And offer a sacrifice of thanksgiving with leaven, and proclaim and publish the free offerings: for this liketh you, O ye children of Israel, saith the Lord God."

k) **Jonah 2:9** "But I will sacrifice unto thee with the voice of thanksgiving; I will pay that that I have vowed. Salvation is of the Lord."

l) **Colossians 3:15** "And let the peace of God rule in your hearts, to the which also ye are called in one body; and be ye thankful."

m) **Colossians 3:17** "And whatsoever ye do in word or deed, do all in the name of the Lord Jesus, giving thanks to God and the Father by him."

n) **1 Timothy 4:4** "For every creature of God is good, and nothing to be refused, if it be received with thanksgiving:"

o) **Hebrews 12:28** "Wherefore we receiving a kingdom which cannot be moved, let us have grace, whereby we may serve God acceptably with reverence and godly fear:"

* * * * * * *

TIP #26

Welcome MLCs

1A - Life can be filled with challenges. Thus, it is good to be prepared when these challenges come around. One way to be prepared is to be able to welcome MLC's. "MLC" stands for Major Life Challenge. They are the more difficult times in our lives such as the death of a loved one, spouse wanting a divorce, negative diagnosis, job loss, serious injury, relocation, lawsuit, and financial loss. Each of these requires an adjustment in our thinking so we keep our peace of mind.

Question 1: Can you think of a time in your life when you were faced with an MLC? If so, how well did you handle it?

2A - <u>Why "Welcome" MLCs?</u>

At first glance, we might wonder why we would want to welcome one of these events in our lives. We will examine the reasons below.

First, as Christians, God requires us to live by faith. That means that we trust God in every aspect of our lives; this includes the difficult times. Our faith tells us that God can heal a negative situation, or bring good out of it.

a) **Romans 1:17** 'The just shall live by faith'. (Also found in Habakkuk 2:4, Galatians 3:11 and Hebrews 10:38.)

b) **2 Corinthians 12:9** "And he said unto me, My grace is sufficient for thee: for my strength is made perfect in weakness. Most gladly therefore will I rather glory in my infirmities, that the power of Christ may rest upon me."

c) **Ephesians 3:20** "Now unto him that is able to do exceeding abundantly above all that we ask or think, according to the power that worketh in us,"

Question 2: Can you think of a time when your faith helped carry you through a major life challenge?

3A - <u>God Can Replace</u>

Another reason to have faith is that God can *replace* what has been lost, as in the case of Job. We talked briefly about Job in Tip #3 – Admit You Have a Problem.

Job was a very reverent follower of God. Satan told God that surely Job would curse Him if his life were negatively affected. God didn't think so, and He let Satan trouble Job's life to prove His point to Satan.

3B - The first trial was with the loss of farm animals.

Job 1:12-19 "And the LORD said unto Satan, Behold, all that he hath is in thy power; only upon himself put not forth thine hand. So Satan went forth from the presence of the LORD. [13] And there was a day when his sons and his daughters were eating and drinking wine in their eldest brother's house: [14] And there came a messenger unto Job, and said, The oxen were plowing, and the asses feeding beside them: [15] And the Sabeans fell upon them, and took them away; yea, they have slain the servants with the edge of the sword; and I only am escaped alone to tell thee. "

3C - "[16] While he was yet speaking, there came also another, and said, The fire of God is fallen from heaven, and hath burned up the sheep, and the servants, and consumed them; and I only am escaped alone to tell thee. [17] While he was yet speaking, there came also another, and said, The Chaldeans made out three bands, and fell upon the camels, and have carried them away, yea, and slain the servants with the edge of the sword; and I only am escaped alone to tell thee."

3D - Job's second loss was the death of all his children.

"[18] While he was yet speaking, there came also another, and said, Thy sons and thy daughters were eating and drinking wine in their eldest brother's house: [19] And, behold, there came a great wind from the wilderness, and smote the four corners of the house, and it fell upon the young men, and they are dead; and I only am escaped alone to tell thee."

These were terrible losses for Job.

Question 3: Have you ever lost something valuable to you? If so, how did you respond?

4A - <u>Job's Health</u>

Job was then afflicted with boils all over his body.

Job 2:6-8 "And the LORD said unto Satan, Behold, he is in thine hand; but save his life. [7] So went Satan forth from the presence of the LORD, and smote Job with sore boils from the sole of his foot unto his crown. [8] And he took him a potsherd to scrape himself withal; and he sat down among the ashes."

Question 4: Have you ever had a major health problem? If so, how did you handle it?

5A - <u>Job's Relationships</u>

Even Job's wife was no help to him. She told Job to "curse God and die."

Job never cursed God, but he did do something that he shouldn't have – he complained. In fact, the whole of Chapter 3 is a complaint about his misfortune. Following, are four of the verses of Chapter 3 that bear this out.

Job 3:3-6 "Let the day perish wherein I was born, and the night in which it was said, There is a man child conceived. [4] Let that day be darkness; let not God regard it from above, neither let the light shine upon it. [5] Let darkness and the shadow of death stain it; let a cloud dwell upon it; let the blackness of the day terrify it. [6] As for that night, let darkness seize upon it; let it not be joined unto the days of the year, let it not come into the number of the months."

Question 5: Have you ever complained about a problem in your life? If so, would you like to share with us what happened?

6A - <u>God Shows Up</u>

Thirty-six chapters later, after much philosophical talk from Job and his well-meaning friends, God corrected everyone's misunderstandings of why things happened as they did. Job repented, and then God began to bless Job. Job ended up getting twice as much back of what he lost.

> **Job 42:19** "And the LORD turned the captivity of Job, when he prayed for his friends: also the LORD gave Job twice as much as he had before."

The story of Job gives us hope that God can make up for the losses that occur in our lives too.

Question 6: Have you ever experienced a great loss, and then received back more than you lost?

7A - Looking at Job's story, notice who was responsible for Job's loss. Job thought it was God, but it was actually Satan.

> **Job 1:12** "And the LORD said unto Satan, Behold, all that he hath is in thy power; only upon himself put not forth thine hand. So Satan went forth from the presence of the LORD."

Question 7: Have you ever had a loss in your life and blamed God for it?

8A - When Jesus was on earth, He attributed most of the people's problems to the work of Satan.

  a) **Matthew 8:16** "When the even was come, they brought unto him many that were possessed with devils: and he cast out the spirits with his word, and healed all that were sick:"

  b) **Matthew 9:33** "And when the devil was cast out, the dumb spake: and the multitudes marvelled, saying, It was never so seen in Israel."

  c) **Matthew 12:22** "Then was brought unto him one possessed with a devil, blind, and dumb: and he healed him, insomuch that the blind and dumb both spake and saw."

  d) **Matthew 17:18** "And Jesus rebuked the devil; and he departed out of him: and the child was cured from that very hour."

  e) **Luke 13:11,16** "And, behold, there was a woman which had a spirit of infirmity eighteen years, and was bowed together, and could in no wise lift up herself. ¹⁸ And ought not this woman, being a daughter of Abraham, whom Satan hath bound, lo, these eighteen years, be loosed from this bond on the sabbath day?"

Question 8: Do you think your problems have come because of Satan?

9A - <u>What if it's My Fault?</u>

Sometimes our losses in life are brought about by our own poor choices. However, just because we sometimes make poor choices doesn't mean God won't help us. He responds to our faith, not because we always do everything right. Thus, we don't have to be discouraged with our mistakes; we can show God that we are trusting Him, and we become candidates for His help, even if we caused the problem.

Mark 11:24 "Therefore I say unto you, <u>What things soever</u> ye desire, when ye pray, believe that ye receive them, and ye shall have them."

Question 9: What can you do to show God that you are trusting Him to solve your present problem?

10A - <u>Other Reasons to Welcome MLC's</u>

As mentioned above, the first reason is to see the challenge as a way to stretch our faith. We sometimes need difficulties to help us grow spiritually.

Secondly, our correct responses to our challenges can bring pleasure to God as He sees us trust him every step of the way. We believe that no problem is too big for us when we have Jesus by our side, guiding us, and even praying for us. See below.

Romans 8:34 "Who *is* he that condemneth? *It is* Christ that died, yea rather, that is risen again, who is even at the right hand of God, who also maketh intercession for us."

10B - Thirdly, we welcome MLC's because they teach us how to be victorious even though we have problems. Circumstances don't have to dictate how we feel. They force us to learn how to cast all our cares onto God. See the verses below.

a) **Psalm 55:22** "Cast thy burden upon the Lord, and he shall sustain thee: he shall never suffer the righteous to be moved."

b) **Philippians 4:6** "Be careful for nothing; but in every thing by prayer and supplication with thanksgiving let your requests be made known unto God."

c) **1 Peter 5:7** "Casting all your care upon him; for he careth for you."

10C - Fourthly, we welcome MLC's because after God delivers us, we'll have a powerful testimony to share with others who may be going through a similar challenge. In fact, our MLC can be the launch pad for a far-reaching ministry. Millions of people can be helped because of the victory we have found while going through a serious challenge.

10D - Fifthly, we welcome MLC's because we're simply curious about how God is going to deliver us. We picture ourselves as a bystander, someone on the outside looking in, observing how God is going to "fix" this situation at hand. This mindset helps us not to get overly engrossed in our problems.

10E - For any life challenge, it is good not to get overly stressed about it, but rather to trust God to solve it; even more so when it is a Major Life Challenge. True, there may be things we have to do to help solve our problem, but our primary focus is on God to solve it. This makes us candidates for His supernatural help.

10F - Remember that our peace is a reflection of our faith. When we have peace about a situation, we know our faith is intact. The following scriptures give us a sense of peace when we truly believe Jesus is in the middle of our life challenge.

10G - **John 14:1-12** "Let not your heart be troubled: ye believe in God, believe also in me. ² In my Father's house are many mansions: if it were not so, I would have told you. I go to prepare a place for you. ³ And if I go and prepare a place for you, I will come again, and receive you unto myself;

that where I am, there ye may be also. ⁴And whither I go ye know, and the way ye know. ⁵Thomas saith unto him, Lord, we know not whither thou goest; and how can we know the way? ⁶Jesus saith unto him, I am the way, the truth, and the life: no man cometh unto the Father, but by me. ⁷If ye had known me, ye should have known my Father also: and from henceforth ye know him, and have seen him."

10H - "⁸Philip saith unto him, Lord, show us the Father, and it sufficeth us. ⁹Jesus saith unto him, Have I been so long time with you, and yet hast thou not known me, Philip? he that hath seen me hath seen the Father; and how sayest thou then, Show us the Father? ¹⁰Believest thou not that I am in the Father, and the Father in me? the words that I speak unto you I speak not of myself: but the Father that dwelleth in me, he doeth the works."

10J - "¹¹Believe me that I am in the Father, and the Father in me: or else believe me for the very works' sake. ¹²Verily, verily, I say unto you, He that believeth on me, the works that I do shall he do also; and greater works than these shall he do; because I go unto my Father. ¹³And whatsoever ye shall ask in my name, that will I do, that the Father may be glorified in the Son. ¹⁴If ye shall ask any thing in my name, I will do it."

Question 10: Can you recall a stressful situation in which you had complete peace that God was right beside you, helping you get through the ordeal?

11A - <u>Final Reason</u>

The final reason we want to welcome major life challenges is that the way we go through them becomes a testimony of the reality of Jesus and His help. People will take notice when they see us go through a challenge peacefully, knowing that they, themselves, would have difficulty going through it. That helps prove the reality of Jesus Christ, and it may be enough for some people to consider making Jesus the Lord of their lives. Don't be afraid of MLC's, instead welcome them. Squeeze out every bit of good that is in them.

Question 11: Can you think of a time when you went through a difficult situation with grace and peace? Did someone comment on how well you went through it?

12A – MLCs can be difficult to go through, but they can also lead us to some amazing growth spiritually.

* * * * * * *

TIP #27

Resolve Delayed Maturity

When I was a child, I spake as a child, I understood as a child, I thought as a child: but when I became a man, I put away childish things. 1 Corinthians 13:11

1A - It is important for us to attain maturity in all aspects of our life. This is because we influence those around us. If people see us engage in certain behaviors, they will consider doing them as well. Thus it is essential to model maturity - emotionally, intellectually, behaviorally and spiritually. A healthy, thriving society depends on it.

1B - Who is This Tip For?

This Tip is primarily written for young people. Knowing vital information when we are young means we won't have to struggle through some pitfalls that catch young people off guard in today's society. This Tip will also alert us to weaknesses we may not know we have. Knowing our weaknesses, early in life, means we can guard them and work on them before they develop into unmanageable problems later in life.

Finally, knowing what a well-adjusted life looks like, early on, will better prepare us to raise our children successfully when that time comes.

Question 1: Can you think of any young people who are presently struggling in life?

2A - Delayed Maturity

Sometimes unhappiness is linked to areas of our lives that are not fully matured. Delayed maturity can come from early childhood trauma. It can also come from an unhealthy home environment growing up. Thirdly, it can from people we associate with during our adolescent and young adult years. Whatever the cause, delayed maturity can hinder us from developing inner peace, and from building friendships with emotionally healthy peers.

2B - Delayed Maturity is Common

Since it is difficult for anyone to go through childhood and adolescence without some form of negative influence, at home, at school, or within the community, most everyone has delayed maturity to some extent.

Question 2: Can you think of someone who has delayed maturity?

3A - <u>Making a Commitment</u>

The apostle Paul was confronted with this challenge at some point in his life. In our theme verse, it appears he made a conscientious decision to live in maturity. Here it is again.

> **1 Corinthians 13:11** "When I was a child, I spake as a child, I understood as a child, I thought as a child: but when I became a man, I put away childish things."

For our good and the good of those around us, we too can make a conscientious decision that we will live in maturity in every area of our life. God gives us the power of choice. We can choose to make life decisions that lead us to success in all areas our lives. This is one of them.

3B - <u>Childhood Trauma</u>

One of the causes of delayed maturity is childhood trauma. Some examples of childhood trauma are assault, molestation, severe teasing, neglect, and other forms of mental, physical, and emotional abuse. Depending on a child's ability to process trauma, the result can be overwhelming fear that prevents the child from returning to a natural state of calm in their minds. Such ongoing stress can prevent normal emotional growth, thus, delaying their maturity.

Question 3: Can you think of someone who experienced childhood trauma? If so, are there any lingering effects from their past trauma in their life today?

4A - <u>Observations</u>

Occasionally, people will comment on our behavior peculiarities. Sometimes, we mistakenly embrace these peculiarities with a sense of pride, and carry on the behavior. For those of us unsure of our identities, these peculiarities can fill our need for individuality, but in an unhealthy way. We don't realize that the trait that people are noticing in us can hold us back from fully maturing. It is wise to take note of what others are saying about us. Their unwelcome observations may sting, but they illuminate our blind spots and alert us to some self-development needed in our lives.

4B - <u>Compare</u>

One way for us to detect if delayed maturity has affected our life can be by comparing our lives with other people's lives in our age group. To do so, we could compare aspects such as the level of inner peace, social skills, educational achievements, and career success.

This method can be deceiving, however, in that, if the people we are comparing ourselves to, are also lacking in maturity, then the determinations we make about ourselves will not be accurate.

Question 4: Based on successful people in your age range, how do you compare with them as far as level of inner peace, social skills, educational achievements, and career success?

5A - One way to detect delayed maturity in us can be if we tend to be gullible; easily lead away from truth.

Question 5: Can you think of anyone who is easily lead away from truth?

Tip #27 – Resolve Delayed Maturity

6A - Disrespect

Another way to detect delayed maturity in us can be by examining the comments people make toward us. If we have delayed maturity, we may sometimes be teased or disrespected. It might be difficult for us to see the disrespect since it may have been happening to us our whole life. We may need to ask a trusted person to help us see if there is any disrespect in what others are saying to us. If any exists, we may need to adopt new ways of acting and responding to those who disrespect us.

At this point, we may also want to determine if we are disrespecting ourselves. If so, we'll want to make changes to how we view ourselves, as well.

Question 6: Can you think of any adults who are frequently teased or disrespected? Do you feel they might have delayed maturity?

7A - Respect and Christianity

As Christians, we need to aim for maximum respect. People may not agree with our faith stance, but they should respect us for our commitment to living a godly life. Below are some related verses.

a) **1 Corinthians 4:1** "Let a man so account of us, as of the ministers of Christ, and stewards of the mysteries of God."

b) **1 Timothy 4:12** "Let no man despise thy youth; but be thou an example of the believers, in word, in conversation, in charity, in spirit, in faith, in purity."

c) **Titus 2:15** "These things speak, and exhort, and rebuke with all authority. Let no man despise thee."

7B - Enabling

Sometimes we enable people to carry on in their delayed maturity. For reasons of respect or sympathy, we may detect where people are emotionally, and we lower ourselves to their level of maturity. Doing this permits them to carry on acting the way they do.

7C - Enabling people in this way is particularly hurtful in the church of Jesus Christ. When we communicate the gospel message, it ought to come from a position of maturity. Otherwise, people may not respect the message we give.

Question 7: Can you think of anyone with delayed maturity with whom you lowered yourself to their level of maturity? Can you tell us about it?

8A - Communication

Another way to detect our delayed maturity can be in the content of our communications. In our desire to relate well with others, we can sometimes share too much information about our personal lives.

For example, in a job setting, it is best to present a professional persona that rarely goes into detail about our personal affairs.

Below are some Bible verses about talking too much.

a) **Proverbs 10:19** "In the multitude of words there wanteth not sin: but he that refraineth his lips is wise."

b) **Proverbs 17:28** "Even a fool, when he holdeth his peace, is counted wise: and he that shutteth his lips is esteemed a man of understanding."

c) **Proverbs 21:23** "Whoso keepeth his mouth and his tongue keepeth his soul from troubles."

d) **Proverbs 29:20** "Seest thou a man that is hasty in his words? there is more hope of a fool than of him."

e) **James 1:19** "Wherefore, my beloved brethren, let every man be swift to hear, slow to speak, slow to wrath:"

For more on this subject see Tip #7 – Speak Right Words.

Question 8: Can you think of any adults who share too much personal information? Do you feel they might have delayed maturity?

9A - Speaking Skills

Another way to detect our delayed maturity can be if we have difficulty speaking to people, or have trouble talking to groups of people. Fear can prevent us from developing into calm, pleasant, enjoyable communicators.

Below are Bible verses about not fearing man.

a) **Deuteronomy 1:17** "Ye shall not respect persons in judgment; but ye shall hear the small as well as the great; ye shall not be afraid of the face of man; for the judgment is God's: and the cause that is too hard for you, bring it unto me, and I will hear it."

b) **1 Samuel 15:24** "And Saul said unto Samuel, I have sinned: for I have transgressed the commandment of the LORD, and thy words: because I feared the people, and obeyed their voice."

c) **Proverbs 29:25** "The fear of man bringeth a snare: but whoso putteth his trust in the LORD shall be safe."

d) **Isaiah 51:12** "I, even I, am He who comforts you Who are you that you are afraid of man who dies And of the son of man who is made like grass,"

9B - Help with Speaking

A great organization that helps people become better communicators is Toastmasters. There are likely Toastmasters clubs near where you live. To find out where, go to www.toastmasters.org.

Question 9: Can you think of someone who has a speech impediment, or has trouble speaking to groups of people?

10A - Anger

Another way to detect delayed maturity in us can be if our personality is dominated by anger. As adults, we want to communicate in a respectful, mature way, without anger.

Here are two Bible verses telling us to avoid getting angry.

a) **Psalms 37:8** "Cease from anger, and forsake wrath: fret not thyself in any wise to do evil."

b) **Ephesians 4:31** "Let all bitterness, and wrath, and anger, and clamour, and evil speaking, be put away from you, with all malice:"

For more information on anger, see Tip #18 - Eliminate Anger.

Question 10: Can you think of anyone who struggles with excessive anger? Do you feel they may have delayed maturity?

11A - Complaining and Being Critical

Another way to detect delayed maturity in us can be if we criticize and complain. As an adult, we want to avoid being critical and complaining. Criticizing and complaining is a quick way to lose good people as friends, and can hinder making new friends. An excellent book on this subject is: *How to Win Friends and Influence People by Dale Carnegie.*

For more on eliminating complaining, see Tip #7 – Speak Right Words, and Affirmation #4 – I Only Speak Right Words.

Below are some scriptures about not complaining.

a) **Numbers 11:1-4** "And when the people complained, it displeased the LORD: and the LORD heard it; and his anger was kindled; and the fire of the LORD burnt among them, and consumed them that were in the uttermost parts of the camp."

b) **1 Corinthians 10:10** "Neither murmur ye, as some of them also murmured (complained), and were destroyed of the destroyer."

c) **Philippians 2:14** "Do all things without murmurings (complaining) and disputings:"

Question 11: Can you think of any adults who have a problem with being critical or complaining? Do you feel they may have delayed maturity?

12A - Confidentiality

Another way to detect delayed maturity in us can be if we break confidentiality. This is a serious breach of trust. A mature person considers confidentiality before talking about other people.

The Bible talks about this problem in the verses below.

a) **Psalms 101:5** "Whoso privily slandereth his neighbour, him will I cut off: him that hath an high look and a proud heart will not I suffer."

b) **Proverbs 11:13** "A talebearer revealeth secrets: but he that is of a faithful spirit concealeth the matter."

c) **Proverbs 17:9** "He that covereth a transgression seeketh love; but he that repeateth a matter separateth very friends."

d) **Proverbs 20:19** "He that goeth about as a talebearer revealeth secrets: therefore meddle not with him that flattereth with his lips."

e) **1 Timothy 5:13** "And withal they learn to be idle, wandering about from house to house; and not only idle, but tattlers also and busybodies, speaking things which they ought not."

Question 12: Can you think of any adults who easily break confidentiality? Do you feel they might have delayed maturity?

13A - Lying

Another way to detect delayed maturity in us can be if we lie. In Tip #7 – Speak Right Words, we list 11 verses that caution us against lying.

Question 13: Can you think of anyone who frequently lies? Do you feel they have delayed maturity?

14A - Entitlement Syndrome

Another way to detect delayed maturity in us may be if we think we are entitled to things. We're not happy until we get what's coming to us. Children will have temper tantrums when they don't get what they want. Adults can sometimes think, act and speak out when they don't get what they want. It can even happen in a Christian context, "I'm God's child, so I deserve thus and thus." When things don't go the way we would like, we should be gracious about it, and trust God to bring things our way in His time.

Question 14: Can you think of anyone who feels the world owes them this or that? Do you feel they have delayed maturity?

15A - Poor Work Attitude

Another way to detect delayed maturity in us can be if we are not giving a 100% at our jobs. One of the reasons we show poor performance on our jobs is that our attitude is negative. A successful worker is one who offers top notch service while on the job. A way to brighten our attitude is to think of our job as a "close personal friend", and that we get to visit that "friend" every day.

Question 15: Can you think of anyone who doesn't want to work or has a negative attitude at work? If so, do you think their poor attitude is rooted in past trauma?

16A - Dress and Hygiene

Another way to detect delayed maturity in us can be how we dress, and how well we maintain our hygiene. We should seek to present ourselves well in public, remembering that we influence those around us. We should take care of our looks and hygiene without getting obsessed about our looks or how people view us.

Question 16: Can you think of any adults who frequently dress shabbily, or do not maintain their hygiene? Do you feel they might have delayed maturity?

17A - <u>Family Needs</u>

Another way to determine delayed maturity in us can be if we are not meeting all the needs of our family. We may have the time and ability to meet these needs, but we prefer to focus on other interests in our life. The Bible has strong words against this behavior.

- a) **Ephesians 5:25** "Husbands, love your wives, even as Christ also loved the church, and gave himself for it;"

- b) **Ephesians 5:33** "Nevertheless let every one of you in particular so love his wife even as himself; and the wife see that she reverence her husband."

- c) **1 Timothy 5:8** "But if any provide not for his own, and specially for those of his own house, he hath denied the faith, and is worse than an infidel."

- d) **1 Peter 3:7** "Likewise, ye husbands, dwell with them according to knowledge, giving honour unto the wife, as unto the weaker vessel, and as being heirs together of the grace of life; that your prayers be not hindered."

Question 17: Can you think of any adults who aren't meeting the needs of their family members adequately? Do you feel they might have delayed maturity?

18A - <u>Financial Responsibility</u>

Another way to detect delayed maturity in us can be with the spending of our finances. As a responsible adult, we want to live within our means, financially. Preferably, we want to live debt free. Living under a load of debt can impact our happiness. Thus we need to have wisdom in budgeting and using our finances.

The Bible cautions us to stay clear of debt as stated below.

- a) **Deuteronomy 15:6** "For the Lord thy God blesseth thee, as he promised thee: and thou shalt lend unto many nations, but thou shalt not borrow; and thou shalt reign over many nations, but they shall not reign over thee."

- b) **Proverbs 22:7** "The rich ruleth over the poor, and the borrower is servant to the lender."

- c) **Luke 14:28** "For which of you, intending to build a tower, sitteth not down first, and counteth the cost, whether he have sufficient to finish it?"

- d) **Romans 13:8** "Owe no man anything, but to love one another: for he that loveth another hath fulfilled the law."

18B - Retirement planning is also important for our financial health. As a responsible adult, we need to plan for our retirement. Thus we need to budget and invest so that when the time comes when we can no longer work, finances will be there to carry us through for the rest of our lives.

- a) **Proverbs 13:22** "A good man leaveth an inheritance to his children's children: and the wealth of the sinner is laid up for the just."

- b) **1 Timothy 5:8** "But if any provide not for his own, and specially for those of his own house, he hath denied the faith, and is worse than an infidel."

Question 18: Can you think of anyone who misspends their finances or neglects to plan for retirement? Do you feel they might have delayed maturity?

19A - Another way to detect delayed maturity in us can be if we have multiple adult partners. It is best to make a commitment to one individual, to be faithful to that person, for life. We do this for our mutual good, the good of our family, and the good of society.

A helpful question to ask ourselves can be: "What would the world be like if everybody lived the way I live?"

Here are some Bible verses on being faithful to one spouse.

a) **Ephesians 5:25** "Husbands, love your wives, even as Christ also loved the church, and gave himself for it;"

b) **Ephesians 5:33** "Nevertheless let every one of you in particular so love his wife even as himself; and the wife see that she reverence her husband."

c) **1 Peter 3:7** "Likewise, ye husbands, dwell with them according to knowledge, giving honour unto the wife, as unto the weaker vessel, and as being heirs together of the grace of life; that your prayers be not hindered."

Question 19: Can you think of any adults who are not committed to one spouse? Do you feel they might have delayed maturity?

20A - Final Notes

If you see someone who is delayed in their maturity, make it a consideration to befriend that individual and keep in touch with them. When the time comes for them to make important decisions in their life, you can be there to offer insight that may not be evident to them, thus helping them to prevent a crisis in their life.

Romans 15:1 "We then that are strong ought to bear the infirmities of the weak, and not to please ourselves."

20B - Wikipedia has a good definition of psychological maturity:

"Psychological maturity is the ability to respond to the environment in an appropriate manner. This response is generally learned rather than instinctive."

With God's help, we can learn how to develop into mature individuals who, in turn, become excellent examples for others to follow.

* * * * * * *

Disclaimer
"Toastmasters International® and all other Toastmasters International trademarks and copyrights are the sole property of Toastmasters International. This book is the opinion of the authors and is independent of Toastmasters International. It is not authorized by, endorsed by, sponsored by, affiliated with, or otherwise approved by Toastmasters International."

Tip #28

Sing

1A - According to a number of sources*, singing can help us overcome anxiety and depression. One such write-up is the August 16, 2013, *Time Magazine* article entitled, "Singing Changes Your Brain." See quotes below.

> *"When you sing, musical vibrations move through you, altering your physical and emotional landscape. Group singing, for those who have done it, is the most exhilarating and transformative of all. It takes something incredibly intimate, a sound that begins inside you, shares it with a roomful of people and it comes back as something even more thrilling: harmony."*

1B - The article goes on to say, *"The elation may come from endorphins, a hormone released by singing, which is associated with feelings of pleasure. Or it might be from oxytocin, another hormone released during singing, which has been found to alleviate anxiety and stress. Oxytocin also enhances feelings of trust and bonding, which may explain why still more studies have found that singing lessens feelings of depression and loneliness."*

1C - A recent study even attempts to make the case that *"music evolved as a tool of social living,"* and that the pleasure that comes from singing together is our evolutionary reward for coming together cooperatively, instead of hiding alone.

Question 1: Have you experienced an improvement in your mood as a result of singing? What is your favorite style of music?

2A - <u>Singing "Plus God."</u>

Singing is a powerful force for good. Now, couple it to God's truths, and we have the potential for huge improvement in our mood. Here are two Bible examples of the power of singing:

In the Book of 2 Chronicles, we see how singing caused the Israelites to win a war.

2 Chronicles 20:21,22 "And when he had consulted with the people, he appointed singers unto the LORD, and that should praise the beauty of holiness, as they went out before the army, and to say, Praise the LORD; for his mercy endureth for ever. ²² And when they began to sing and to praise, the

LORD set ambushments against the children of Ammon, Moab, and mount Seir, which were come against Judah; and they were smitten."

2B - In Acts 16, we see how singing praises to God opened prison doors where Paul and Silas were imprisoned for preaching the gospel.

> **Acts 16:22-26** "And the multitude rose up together against them: and the magistrates rent off their clothes, and commanded to beat them. [23] And when they had laid many stripes upon them, they cast them into prison, charging the jailor to keep them safely: [24] Who, having received such a charge, thrust them into the inner prison, and made their feet fast in the stocks. [25] And at midnight Paul and Silas prayed, and sang praises unto God: and the prisoners heard them. [26] And suddenly there was a great earthquake, so that the foundations of the prison were shaken: and immediately all the doors were opened, and every one's bands were loosed."

Question 2: Do you have any stories of how singing has helped you?

3A - There are many references in the Bible about singing. The following are scripture references highlighting the importance of singing.

Old Testament References

a) **Psalm 13:6** "I will sing unto the LORD, because he hath dealt bountifully with me."

b) **Psalm 59:16** "But I will sing of thy power; yea, I will sing aloud of thy mercy in the morning: for thou hast been my defence and refuge in the day of my trouble."

c) **Psalm 95:1,2** "O come, let us sing unto the LORD: let us make a joyful noise to the rock of our salvation. [2] Let us come before his presence with thanksgiving, and make a joyful noise unto him with psalms."

d) **Psalm 100:1,2** "(A Psalm of praise.) Make a joyful noise unto the LORD, all ye lands. [2] Serve the LORD with gladness: come before his presence with singing."

e) **Psalm 104:33** "I will sing unto the LORD as long as I live: I will sing praise to my God while I have my being."

f) **Psalm 147:1** "Praise ye the LORD: for it is good to sing praises unto our God; for it is pleasant; and praise is comely."

New Testament References

g) **1 Corinthians 14:15** "What is it then? I will pray with the spirit, and I will pray with the understanding also: I will sing with the spirit, and I will sing with the understanding also."

h) **Ephesians 5:19** "Speaking to yourselves in psalms and hymns and spiritual songs, singing and making melody in your heart to the Lord;"

i) **Colossians 3:16** "Let the word of Christ dwell in you richly in all wisdom; teaching and admonishing one another in psalms and hymns and spiritual songs, singing with grace in your hearts to the Lord."

j) **James 5:13** "Is any among you afflicted? let him pray. Is any merry? let him sing psalms."

3B - Martin Luther Highly Endorsed Singing

It may be interesting to know that the great reformer of the church, Martin Luther (1483-1546), highly endorsed singing praises to God. He wrote these words:

"When man's natural ability is whetted and polished to the extent that it becomes an art, then do we note with great surprise the great and perfect wisdom of God in music, which is, after all, His product and His gift; we marvel when we hear music in which one voice sings a simple melody, while three, four, or five other voices play and trip lustily around the voice that sings its simple melody and adorn this simple melody wonderfully with artistic musical effects, thus reminding us of a heavenly dance where all meet in a spirit of friendliness, caress, and embrace. . . ."

3C - *"A person who gives this some thought and yet does not regard it [music] as a marvelous creation of God, must be a clodhopper indeed and does not deserve to be called a human being; he should be permitted to hear nothing but the braying of asses and the grunting of hogs."* (Luther, "Preface to Georg Rhau's Symphoniae iucundae," LW 53, cited by Buszin in "Luther on Music," The Musical Quarterly 32, no. 1 [1946]: 85)

3D - God Sings Over You

It may surprise us to know that God sings over us.

Zephaniah 3:17 "The LORD thy God in the midst of thee is mighty; he will save, he will rejoice over thee with joy; he will rest in his love, he will joy over thee with singing."

Question 3: Do you sing to the Lord in your daily walk with Him?

4A - An Act of Faith

Singing can be an act of faith. If we are feeling so low that all we want to do is go to bed and pull the covers over us, we can begin to sing God's praises. That is an act of faith, and it gets God's attention.

Here are verses about using our will to sing praises to God.

a) **Numbers 21:17** "Then Israel sang this song, Spring up, O well; **sing** ye unto it:"

b) **Judges 5:3** "Hear, O ye kings; give ear, O ye princes; I, even I, will **sing** unto the Lord; I will **sing** praise to the Lord God of Israel."

c) **2 Samuel 22:50** "Therefore I will give thanks unto thee, O Lord, among the heathen, and I will **sing** praises unto thy name."

d) **Psalm 7:17** "I will praise the Lord according to his righteousness: and will **sing** praise to the name of the Lord most high."

e) **Psalm 9:2** "I will be glad and rejoice in thee: I will **sing** praise to thy name, O thou most High."

f) **Psalm 18:49** "Therefore will I give thanks unto thee, O Lord, among the heathen, and **sing** praises unto thy name."

g) **Psalm 27:6** "And now shall mine head be lifted up above mine enemies round about me: therefore will I offer in his tabernacle sacrifices of joy; I will **sing**, yea, I will **sing** praises unto the Lord."

h) **Psalm 30:12** "To the end that my glory may **sing** praise to thee, and not be silent. O Lord my God, I will give thanks unto thee for ever."

i) **Psalm 57:7** "My heart is fixed, O God, my heart is fixed: I will **sing** and give praise."

j) **Psalm 57:9** "I will praise thee, O Lord, among the people: I will **sing** unto thee among the nations."

k) **Psalm 59:16** "But I will **sing** of thy power; yea, I will **sing** aloud of thy mercy in the morning: for thou hast been my defence and refuge in the day of my trouble."

l) **Psalm 59:17** "Unto thee, O my strength, will I **sing**: for God is my defence, and the God of my mercy."

m) **Psalm 61:8** "So will I **sing** praise unto thy name for ever, that I may daily perform my vows."

n) **Psalm 71:22** "I will also praise thee with the psaltery, even thy truth, O my God: unto thee will I **sing** with the harp, O thou Holy One of Israel."

o) **Psalm 75:9** "But I will declare for ever; I will **sing** praises to the God of Jacob."

p) **Psalm 89:1** "I will **sing** of the mercies of the Lord for ever: with my mouth will I make known thy faithfulness to all generations."

q) **Psalm 101:1** "I will **sing** of mercy and judgment: unto thee, O Lord, will I **sing**."

r) **Psalm 108:1** "O God, my heart is fixed; I will **sing** and give praise, even with my glory."

s) **Psalm 108:3** "I will praise thee, O Lord, among the people: and I will **sing** praises unto thee among the nations."

t) **Psalm 146:2** "While I live will I praise the Lord: I will **sing** praises unto my God while I have any being."

Question 4: Have you ever forced yourself to sing when you didn't feel like singing?

5A - <u>Sing With Might!</u>

a) **1 Chronicles 13:8** "And David and all Israel played before God with all their might, and with singing, and with harps, and with psalteries, and with timbrels, and with cymbals, and with trumpets."

b) **2 Chronicles 30:21** "And the children of Israel that were present at Jerusalem kept the feast of unleavened bread seven days with great gladness: and the Levites and the priests praised the Lord day by day, singing with loud instruments unto the Lord."

c) **Nehemiah 12:42** "And Maaseiah, and Shemaiah, and Eleazar, and Uzzi, and Jehohanan, and Malchijah, and Elam, and Ezer. And the singers sang loud, with Jezrahiah their overseer."

Tip #28 – Sing

    d) **Psalm 51:14** "Deliver me from bloodguiltiness, O God, thou God of my salvation: and my tongue shall **sing** aloud of thy righteousness."

    e) **Psalm 71:23** "My lips shall greatly rejoice when I **sing** unto thee; and my soul, which thou hast redeemed."

    f) **Psalm 138:1** "I will praise thee with my whole heart: before the gods will I **sing** praise unto thee."

Question 5: Have you ever sung praise to God with all your might?

6A - <u>Sing About God's Past Works</u>

    a) **Exodus 15:1** "Then sang Moses and the children of Israel this song unto the Lord, and spake, saying, I will **sing** unto the Lord, for he hath triumphed gloriously: the horse and his rider hath he thrown into the sea."

    b) **1 Chronicles 16:9** "**Sing** unto him, **sing** psalms unto him, talk ye of all his wondrous works."

    c) **Psalm 13:6** "I will **sing** unto the Lord, because he hath dealt bountifully with me."

    d) **Psalm 21:13** "Be thou exalted, Lord, in thine own strength: so will we **sing** and praise thy power."

Question 6: Have you ever sung praise to God for the things He has done in the past?

7A - <u>Sing Until Something Happens</u>

    2 Chronicles 5:13 "It came even to pass, as the trumpeters and **sing**ers were as one, to make one sound to be heard in praising and thanking the Lord; and when they lifted up their voice with the trumpets and cymbals and instruments of musick, and praised the Lord, saying, For he is good; for his mercy endureth for ever: that then the house was filled with a cloud, even the house of the Lord;"

7B - <u>Tell People to Sing</u>

    a) **Numbers 21:17** "Then Israel sang this song, Spring up, O well; **sing** ye unto it:"

    b) **1 Chronicles 16:23** "**Sing** unto the Lord, all the earth; shew forth from day to day his salvation."

    c) **Psalm 9:11** "**Sing** praises to the Lord, which dwelleth in Zion: declare among the people his doings."

    d) **Psalm 30:4** "**Sing** unto the Lord, O ye saints of his, and give thanks at the remembrance of his holiness."

    e) **Psalm 33:3** "**Sing** unto him a new song; play skilfully with a loud noise."

    f) **Psalm 47:6** "**Sing** praises to God, **sing** praises: **sing** praises unto our King, **sing** praises."

    g) **Psalm 47:7** "For God is the King of all the earth: **sing** ye praises with understanding."

    h) **Psalm 66:2** "**Sing** forth the honour of his name: make his praise glorious."

    i) **Psalm 68:4** "**Sing** unto God, **sing** praises to his name: extol him that rideth upon the heavens by his name Jah, and rejoice before him."

    j) **Psalm 68:32** "**Sing** unto God, ye kingdoms of the earth; O **sing** praises unto the Lord; Selah:"

k) **Psalm 92:1** "It is a good thing to give thanks unto the Lord, and to **sing** praises unto thy name, O Most High:"

l) **Psalm 96:2** "**Sing** unto the Lord, bless his name; shew forth his salvation from day to day. "

m) **Psalm 98:5** "**Sing** unto the Lord with the harp; with the harp, and the voice of a psalm."

n) **Psalm 105:2** "**Sing** unto him, **sing** psalms unto him: talk ye of all his wondrous works."

o) **Psalm 135:3** "Praise the Lord; for the Lord is good: **sing** praises unto his name; for it is pleasant."

p) **Psalm 147:1** "Praise ye the Lord: for it is good to **sing** praises unto our God; for it is pleasant; and praise is comely."

q) **Psalm 147:7** "**Sing** unto the Lord with thanksgiving; **sing** praise upon the harp unto our God:"

r) **Isaiah 12:5** "**Sing** unto the Lord; for he hath done excellent things: this is known in all the earth."

s) **Isaiah 44:23** "**Sing**, O ye heavens; for the Lord hath done it: shout, ye lower parts of the earth: break forth into **sing**ing, ye mountains, O forest, and every tree therein: for the Lord hath redeemed Jacob, and glorified himself in Israel."

t) **Isaiah 54:1** "**Sing**, O barren, thou that didst not bear; break forth into **sing**ing, and cry aloud thou that didst not travail with child: for more are the children of the desolate than the children of the married wife, saith the Lord."

u) **Jeremiah 20:13** "**Sing** unto the Lord, praise ye the Lord: for he hath delivered the soul of the poor from the hand of evildoers."

v) **Zechariah 2:10** "**Sing** and rejoice, O daughter of Zion: for, lo, I come, and I will dwell in the midst of thee, saith the Lord."

w) **Psalm 95:1** "O come, let us **sing** unto the Lord: let us make a joyful noise to the rock of our salvation."

Question 7: Have you ever suggested to people that they sing to God?

8A - <u>Sing with Instruments</u>

a) **Psalm 33:2** "Praise the Lord with harp: **sing** unto him with the psaltery and an instrument of ten strings."

b) **Psalm 33:3** "**Sing** unto him a new song; play skilfully with a loud noise."

c) **Psalm 87:7** "As well the singers as the players on instruments shall be there: all my springs are in thee."

d) **Psalm 149:3** "Let them praise his name in the dance: let them **sing** praises unto him with the timbrel and harp."

Question 8: Do you play a musical instrument to God? If yes, what do you play?

9A - Sing a New Song

a) **Psalm 33:3** "**Sing** unto him a new song; play skillfully with a loud noise."

b) **Psalm 96:1** "O **sing** unto the Lord a new song: **sing** unto the Lord, all the earth."

c) **Psalm 98:1** "O **sing** unto the Lord a new song; for he hath done marvellous things: his right hand, and his holy arm, hath gotten him the victory."

d) **Psalm 144:9** "I will **sing** a new song unto thee, O God: upon a psaltery and an instrument of ten strings will I **sing** praises unto thee."

e) **Psalm 149:1** "Praise ye the Lord. **Sing** unto the Lord a new song, and his praise in the congregation of saints."

f) **Isaiah 42:10** "**Sing** unto the Lord a new song, and his praise from the end of the earth, ye that go down to the sea, and all that is therein; the isles, and the inhabitants thereof."

9B - Singing and Joy

a) **Psalm 67:4** "O let the nations be glad and **sing** for joy: for thou shalt judge the people righteously, and govern the nations upon earth. Selah."

b) **Psalm 100:2** "Serve the Lord with gladness: come before his presence with **sing**ing."

c) **Psalm 126:2** "Then was our mouth filled with laughter, and our tongue with **sing**ing: then said they among the heathen, The Lord hath done great things for them."

d) **Isaiah 49:13** "**Sing**, O heavens; and be joyful, O earth; and break forth into **sing**ing, O mountains: for the Lord hath comforted his people, and will have mercy upon his afflicted."

e) **Isaiah 51:11** "Therefore the redeemed of the Lord shall return, and come with **sing**ing unto Zion; and everlasting joy shall be upon their head: they shall obtain gladness and joy; and sorrow and mourning shall flee away."

f) **Isaiah 52:9** "Break forth into joy, **sing** together, ye waste places of Jerusalem: for the Lord hath comforted his people, he hath redeemed Jerusalem."

g) **Isaiah 55:12** "For ye shall go out with joy, and be led forth with peace: the mountains and the hills shall break forth before you into **sing**ing, and all the trees of the field shall clap their hands."

h) **Zephaniah 3:14** "**Sing**, O daughter of Zion; shout, O Israel; be glad and rejoice with all the heart, O daughter of Jerusalem."

Question 9: Have you ever sung to God with great joy?

*Articles on Singing:
https://www.sciencedaily.com/releases/2017/12/171221101402.htm
https://www.psychologytoday.com/gb/blog/the-athletes-way/201811/feeling-lonely-singing-could-be-joyful-remedy
https://www.rhinegold.co.uk/music_teacher/31600/

* * * * * * *

TIP #29

Join a Church

1A - In this Tip, we are going to see that the Christian church is the center of the community. We will also look at the purpose of the church, part of which, is to show us how to live above anxiety and depression.

Not every congregation meets in a public building, but wherever a church meets, that is the focus of all of heaven. See below.

Hebrews 12:1 "Wherefore seeing we also are compassed about with so great a cloud of witnesses, let us lay aside every weight, and the sin which doth so easily beset us, and let us run with patience the race that is set before us,"

Thus, heaven has the greatest "reality show" in the universe. They are watching us GO!

1B - <u>How the Church Got Started</u>

After God, the Father, resurrected Jesus from the dead, Jesus commissioned His disciples to go and preach the Gospel of forgiveness through Christ Jesus throughout the whole world.

Mark 16:15, "And he said unto them, Go ye into all the world, and preach the gospel to every creature."

1C - Before the disciples were to evangelize the world Jesus had them wait for the Holy Spirit to empower them.

Acts 2:1-4 "And when the day of Pentecost was fully come, they were all with one accord in one place. ² And suddenly there came a sound from heaven as of a rushing mighty wind, and it filled all the house where they were sitting. ³ And there appeared unto them cloven tongues like as of fire, and it sat upon each of them. ⁴ And they were all filled with the Holy Ghost, and began to speak with other tongues, as the Spirit gave them utterance."

Since then the church has grown in number, and in knowledge of the scriptures.

1D - <u>Esteem Mature Christians</u>

In a local church, we can meet some amazing people, individuals who are eager to help us mature in our walk with God. Remember to value these people. We may not see their real value at the time, but years later we will see how instrumental they were in helping us grow spiritually.

a) **Proverbs 27:17** "Iron sharpeneth iron; so a man sharpeneth the countenance of his friend."

b) **1 Timothy 5:17** "Let the elders that rule well be counted worthy of double honour, especially they who labour in the word and doctrine."

Question 1: Have you ever been inspired by someone in your church? If so, how did they help you?

2A - <u>Churches and Unbelievers</u>

As the church mobilizes its members, unbelievers will begin attending church services. Wise churches will always present the simple story of salvation through Christ at the end of the service to give unbelievers the opportunity to receive Jesus as their personal Savior. Once they accept Jesus, they can begin enjoying the benefits of connection to a local church.

2B - <u>New Believers</u>

Something to note about churches is, although they have some great people as members, churches that are growing will also have people who are just at the beginning of their spiritual growth. This means that there may be people who have come into the church with various negative habits, behaviors, and mindsets. As we get to know these new members, we might be negatively affected and hurt by them. This is normal. When this happens, it is best for us to forgive the person who has hurt us. We need to remember that we, ourselves, were once new believers, with problems needing help from our Savior, and His church. We will want to quickly forgive these people so we can continue our growth in Christ.

Question 2: Have you ever been hurt by someone in your church? If so, how did it affect you, and what did you learn from it?

3A - Some people say they don't need to be part of a local church, but the Bible tells us not to neglect meeting together.

Hebrews 10:25 "Not forsaking the assembling of ourselves together, as the manner of some is; but exhorting one another: and so much the more, as ye see the day approaching."

Question 3: Do you know an Christians who do not attend a local church?

4A - In the scripture below we see that Jesus intends to build a community of believers, and called it His church. His intention is for the church to be strong and victorious.

Matthew 16:18 "And I say also unto thee, That thou art Peter, and upon this rock I will build my church; and the gates of hell shall not prevail against it."

Question 4: Do you know of a church which is vibrant and victorious?

5A - The Bible tells us to be watchful of people who try to bring discord into the church.

Romans 16:17 "Now I beseech you, brethren, mark them which cause divisions and offences contrary to the doctrine which ye have learned; and avoid them."

Question 5: Can you think of anyone who tends to bring division to a church?

6A - The Bible refers to the church as the body of Christ.

- a) **Romans 12:5** "So we, being many, are one body in Christ, and every one members one of another."

- b) **1 Corinthians 12:27** "Now ye are the body of Christ, and members in particular."

- c) **Ephesians 4:12** "For the perfecting of the saints, for the work of the ministry, for the edifying of the body of Christ:"

- d) **Ephesians 4:16** "From whom the whole body fitly joined together and compacted by that which every joint supplieth, according to the effectual working in the measure of every part, maketh increase of the body unto the edifying of itself in love."

6B - Since the church is the Body of Christ, the church should know what is important to Jesus. Preaching and teaching the gospel of salvation is what is important to Jesus. See below.

- a) **Matthew 10:32** "Whosoever therefore shall confess me before men, him will I confess also before my Father which is in heaven."

- b) **Matthew 28:19** "Go ye therefore, and teach all nations, baptizing them in the name of the Father, and of the Son, and of the Holy Ghost:"

- c) **Mark 16:15** "And he said unto them, Go ye into all the world, and preach the gospel to every creature."

- d) **Luke 14:23** "And the lord said unto the servant, Go out into the highways and hedges, and compel them to come in, that my house may be filled."

- e) **John 3:3** "Jesus answered and said unto him, Verily, verily, I say unto thee, Except a man be born again, he cannot see the kingdom of God."

- f) **John 3:5** "Jesus answered, Verily, verily, I say unto thee, Except a man be born of water and the Spirit, he cannot enter into the kingdom of God."

- g) **John 15:16** "Ye have not chosen me, but I have chosen you, and ordained you, that ye should go and bring forth fruit, and [that] your fruit should remain: that whatsoever ye shall ask of the Father in my name, he may give it you."

Question 6: Can you tell us of a church where preaching the gospel is a priority?

7A - <u>A Unique Term</u>

Jesus used a unique term when talking about how people make it to heaven after they die. He said that a person needs to be "born again."

John 3:3 "Jesus answered and said unto him, Verily, verily, I say unto thee, Except a man be <u>born again</u>, he cannot see the kingdom of God."

7B - Heaven is a place without sin, and only sinless people can get to heaven. An marvelous attribute with man is that we have freedom of choice – we can choose to do right, but we can also choose to do wrong. All of us, at some point in our lives, have chosen wrongly – we have sinned. The Bible tells us that only blood can take away sin.

a) **Leviticus 17:11** "For the life of the flesh is in the blood: and I have given it to you upon the altar to make an atonement for your souls: for it is the blood that maketh an atonement for the soul."

b) **Hebrews 9:22** "And almost all things are by the law purged with blood; and without shedding of blood is no remission."

7C - We become born again when we admit we have sinned, and we acknowledge what Jesus did on the cross for us personally – Jesus took the punishment for our sin by allowing Himself to be nailed on the cross.

It's at the cross that a great exchange took place. The Apostle Paul tells us what God did when Christ died.

2 Corinthians 5:21 "For he hath made him to be sin for us, who knew no sin; that we might be made the righteousness of God in him."

7D - Jesus became sin for us so that we might become righteous (sinless) in God's sight. Our sin killed Jesus. But then God miraculously resurrected Jesus on the third day, and now we can all be forgiven of sin. We can also learn how to live free of sin, and be ready for heaven. Our old life of sin dies, and our new life in Christ begins – hence the term, "born again."

Question 7: Can you tell us of a church that uses the term "born again" when speaking to unbelievers about becoming a Christian?

8A - <u>Church Outreach</u>

The most important part of human life is making it to heaven, thus a church should try to be open as many hours a week as possible so unbelievers can come and find Jesus as Savior. Also, that people can be taught how to live free of all hindrances to happiness. In this way, a church is like a hospital; they help "broken" people.

Indeed, people should be able to come in anytime they feel the need, and be able to speak with someone, or learn how to overcome obstacles in their life.

Question 8: Can you tell us of a church that is open many hours a week, teaching people principles that help them know God, and how to overcome obstacles in their life?

9A - In addition to making the church available throughout the week, a church should have community events that give people in the community an opportunity to hear the Gospel message. Most churches offer a week-long Vacation Bible School during the summer. Some churches will rent a band shell in a park and provide a "Church-in-the-Park" experience. Some churches have live theater presentations during Christmas or Easter.

9B - An effective way for a church to present the gospel is when churches work together on a community outreach event. Jesus prayed that such meetings would be held, so that the world would believe that God sent Jesus.

John 17:21 "That they all may be one; as thou, Father, art in me, and I in thee, that they also may be one in us: that the world may believe that thou hast sent me."

Question 9: What methods of sharing the gospel have you seen churches use?

10A - In addition to sharing the good news of the gospel, the church should be able to help the community in practical ways. See below.

- a) **Matthew 5:42** "Give to him that asketh thee, and from him that would borrow of thee turn not thou away."

- b) **Matthew 25:35** "For I was an hungred, and ye gave me meat: I was thirsty, and ye gave me drink: I was a stranger, and ye took me in:"

- c) **Matthew 25:44-45** "Then shall they also answer him, saying, Lord, when saw we thee an hungred, or athirst, or a stranger, or naked, or sick, or in prison, and did not minister unto thee? [45] Then shall he answer them, saying, Verily I say unto you, Inasmuch as ye did it not to one of the least of these, ye did it not to me."

- d) **Ephesians 4:28** "Let him that stole steal no more: but rather let him labour, working with his hands the thing which is good, that he may have to give to him that needeth."

- e) **Hebrews 13:16** "But to do good and to communicate forget not: for with such sacrifices God is well pleased."

Question 10: In what ways have you seen churches help people in the community?

11A - Church "In-Reach"

In addition to reaching out to help unbelievers, a church should be helping people who are already members of the church. Here are some verses on the church helping its members.

- a) **Acts 20:35** "I have shewed you all things, how that so labouring ye ought to support the weak, and to remember the words of the Lord Jesus, how he said, It is more blessed to give than to receive."

- b) **Romans 15:1** "We then that are strong ought to bear the infirmities of the weak, and not to please ourselves."

- c) **Galatians 6:2** "Bear ye one another's burdens, and so fulfil the law of Christ."

- d) **Galatians 6:10** "As we have therefore opportunity, let us do good unto all men, especially unto them who are of the household of faith."

- e) **Philippians 2:4** "Look not every man on his own things, but every man also on the things of others."

- f) **Hebrews 13:16** "But to do good and to communicate forget not: for with such sacrifices God is well pleased."

- g) **James 2:15-17** "If a brother or sister be naked, and destitute of daily food, [16] And one of you say unto them, Depart in peace, be ye warmed and filled; notwithstanding ye give them not those things which are needful to the body; what doth it profit? [17] Even so faith, if it hath not works, is dead, being alone."

- h) **1 John 3:17** "But whoso hath this world's good, and seeth his brother have need, and shutteth up his bowels of compassion from him, how dwelleth the love of God in him?"

11B - As members of the Body of Christ, we are one body, and are to share the joys and the pains of our brothers and sisters in Christ. Social media makes it easy for us to stay connected with our church family and lets us know when help is needed.

Question 11: In what ways have you seen churches help its members?

12A - An effective way to meet the many needs of church members is to organize them into groups that meet outside of church meetings. There are various names given to these groups, for example, Home Groups, Home Fellowships, Life Groups, Connect Groups. These groups offer a relaxed atmosphere to get to know one another and to learn about Christ. They also provide immediate, close-to-home care when someone is struggling.

   a) **1 Corinthians 12:26** "And whether one member suffer, all the members suffer with it; or one member be honoured, all the members rejoice with it."

   b) **Hebrews 13:5** "Remember them that are in bonds, as bound with them; and them which suffer adversity, as being yourselves also in the body."

Question 12: Do you know of any churches that have weekly home groups? Have you ever been helped by a home group?

13A - <u>Supporting the Church Financially</u>

Donating money can be a delicate issue. A wise church will be thrifty and transparent with their finances so that if a financial matter arises, it can be quickly resolved, so the church can get back to the job of spreading the Gospel.

Question 13: Can you think of a church that publishes an annual report on how donations were allocated?

14A - <u>The Love of Giving</u>

There is something about Jesus that makes people want to give. Zacchaeus, the despised tax collector, felt it. One day he climbed a tree to watch Jesus walk by. Jesus spotted him and said, *"Zacchaeus, make haste, and come down; for to day I must abide at thy house."* (**Luke 19:5**) That brief time with Jesus prompted Zacchaeus to give away a large sum of money.

   Luke 19:8 "And Zacchaeus stood, and said unto the Lord: Behold, Lord, the half of my goods I give to the poor; and if I have taken anything from any man by false accusation, I restore him fourfold."

14B - Other people gave more than Zacchaeus. The Apostles gave up everything to follow Him.

   Matthew 19:27 "Then answered Peter and said unto him, Behold, we have forsaken all, and followed thee; what shall we have therefore?"

Indeed, one way to spot a child of God is by their generosity.

Question 14: Have you ever felt the desire to give to God, or give to help others?

15A - God has instituted a method of meeting the needs of a local church called tithing. The tithing principle is one in which a person gives to God 10% of any profit they earn. This principle started with Abraham. The Bible says that after a war Abraham paid tithes to Melchizedek.

Genesis 14:19-20 "And he blessed him, and said, Blessed be Abram of the most high God, possessor of heaven and earth: [20] And blessed be the most high God, which hath delivered thine enemies into thy hand. And he gave him tithes of all."

15B - Many people believe Melchisedek was a type of Jesus because he had no beginning and no end. See verses below.

Hebrews 7:1-6 "For this Melchisedek, king of Salem, priest of the most high God, who met Abraham returning from the slaughter of the kings, and blessed him; [2] To whom also Abraham gave a tenth part of all; first being by interpretation King of righteousness, and after that also King of Salem, which is, King of peace; [3] Without father, without mother, without descent, having neither beginning of days, nor end of life; but made like unto the Son of God; abideth a priest continually."

15C - "[4] Now consider how great this man was, unto whom even the patriarch Abraham gave the tenth of the spoils. [5] And verily they that are of the sons of Levi, who receive the office of the priesthood, have a commandment to take tithes of the people according to the law, that is, of their brethren, though they come out of the loins of Abraham: [6] But he whose descent is not counted from them received tithes of Abraham, and blessed him that had the promises."

15D - 430 years later, God gave the Levitical Law to Israel, which was a list of rules for God's people to live by. This included tithing.

a) **Leviticus 27:30** "And all the tithe of the land, whether of the seed of the land, or of the fruit of the tree, is the LORD's: it is holy unto the LORD."

b) **Leviticus 27:32** "And concerning the tithe of the herd, or of the flock, even of whatsoever passeth under the rod, the tenth shall be holy unto the LORD."

15E - 1500 years after that, we see that Jesus endorsed tithing.

a) **Matthew 23:23** "Woe unto you, scribes and Pharisees, hypocrites! for ye pay tithe of mint and anise and cummin, and have omitted the weightier matters of the law, judgment, mercy, and faith: these ought ye to have done, and not to leave the other undone."

b) **Luke 11:42** "But woe unto you, Pharisees! for ye tithe mint and rue and all manner of herbs, and pass over judgment and the love of God: these ought ye to have done, and not to leave the other undone."

Question 15: Can you tell us of a church that teaches the principle of tithing?

16A - <u>The Promise of Blessing</u>

In the following verse we see that God issues us a challenge.

Malachi 3:10 "Bring ye all the tithes into the storehouse, that there may be meat in mine house, and <u>prove me</u> now herewith, saith the LORD of hosts, if I will not open you the windows of heaven, and pour you out a blessing, that there shall not be room enough to receive it."

16B - Verse 10 says *"...prove me now herewith, saith the LORD of hosts, if I will not open you the windows of heaven, and pour you out a blessing, that there shall not be room enough to receive it."* God wants us to tithe so we can help others. Helping others is a good enough reward to do so, but God doesn't stop there. He says He will bless us if we tithe. Many people testify that their lives have been blessed financially, and in other ways, because of tithing. That is wonderful, but this isn't why we tithe. We tithe because God tells us to tithe.

16C - Here are other scriptures on blessings that come from giving.

  a) **Proverbs 11:24** "There is that scattereth, and yet increaseth; and there is that withholdeth more than is meet, but it tendeth to poverty."

  b) **Luke 6:38** "Give, and it shall be given unto you; good measure, pressed down, and shaken together, and running over, shall men give into your bosom. For with the same measure that ye mete withal it shall be measured to you again."

  c) **2 Corinthians 9:6** "But this I say, He which soweth sparingly shall reap also sparingly; and he which soweth bountifully shall reap also bountifully."

  d) **2 Corinthians 9:7,8** "Every man according as he purposeth in his heart, so let him give; not grudgingly, or of necessity: for God loveth a cheerful giver. And God is able to make all grace abound toward you; that ye, always having all sufficiency in all things, may abound to every good work:"

Question 16: Do you know people who have been blessed by tithing?

17A - New Testament Giving

Nothing is said about tithing after Jesus was resurrected, but people in the 1st-century church gave much more than the tithe.

  Acts 4:36-37 "And Joses, who by the apostles was surnamed Barnabas, (which is, being interpreted, The son of consolation,) a Levite, and of the country of Cyprus, ^{37} Having land, sold it, and brought the money, and laid it at the apostle's feet."

17B - Communal Living

The New Testament church was a beautiful picture of peace and love amongst its members, with everyone sharing what they had with those in need.

  a) **Acts 2:44-45** "And all that believed were together, and had all things common; ^{45} And sold their possessions and goods, and parted them to all men, as every man had need."

  b) **Acts 4:32** "And the multitude of them that believed were of one heart and of one soul: neither said any *of them* that ought of the things which he possessed was his own; but they had all things common."

  c) **Acts 4:34-35** "Neither was there any among them that lacked: for as many as were possessors of lands or houses sold them, and brought the prices of the things that were sold, ^{35} And laid *them* down at the apostles' feet: and distribution was made unto every man according as he had need."

  d) **2 Corinthians 8:13-15** "For I mean not that other men be eased, and ye burdened: ^{14} But by an equality, that now at this time your abundance may be a supply for their want, that their abundance also may be a supply for your want: that there may be equality: ^{15} As it is written, He that had gathered much had nothing over; and he that had gathered little had no lack."

Question 17: Can you tell us of a church that has a communal feel when it comes to sharing?

18A - <u>A Store House</u>

The Bible says that if church members are tithing, their church needs to have a "storehouse" – a place where people can come when they are in need. The following scriptures show the importance of tithing and of having a storehouse.

> **Malachi 3:8-10** "Will a man rob God? Yet ye have robbed me. But ye say, Wherein have we robbed thee? In tithes and offerings. ⁹ Ye are cursed with a curse: for ye have robbed me, even this whole nation. ¹⁰ Bring ye all the tithes into the <u>storehouse</u>, that there may be meat in mine house, and prove me now herewith, saith the LORD of hosts, if I will not open you the windows of heaven, and pour you out a blessing, that there shall not be room enough to receive it."

Question 18: Can you think of a church that has a "storehouse" from which to give to those in need?

19A - <u>First Century Church Needs</u>

The 1ˢᵗ-century church had great needs. They were feeding the poor and sending groups of people all over the world to spread the Good News of Jesus Christ. The Apostle Paul had to do everything in his power to meet the many needs. Here is a strategy he used: He offered his preaching for free. He didn't want people to think he was preaching the gospel to make money. The following scriptures reveal this mindset.

> a) **1 Corinthians 9:18** "What is my reward then? Verily that, when I preach the gospel, I may make the gospel of Christ without charge, that I abuse not my power in the gospel."
>
> b) **1 Thessalonians 2:9** "For ye remember, brethren, our labour and travail; for laboring night and day, because we would not be chargeable unto any of you, we preached unto you the gospel of God."
>
> c) **2 Thessalonians 3:8** "Neither did we eat any man's bread for nought; but wrought with labour and travail night and day, that we might not be chargeable to any of you:"

Question 19: Do you know of a church that is sensitive to people's tendency to think *"churches only want your money"*?

20A - Paul could preach the Gospel for free because he was a tent-maker by trade.

> **Acts 18:3** "And because he was of the same craft, he abode with them, and wrought: for by their occupation they were tentmakers."

Question 20: Do you know of anyone who funds their own Christian ministry?

21A - <u>Financial Gain and Godliness</u>

In Paul's day, some people taught that having great wealth was a sign of Godliness. Paul refuted that belief extensively.

> **1 Timothy 6:5-11** "Perverse disputings of men of corrupt minds, and destitute of the truth, supposing that gain is godliness: from such withdraw thyself. ⁶ But godliness with contentment is great gain." ⁷ For we brought nothing into this world, and it is certain we can carry nothing out.⁸ And having food and raiment let us be therewith content. ⁹ But they that will be rich fall into temptation and a snare, and into many foolish and hurtful lusts, which drown men in destruction and perdition. ¹⁰ For the love of money is the root of all evil: which while some coveted after, they have erred from

the faith, and pierced themselves through with many sorrows. [11] But thou, O man of God, flee these things; and follow after righteousness, godliness, faith, love, patience, meekness."

21B - <u>Two Opponents</u>

Is it wrong to be a wealthy Christian? No, but Jesus told us that wealth can be a god in our lives. He said that we cannot serve, both, God and money.

Matthew 6:24 "No man can serve two masters: for either he will hate the one, and love the other; or else he will hold to the one, and despise the other. Ye cannot serve God and mammon."

21C - Money is not our friend. It seeks to displace God in our lives. We must be careful. We can be at a time in our lives when we are enthralled with God, and busy doing things to further His kingdom, and all of a sudden we get a desire to buy something, or we get a better job offer, or we get a business idea. These are not bad things, but they *can* affect our commitment for God. A person's zeal for God is their most valuable possession. And the devil will go after it, and steal it in any way he can. Here are verses related to losing our focus for God.

a) **Revelation 2:4-5** "Nevertheless I have somewhat against thee, because thou hast left thy first love. [5] Remember therefore from whence thou art fallen, and repent, and do the first works;"

b) **Revelation 3:16** "So then because thou art lukewarm, and neither cold nor hot, I will spue thee out of my mouth."

21D - Jesus addresses the issue of money on a number of occasions. Let's look at the following verses to get a sense of what money is from Jesus's perspective.

Below, we read how Jesus advised people not to hoard their wealth, but instead to use their money to help others.

a) **Matthew 6:19-21** "Lay not up for yourselves treasures upon earth, where moth and rust doth corrupt, and where thieves break through and steal: [20] But lay up for yourselves treasures in heaven, where neither moth nor rust doth corrupt, and where thieves do not break through nor steal: [21] For where your treasure is, there will your heart be also."

b) **Luke 12:20,21** "But God said unto him, Thou fool, this night thy soul shall be required of thee: then whose shall those things be, which thou hast provided? [21] So is he that layeth up treasure for himself, and is not rich toward God."

c) **Luke 12:33** "Sell that ye have, and give alms; provide yourselves bags which wax not old, a treasure in the heavens that faileth not, where no thief approacheth, neither moth corrupteth."

21E - Below, we read how hard it is for a rich man to enter into the kingdom of heaven.

Matthew 19:23,24 "Then said Jesus unto his disciples, Verily I say unto you, That a rich man shall hardly enter into the kingdom of heaven. [24] And again I say unto you, It is easier for a camel to go through the eye of a needle, than for a rich man to enter into the kingdom of God."

21F - Following, we read how Jesus warns people who are rich.

Luke 6:24,25 "But woe unto you that are rich! for ye have received your consolation. [25] Woe unto you that are full! for ye shall hunger. Woe unto you that laugh now! for ye shall mourn and weep."

21G - Below, we read how Jesus advised people to be content with their wages.

> **Luke 3:14** "And the soldiers likewise demanded of him, saying, And what shall we do? And he said unto them, Do violence to no man, neither accuse any falsely; and be content with your wages."

21H - In Matthew 21:12, Mark 11:15 and John 2:15, we see how Jesus flipped over the tables of the money-changers in the temple.

> **Matthew 21:12,13** "And Jesus went into the temple of God, and cast out all them that sold and bought in the temple, and overthrew the tables of the moneychangers, and the seats of them that sold doves, [13] And said unto them, It is written, My house shall be called the house of prayer; but ye have made it a den of thieves."

21J - Jesus did not think to highly of money, in fact He despised it. Does that mean we aren't supposed to have a savings account or a retirement plan? It can be wise to have these, so it is a delicate question, and can only be answered by each person individually. As we take time to pray and grow close to God, we will learn how to hear His voice. This will help us see where we should allocate our financial resources.

21K - In the final scene of the movie *Schindler's List*, in which Schindler is surrounded by the 1,100 people he saved from Nazi concentration camps, he says slowly and painfully, *"I could have got more out. I could have sold that car and got ten more people out." "And this pin, it is gold. I could have sold it and got two more people out..."* It is a solemn scene, and it illustrates the love and commitment he had developed to help the Jewish people in need.

21L - What is written on *our* 'Schindler's list'? What are *our* priorities? What do we aspire to do with our lives? May our 'Schindler's list' be filled with noble goals and achievements, so that when we come face to face with God, we will stand unashamed, hoping only to hear the words, "Well done, good and faithful servant."

> **Matthew 25:21** "His lord said unto him, Well done, thou good and faithful servant: thou hast been faithful over a few things, I will make thee ruler over many things: enter thou into the joy of thy lord."

21M - May each of us be "God-conscious" and "others-conscious" so that God can use us to help those in need. And may those responsible for distributing funds for operating church ministries do it wisely. May those who receive these funds, do their jobs well so that many will be helped, and many will hear the Good News of what Jesus did for them, and be challenged to give their lives to Christ, and be saved.

Question 22: Do you know of a church that is watchful of how they spend their money? Do they have a deep desire to share the Gospel message with unsaved people?

22A - Joining a great church can have a wonderful effect on our lives, ushering us toward happiness and fruitfulness in every area of our lives.

* * * * * * *

The Happiness Basics
Meeting Start

The numbered paragraphs below are to be read by the participants in the meeting. They will direct the content of the conversation during the meeting. The Chairperson will read their own parts marked in ***bold italics** font,* and the meeting participants will read their parts marked in **Bold Arial** font, such as **First Speaker**.

1 - *Chairperson: Welcome everyone to the Victory Tips Recovery Group! My name is ____(Chairperson name)___ , and I will be the Chairperson for our meeting. Before we start, please turn off the ringers on your cell phone. Also, please try to limit background noise during the call. Use the Mute feature if need be.*

2 - *Chairperson: Do we have any new visitors?* *[If so, kindly acknowledge and thank them for joining in, and ask who wants to participate or just listen in.]* ***Our meetings have two main sections: The Happiness Basics, and the Happiness Tips. As we go through the program, I will read from the bold italics text marked 'Chairperson', and I will call on others who wish to have Speaker Roles by reading from the*** **Bold Arial** ***font text. Please keep your comments to about thirty seconds so everyone has a chance to speak. The last fifteen minutes are reserved for Prayer Requests and members praying for each other. We should finish in 90 min.***

3 - *Chairperson: So, let's get started!* *[Chairperson or attendee reads the Recovery Prayer below].*

Recovery Prayer

"Dear God, thank you for giving us your Word to heal us. We joyfully dedicate this time to renew our minds to the truths in your Word. With your help we will use your Word to bring down strongholds of fear and deception. We agree that your Word is a light to our path and it leads us to a place of peace, confidence and happiness. We thank you in advance for everything you have done for us, and will do in our lives. You have made our future bright, and we praise you for this. In Jesus's name. Amen."

4 - *Chairperson: This program promotes confidentiality. We teach its importance so those unfamiliar with it can learn about it and begin abiding by it. Whatever is said in the group stays in the group. Here to read our Confidentiality Commitment is our first speaker ____(Speaker name)____ .*

5 - Confidentiality Speaker: Thank you, ____(Chairperson name)____ .

We value your confidentiality. Whatever we hear you say at a group or in private conversation we promise not to repeat to anyone. This includes your contact information. We will never share any information about you without your permission.

6 - *Chairperson: Thank you, ____(Speaker name)____ .* *[Chairperson now asks each person who wants to participate if they have any Praise Reports.]*

7 - *Chairperson: We will now give a quick overview of how to achieve happiness by using the Happiness Basics. God wants us to be Happy. To talk more about this, is our Happiness Speaker, ___(Speaker name)__ .*

8 – Happiness Speaker: Thank you, ____(Chairperson name)___ . Indeed, God wants us to enjoy our journey in life, as seen in the following verses. I will pick one randomly to read, and speak briefly on how it applies to God wanting us to be happy. The verse I choose is _____ .

1) **Psalm 19:8** "The statutes of the Lord are right, <u>rejoicing the heart</u>: the commandment of the Lord is pure, <u>enlightening the eyes</u>."

2) **Psalm 28:7** "The Lord is my strength and my shield; my heart trusted in him, and I am helped: therefore <u>my heart greatly rejoiceth</u>; and with my song will I praise him."

3) **Psalm 30:11,12** "Thou hast turned for me my <u>mourning into dancing</u>: thou hast put off my sackcloth, and girded me with <u>gladness</u>;¹² To the end that <u>my glory may sing praise</u> to thee, and not be silent. O Lord my God, I will give thanks unto thee for ever."

4) **Psalm 32:11** "<u>Be glad in the Lord, and rejoice</u>, ye righteous: and <u>shout for joy</u>, all ye that are upright in heart."

5) **Psalm 64:10** "<u>The righteous shall be glad in the Lord</u>, and shall trust in him; and all the upright in heart <u>shall glory</u>."

6) **Psalm 89:16** "In thy name <u>shall they rejoice all the day</u>: and in thy righteousness shall they be exalted."

7) **Psalm 97:11** "Light is sown for the righteous, and <u>gladness for the upright in heart</u>."

8) **Ecclesiastes 2:26** "For God giveth to a man that is good in his sight wisdom, and knowledge, and <u>joy</u>:"

9) **Ecclesiastes. 5:19** "Every man also to whom God hath given riches and wealth, and hath given him power to eat thereof, and to take his portion, and to <u>rejoice in his labour</u>; this is the gift of God."

10) **Ecclesiastes. 11:8** "But if a man live many years, and <u>rejoice in them all</u>…"

11) **Luke 10:20** "*(Jesus speaking)* Notwithstanding in this rejoice not, that the spirits are subject unto you; <u>but rather rejoice</u>, because your names are written in heaven."

12) **John 10:10** "*(Jesus speaking)* The thief cometh not, but for to steal, and to kill, and to destroy: <u>I am come that they might have life, and that they might have it more abundantly</u>."

13) **John 15:11** "*(Jesus speaking)* These things have I spoken unto you, <u>that my joy might remain in you, and that your joy might be full</u>."

14) **Acts 2:25, 26** "For David speaks concerning him, I foresaw the Lord always before my face, for he is on my right hand, that I should not be moved: <u>Therefore did my heart rejoice, and my tongue was glad</u>; moreover also my flesh shall rest in hope:"

15) **Romans 15:13** "Now the God of hope <u>fill you with all joy</u> and peace in believing, that ye may abound in hope, through the power of the Holy Ghost."

16) **1 Corinthians 15:57** "But thanks be to God, <u>which gives us the victory through our Lord Jesus Christ</u>."

17) **2 Corinthians 2:14** "Now thanks be unto God, which <u>always causes us to triumph in Christ</u>,…"

18) **Galatians 5:22** "But the fruit of the Spirit is love, <u>joy</u>, peace, longsuffering *(patience)*, gentleness, goodness, faith, meekness, temperance *(self-control):"*

19) **Philippians 1:25** "And having this confidence, I know that I shall abide and continue with you all for your furtherance and <u>joy of faith</u>;"

20) **Philippians 4:4** "<u>Rejoice in the Lord always</u>: and again I say, <u>Rejoice</u>."

21) **1 Thessalonians 5:16** "<u>Rejoice evermore</u>."

22) **1 John 1:4** "And these things write we unto you, that your joy may be full."

23) **2 John 1:12** "Having many things to write unto you, I would not write with paper and ink: but I trust to come unto you, and speak face to face, that our joy may be full."

9 - Happiness Speaker: So, God wants us to be happy. We can even be happy when we have problems in our lives. From the verses below, I will pick one randomly to read, and speak briefly on how it applies to us being happy even when we have problems in our lives. The verse I choose is _____.

1) **Psalm 27:6** "And now shall mine head be lifted up above mine enemies round about me: therefore will I offer in his tabernacle sacrifices of joy; I will sing, yea, I will sing praises unto the LORD."

2) **Psalm 119:143** "Trouble and anguish have taken hold on me: yet thy commandments are my delights."

3) **Luke 6:22,23** "Blessed are ye, when men shall hate you, and when they shall separate you from their company, and shall reproach you, and cast out your name as evil, for the Son of man's sake. ^{23} Rejoice ye in that day, and leap for joy: for, behold, your reward is great in heaven: for in the like manner did their fathers unto the prophets."

4) **John 16:33** *(Jesus speaking)* "These things I have spoken unto you, that in me ye might have peace. In the world ye shall have tribulation: but be of good cheer; I have overcome the world."

5) **Romans 5:3-5a** "And not only so, but we glory in tribulations also: knowing that tribulation worketh patience; ^{4} And patience, experience; and experience, hope: ^{5} And hope maketh not ashamed;"

6) **Romans 8:18** "For I reckon that the sufferings of this present time are not worthy to be compared with the glory which shall be revealed in us."

7) **Romans 8:28** "And we know that all things work together for good to them that love God, to them who are the called according to his purpose."

8) **2 Corinthians 4:17** "For our light affliction, which is but for a moment, works for us a far more exceeding and eternal weight of glory;"

9) **2 Corinthians 7:4** "Great is my boldness of speech toward you, great is my glorying of you: I am filled with comfort, I am exceeding joyful in all our tribulation."

10) **2 Corinthians 12:9,10** *(In this passage, Paul was troubled by a 'thorn in his flesh.')* "And he *(Jesus)* said unto me, "My grace is sufficient for you: for my strength is made perfect in weakness." *(Paul speaking)* Most gladly therefore will I rather glory *(rejoice)* in my infirmities (problems), that the power of Christ may rest upon me. ^{10} Therefore I take pleasure in infirmities, in reproaches *(hardships),* in necessities, in persecutions, in distresses for Christ's sake: for when I am weak, then am I strong."

11) **Colossians 1:11** "Strengthened with all might, according to his glorious power, unto all patience and longsuffering *(enduring injury or trouble)* with joyfulness;"

12) **James 1:2** "My brethren, count it all joy when you fall into divers temptations *(various trials);*"

13) **1 Peter 1:6** "Wherein you greatly rejoice, though now for a season, if need be, you are in heaviness through manifold temptations" *(many problems):*

14) **1 Peter 3:14** "But and if ye suffer for righteousness' sake, <u>happy are ye</u>: and be not afraid of their terror, neither be troubled;"

15) **1 Peter 4:12,13** "Beloved, think it not strange concerning the fiery trial which is to try you, as though some strange thing happened unto you: ¹³But <u>rejoice, inasmuch as ye are partakers of Christ's sufferings</u>; that, when his glory shall be revealed, <u>ye may be glad also with exceeding joy</u>."

16) **1 Peter 4:14** "<u>If ye be reproached for the name of Christ, happy are ye</u>; for the spirit of glory and of God resteth upon you: on their part he is evil spoken of, but on your part he is glorified."

10 - Happiness Speaker: So even in troubles, we can be happy! Back to you, _(Chairperson name)_ .

11 - *Chairperson: Thank you, ____(Speaker name)____ . So, it is God's will that we be happy, but it goes deeper than that. God wants us to be strong in our spirit. Here to tell us more on that is our Strong Speaker, ____(Speaker name)____ .*

12 - Strong Speaker: Thank you, ____(Chairperson name)____ . Indeed, God wants people to be strong in spirit, and from the verses below, I will pick one randomly to read, and speak briefly on how it applies to us being strong in our spirit. The verse I choose is _____ .

1) **Joshua 1:6** "<u>Be strong</u> and of a good courage: for unto this people shalt thou divide for an inheritance the land, which I sware unto their fathers to give them."

2) **Joshua 1:7** "Only <u>be thou strong</u> and very courageous, that thou mayest observe to do according to all the law, which Moses my servant commanded thee: turn not from it to the right hand or to the left, that thou mayest prosper withersoever thou goest."

3) **Joshua 1:9** "Have not I commanded thee? <u>Be strong</u> and of a good courage; be not afraid, neither be thou dismayed: for the LORD thy God is with thee whithersoever thou goest."

4) **2 Samuel 22:33** "<u>God is my strength</u> and power: and he maketh my way perfect."

5) **2 Samuel 22:40** "For thou hast <u>girded me with strength</u> to battle: them that rose up against me hast thou subdued under me."

6) **Psalm 31:24** "Be of <u>good courage</u>, and he shall <u>strengthen your heart</u>, all ye that hope in the LORD."

7) **Proverbs 24:5** "<u>A wise man is strong</u>; yea, <u>a man of knowledge increaseth strength</u>."

8) **Romans 8:37** "Nay, in all these things <u>we are more than conquerors</u> through him that loved us."

9) **1 Corinthians 16:13** "Watch ye, stand fast in the faith, quit you (act) like men, <u>be strong</u>."

10) **Ephesians 1:19** "That you may know…what is <u>the exceeding greatness of his power to us-ward</u> who believe, according to the working of his mighty power,"

11) **Ephesians 3:16** "That he would grant you, according to the riches of his glory, to be <u>strengthened with might</u> by his Spirit in the inner man;"

12) **Ephesians 3:20** "Now unto him that is able to do exceeding abundantly above all that we ask or think, <u>according to the power that worketh in us</u>,"

13) **Ephesians 6:10-11** "Finally, my brethren, be strong in the Lord, and in the power of his might. [11] Put on the whole armour of God, that ye may be able to stand against the wiles of the devil."

14) **Philippians 4:13** "I can do all things through Christ which strengtheneth me."

15) **Colossians 1:10-11** "That ye might walk worthy of the Lord unto all pleasing, being fruitful in every good work, and increasing in the knowledge of God; [11] Strengthened with all might, according to his glorious power, unto all patience and longsuffering with joyfulness; "

16) **2 Timothy 1:7** "For God hath not given us the spirit of fear; but of power, and of love, and of a sound mind."

17) **2 Timothy 2:1** "Thou therefore, my son, be strong in the grace that is in Christ Jesus."

18) **1 Peter 5:10** "But the God of all grace, who hath called us unto his eternal glory by Christ Jesus, after that ye have suffered a while, make you perfect, stablish, strengthen, settle you."

13 - Strong Speaker: So, God wants us to be strong emotionally, but it goes deeper than that. God wants us to stand firm and steadfast, and be bold, established, and confident! From the verses below, I will pick one randomly to read, then share briefly on how it ties in to God wanting us to be stedfast, bold, established and confident. The verse I choose is _____.

1) **Psalm 20:8** "They are brought down and fallen: but we are risen, and stand upright."

2) **Psalm 138:3** "In the day when I cried thou answeredst me, and strengthenedst me with strength in my soul."

3) **Proverbs 10:25** "As the whirlwind passeth, so is the wicked no more: but the righteous is an everlasting foundation."

4) **1 Corinthians 15:58** "Therefore, my beloved brethren, be ye steadfast, unmoveable, always abounding in the work of the Lord, forasmuch as ye know that your labour is not in vain in the Lord."

5) **1 Corinthians 16:13** "Watch ye, stand fast in the faith, quit you (act) like men, be strong."

6) **2 Corinthians 5:6,8** "Therefore we are always confident, knowing that, whilst we are at home in the body, we are absent from the Lord: [8] We are confident, I say, and willing rather to be absent from the body, and to be present with the Lord."

7) **2 Corinthians 7:4** "Great is my boldness of speech toward you, great is my glorying of you: I am filled with comfort, I am exceeding joyful in all our tribulation."

8) **Ephesians 3:12** "In whom we have boldness and access with confidence by the faith of him."

9) **Ephesians 3:13** "Wherefore I desire that ye faint not at my tribulations for you, which is your glory."

10) **Ephesians 3:16** "That he would grant you, according to the riches of his glory, to be strengthened with might by his Spirit in the inner man;"

11) **Ephesians 6:13** "Wherefore take unto you the whole armour of God, that ye may be able to withstand in the evil day, and having done all, to stand."

12) **Ephesians. 6:19** "And for me, that utterance may be given unto me, that I may <u>open my mouth boldly</u>, to make known the mystery of the gospel,"

13) **Philippians 1:6** "<u>Being confident</u> of this very thing, that he which hath begun a good work in you will perform it until the day of Jesus Christ:"

14) **Philippians 1:20** "According to my earnest expectation and my hope, that in nothing I shall be ashamed, but that <u>with all boldness</u>, as always, so now also Christ shall be magnified in my body, whether it be by life, or by death."

15) **Philippians 1:27** "Only let your conversation be as it becometh the gospel of Christ: that whether I come and see you, or else be absent, I may hear of your affairs, that ye <u>stand fast</u> in one spirit, with one mind striving together for the faith of the gospel;"

16) **Philippians 4:1** "Therefore, my brethren dearly beloved and longed for, my joy and crown, so <u>stand fast</u> in the Lord, my dearly beloved."

17) **Colossians 1:23** "If ye continue in the faith <u>grounded</u> and <u>settled</u>, and be <u>not moved</u> away from the hope of the gospel, which ye have heard, and which was preached to every creature which is under heaven; whereof I Paul am made a minister;"

18) **Colossians 2:7** "Rooted and built up in him, and <u>stablished in the faith</u>, as ye have been taught, abounding therein with thanksgiving."

19) **1 Thessalonians 3:8** "For now we live, if ye <u>stand fast</u> in the Lord."

20) **1 Thessalonians. 3:13** "To the end he may <u>stablish your hearts</u> unblameable in holiness before God, even our Father, at the coming of our Lord Jesus Christ with all his saints."

21) **2 Thessalonians 2:15** "Therefore, brethren, <u>stand fast</u>, and <u>hold</u> the traditions which ye have been taught, whether by word, or our epistle."

22) **2 Thessalonians 2:16,17** "Now our Lord Jesus Christ himself, and God, even our Father, which hath loved us, and hath given us everlasting consolation and good hope through grace,^{17} Comfort your hearts, and <u>stablish you</u> in every good word and work."

23) **2 Peter 1:12** "Wherefore I will not be negligent to put you always in remembrance of these things, though ye know them, and <u>be established</u> in the present truth."

24) **James 5:8** "Be ye also patient; <u>stablish your hearts</u>: for the coming of the Lord draweth nigh."

14 - Strong Speaker: So, God wants us to stand firm and steadfast, and be bold, established and confident. Back to you, ___(Chairperson name)___.

15 - *Chairperson: Thank you, ___(Speaker name)___. If God's will is for us to be happy and strong, what do you think gets in the way of us experiencing these attributes in our lives? Hosea 4:6 gives us a clue: It says, "My people are destroyed for a lack of knowledge." Knowledge is powerful. Here to help us understand the importance of gathering knowledge is our Knowledge Speaker, __(Speaker name)__.*

16 - Knowledge Speaker: Thank you, ___(Chairperson name)___. God urges us to gain knowledge, and from the verses below, I will pick one randomly to read, and then speak briefly on how it applies to the importance of gathering knowledge. The verse I choose is _____.

1) King Solomon prayed to God for wisdom and knowledge when he was crowned king.

   2 Chronicles 1:9-12 "Now, O LORD God, let thy promise unto David my father be established: for thou hast made me king over a people like the dust of the earth in multitude. ^{10} Give me now wisdom and knowledge, that I may go out and come in before this people: for who can judge this thy people, that is so great? ^{11} And God said to Solomon, Because this was in thine heart, and thou hast not asked riches, wealth, or honour, nor the life of thine enemies, neither yet hast asked long life; but hast asked wisdom and knowledge for thyself, that thou mayest judge my people, over whom I have made thee king: ^{12} Wisdom and knowledge is granted unto thee; and I will give thee riches, and wealth, and honour, such as none of the kings have had that have been before thee, neither shall there any after thee have the like."

2) **Proverbs 2:3-5** "Yea, if thou <u>criest after knowledge</u>, and <u>liftest up thy voice for understanding</u>; ^{4} If thou <u>seekest her as silver</u>, and <u>searchest for her as for hid treasures</u>; ^{5} Then shalt thou understand the fear of the LORD, and find the knowledge of God."

3) **Proverbs 3:13,14** "Happy is the man that <u>findeth wisdom</u>, and the man that <u>getteth understanding</u>. ^{14} For the merchandise of it is better than the merchandise of silver, and the gain thereof than fine gold."

4) **Proverbs 3:20-22** "his <u>knowledge</u> the depths are broken up, and the clouds drop down the dew. ^{21} My son, <u>let not them depart from thine eyes</u>: <u>keep sound wisdom and discretion</u>: ^{22} So shall they be life unto thy soul, and grace to thy neck."

5) **Proverbs 4:1** " Hear, ye children, the instruction of a father, and <u>attend to know understanding</u>."

6) **Proverbs 4:5-7** "<u>Get wisdom, get un</u>derstanding: forget it not; neither decline from the words of my mouth. ^{6} Forsake her not, and she shall preserve thee: love her, and she shall keep thee. ^{7} <u>Wisdom is the principal thing; therefore get wisdom</u>: and with all thy getting <u>get understanding</u>."

7) **Proverbs 4:13** "<u>Take fast hold of instruction</u>; let her not go: keep her; for she is thy life."

8) **Proverbs 8:5** "O ye simple, <u>understand wisdom</u>: and, ye fools, <u>be ye of an understanding heart</u>."

9) **Proverbs 8:10** "<u>Receive my instruction</u>, and not silver; <u>and knowledge</u> rather than choice gold."

10) **Proverbs 16:16** "How much better is it to <u>get wisdom</u> than gold! and to <u>get understanding</u> rather to be chosen than silver!"

11) **Proverbs 18:15** "The heart of the prudent <u>getteth knowledge</u>; and the ear of the wise <u>seeketh knowledge</u>."

12) **Proverbs 23:23** "<u>Buy the truth</u>, and sell it not; also wisdom, and instruction, and understanding."

13) **Proverbs 24:3-5** "Through wisdom is an house builded; and by understanding it is established: ^{4} And by knowledge shall the chambers be filled with all precious and pleasant riches. ^{5} A wise man is strong; yea, a man of knowledge increaseth strength."

14) **Proverbs 24:14** "So shall the knowledge of wisdom be unto thy soul: <u>when thou hast found it</u>, then there shall be a reward, and thy expectation shall not be cut off."

17 - Knowledge Speaker: So knowledge is valuable and vital for healing from anxiety and depression. Back to you, ___(Chairperson name)___ **.**

18 - *Chairperson: Thank you,* ___(Speaker name)___ *. This program places a great emphasis on God's Word as our way toward peace and happiness. Here to help us understand the importance of God's Word is our Word Speaker,* ___(Speaker name)___ *.*

19 - Word Speaker: Thank you, ___(Chairperson name)___ **. God's Word is very important, and from the verses below, I will pick one randomly to read, and speak briefly on how it applies to the importance God's Word. The verse I choose is _____ .**

1) **Psalm 107:20** "He sent his word, and healed them, and delivered them from their destructions."

2) The longest psalm in the Bible is Psalm 119. It has 176 verses! It is 2 ½ times longer than the next longest Psalm. The whole psalm talks about God's Word, how the writer loves God's Word. Do you think God is trying to teach us something about the importance of His Word?

3) **Psalm 138:2** "I will worship toward thy holy temple, and praise thy name for thy lovingkindness and for thy truth: for thou hast magnified thy word above all thy name."

4) **Proverbs 4:4** "He taught me also, and said unto me, Let thine heart retain my words: keep my commandments, and live."

5) **Isaiah 55:11** "So shall my word be that goeth forth out of my mouth: it shall not return unto me void, but it shall accomplish that which I please, and it shall prosper in the thing whereto I sent it."

6) **Luke 6:47-48** "Whosoever cometh to me, and heareth my sayings, and doeth them, I will shew you to whom he is like:^{48} He is like a man which built an house, and digged deep, and laid the foundation on a rock: and when the flood arose, the stream beat vehemently upon that house, and could not shake it: for it was founded upon a rock."

7) **John 1:1** "In the beginning was the Word, and the Word was with God, and the Word was God."

8) **John 8:37** Jesus told us how important God's Word is in John 8:37, saying, "I know that ye are Abraham's seed; but ye seek to kill me, because my word hath no place in you."

9) **John 15:7** Jesus told us how important God's Word is in John 15:7, saying, If ye abide in me, and my words abide in you, ye shall ask what ye will, and it shall be done unto you."

10) **John 17:17** "Sanctify them through thy truth: thy word is truth." *(God's Word is truth. And we know that the truth sets us free!)*

11) **Ephesians 6:17** "And take the helmet of salvation, and the sword of the Spirit, which is the word of God:" *(You have to know the Word before you can use it!)*

20 - Word Speaker: God's Word is important. But, building God's Word into our hearts, is equally important. From the verses below, I will pick one randomly to read, and speak briefly on how it applies to the importance of building God's Word into our hearts. I choose verse _____ .

1) **Exodus 13:9** "And it shall be for a sign unto thee upon thine hand, and for a memorial between thine eyes, that the LORD's law may be in thy mouth: for with a strong hand hath the LORD brought thee out of Egypt."

2) **Deuteronomy 6:6-9** "And these words, which I command thee this day, shall be in thine heart: ⁷ And thou shalt teach them diligently unto thy children, and shalt talk of them when thou sittest in thine house, and when thou walkest by the way, and when thou liest down, and when thou risest up. ⁸ And thou shalt bind them for a sign upon thine hand, and they shall be as frontlets between thine eyes. ⁹ And thou shalt write them upon the posts of thy house, and on thy gates."

3) **Joshua 1:8** "This book of the law shall not depart out of thy mouth; but thou shalt meditate therein day and night, that thou mayest observe to do according to all that is written therein: for then thou shalt make thy way prosperous, and then thou shalt have good success."

4) **Psalm 1:2-3** "But his delight is in the law of the LORD; and in his law doth he meditate day and night. ³ And he shall be like a tree planted by the rivers of water, that bringeth forth his fruit in his season; his leaf also shall not wither; and whatsoever he doeth shall prosper."

5) **Psalm 119:11** "Thy word have I hid in mine heart, that I might not sin against thee." *(Memorizing scripture can help us live free of sin.)*

6) **Proverbs 2:1** "My son, if thou wilt receive my words, and hide my commandments with thee; ² So that thou incline thine ear unto wisdom, and apply thine heart to understanding; ³ Yea, if thou criest after knowledge, and liftest up thy voice for understanding; ⁴ If thou seekest her as silver, and searchest for her as for hid treasures; ⁵ Then shalt thou understand the fear of the LORD, and find the knowledge of God."

7) **Proverbs 4:4** "He taught me also, and said unto me, Let thine heart retain my words: keep my commandments, and live." *(Memorize scripture "and live.")*

8) **Proverbs 4:20,21** "My son, attend to my words; incline thine ear unto my sayings. ²¹ Let them not depart from thine eyes; keep them in the midst of thine heart."

9) **Jeremiah 20:9** "Then I said, I will not make mention of him, nor speak any more in his name. But his word was in mine heart as a burning fire shut up in my bones, and I was weary with forbearing, and I could not stay."

10) **Luke 4:1-4** *Jesus used God's Word to defend himself when he was tempted by the devil:* And Jesus being full of the Holy Ghost returned from Jordan, and was led by the Spirit into the wilderness, ² Being forty days tempted of the devil. And in those days he did eat nothing: and when they were ended, he afterward hungered. ³ And the devil said unto him, If thou be the Son of God, command this stone that it be made bread. ⁴ And Jesus answered, saying, It is written, That man shall not live by bread alone, but by every word of God."

11) **Luke 4:5-8** "Jesus used God's Word to defend himself when he was tempted by the devil: ⁵ And the devil, taking him up into an high mountain, shewed unto him all the kingdoms of the world in a moment of time. ⁶ And the devil said unto him, All this power will I give thee, and the glory of them: for that is delivered unto me; and to whomsoever I will I give it. ⁷ If thou therefore wilt worship me, all shall be thine. ⁸ And Jesus answered and said unto him, Get thee behind me, Satan: for it is written, Thou shalt worship the Lord thy God, and him only shalt thou serve."

12) **Luke 4:9-13** "Jesus used God's Word to defend himself when he was tempted by the devil: ⁹ And he brought him to Jerusalem, and set him on a pinnacle of the temple, and said unto him, If thou be the Son of God, cast thyself down from hence: ¹⁰ For it is written, He shall give his angels charge over thee, to keep thee: ¹¹ And in their hands they shall bear thee up, lest at any time thou dash thy foot against a stone. ¹² And Jesus answering said unto him, It is said, Thou shalt not tempt the Lord thy God. ¹³ And when the devil had ended all the temptation, he departed from him for a season."

13) **Luke 6:43-45** "For a good tree bringeth not forth corrupt fruit; neither doth a corrupt tree bring forth good fruit. [44] For every tree is known by his own fruit. For of thorns men do not gather figs, nor of a bramble bush gather they grapes. [45] A good man out of the <u>good treasure of his heart</u> <u>bringeth forth that which is good</u>; and an evil man out of the evil treasure of his heart bringeth forth that which is evil: for <u>of the abundance of the heart his mouth speaketh</u>."

14) **Luke 6:49** "Jesus tells us what happens when people don't build his Word in their hearts: But he that heareth, and doeth not, is like a man that without a foundation built an house upon the earth; against which the stream did beat vehemently, and immediately it fell; and the ruin of that house was great."

15) **John 1:14** "And <u>the Word was made flesh</u> (Jesus), and dwelt among us, (and we beheld his glory, the glory as of the only begotten of the Father,) full of grace and truth."

16) **John 8:31,32** "Then said Jesus to those Jews which believed on him, <u>If ye continue in my word, then are ye my disciples</u> indeed; And ye shall know the truth, and the truth shall make you free."

17) **Romans 10:8** "But what saith it? <u>The word is nigh (near) thee</u>, even <u>in thy mouth</u>, and <u>in thy heart</u>: that is, the word of faith, which we preach;"

18) **Colossians 3:16** "<u>Let the word of Christ dwell in you richly</u> in all wisdom; teaching and admonishing one another in psalms and hymns and spiritual songs, singing with grace in your hearts to the Lord."

19) **James 1:21** "Wherefore lay apart all filthiness and superfluity of naughtiness, and <u>receive with meekness the engrafted word</u>, which is able to save your souls."

21 - Word Speaker: One cause of emotional pain can be sin. God's Word has an answer for that. From the verses below, I will pick one randomly to read, and speak briefly on how it applies to God having an answer for sin. The verse I choose is number _____.

1) **Psalm 119:2,3** "Blessed are they that <u>keep his testimonies</u>, and that seek him with the whole heart. [3] <u>They also do no iniquity</u>: they walk in his ways."

2) **Psalm 119:9** "<u>Wherewithal shall a young man cleanse his way? by taking heed thereto according to thy word</u>."

3) **Psalm 119:11** "<u>Thy word have I hid in mine heart, that I might not sin against thee</u>."
(*When you memorize God's Word, you are able to recite God's Word throughout your day. By doing so, you are less apt to fall into temptation to sin.*)

4) **Psalm 119:127,128** "Therefore I <u>love thy commandments</u> above gold; yea, above fine gold. [128] Therefore I <u>esteem all thy precepts</u> concerning all things to be right; and <u>I hate every false way</u>."

22 - Word Speaker: Since God's Word is so important, we should ask ourselves: 1) How much time do I spend each day reading and meditating on God's Word? 2) Could it be that my struggles are tied to: a) a lack of interest in God's Word, or b) a lack of understanding of what it teaches about victorious living. Consider praying this prayer: "God, please give me a hunger for your Word." Back to you, ____(Chairperson name)____ .

23 - *Chairperson: Thank you, ____(Speaker name)___ . Three personal attributes we recommend you develop in your life are: Faith, Truth, and Love. Here to help us understand the importance of Faith, is our Faith Speaker, ___(Speaker name)___ .*

24 - Faith Speaker: Thank you, ____(Chairperson name)___ . The attribute of Faith is an amazing tool. It enables us to roll our problems over to God, thus freeing us up to enjoy life while we wait for God to move on our behalf. The following are Biblical principles that can help us live in Faith, and keep us in a state of constant peace. From the principles below, I will pick one randomly to read, and speak, briefly, on how it helps us live by Faith. I choose Principle ____ .

The Principles Of Faith

1) Based on Hebrews Chapter 11, we see that God places a strong emphasis on a person's faith. **Hebrews 11:6** says, *"But without faith it is impossible to please him: for he that cometh to God must believe that he is, and that he is a rewarder of them that diligently seek him."*

2) Based on Galatians 5:6, faith works along side of love. **Galatians 5:6** says, *"For in Jesus Christ neither circumcision availeth any thing, nor uncircumcision; but faith which worketh by love."*

3) Based on James 2:26, faith must be demonstrated. (Belief + Action = Faith) **James 2:26** says, *"For as the body without the spirit is dead, so faith without works is dead also."* **James 2:22** says, *"Seest thou how faith wrought (working together) with his works, and by works was faith made perfect?"*

4) Based on Hebrews 10:35,36, faith must be patient. **Hebrews 10:35,36** says, *"Cast not away therefore your confidence, which hath great recompense of reward. ³⁶ For ye have need of patience, that, after ye have done the will of God, ye might receive the promise."* **Hebrews 6:12** says, *"That ye be not slothful, but followers of them who through faith and patience inherit the promises."*

5) Based on 2 Corinthians 5:7, we do not judge a problem's solvability by how impossible *it looks* or how bad *we feel*. **2 Corinthians 5:7** says, *"For we walk by faith, not by sight:"*

6) Based on Mark 11:24, we believe we have received the thing we have asked for, even before we actually have it. Jesus says, **Mark 11:24** says, *"Therefore I say unto you, What things soever ye desire, when ye pray, believe that ye receive them, and ye shall have them."* **Matthew 21:22** says, *"And all things, whatsoever ye shall ask in prayer, believing, ye shall receive."*

7) Based on James 5:15, we see that faith can heal a sick body. **James 5:15** says, *"And the prayer of faith shall save the sick, and the Lord shall raise him up; and if he have committed sins, they shall be forgiven him."*

8) Based on 1 Timothy 6:12 & Ephesians Chapter 6, we understand that the life of faith is a *fight*. But based on Romans 8:37, we believe we are more than able to win this fight. **1 Timothy 6:12** says, *"Fight the good fight of faith, lay hold on eternal life, whereunto thou art also called, and hast professed a good profession before many witnesses."* **Romans 8:37** says, *"Nay, in all these things we are more than conquerors through him that loved us."*

9) Based on James 1:6-8, we see that people who waiver in their faith shouldn't expect to receive anything from God. **James 1:6-8** says, *"But let him ask in faith, nothing wavering. For he that wavereth is like a wave of the sea driven with the wind and tossed. ⁷ For let not that man think that he shall receive any thing of the Lord. ⁸ A double minded man is unstable in all his ways."*

10) Based on Romans 10:17, faith must be developed. It does not come naturally. It comes from reading and speaking God's Word. **Romans 10:17** *says, "So then faith cometh by hearing, and hearing by the word of God."*

25 - Faith Speaker: This principle helps us with _____. Back to you, ___(Chairperson name)___.

26 - *Chairperson: Thank you, ___(Chairperson name)___. Here to help us understand the importance of Truth, is our Truth Speaker, ___(Speaker name)___.*

27 - Truth Speaker: Thank you, ___(Chairperson name)___. The key verses for the Truth Speaker are John 8:31-32, in which Jesus said to the Jews who had believed in Him: *"If you abide in my word, you are truly my disciples, and you will know the truth, and the truth will set you free."* **Indeed, the Truth *can* set us free! Circumstances take place in our lives that cause us to believe lies. These lies tell us that problems will never change, habits cannot be broken, loved ones will never change, and so on. The antidote to these lies is Truth. For every problem in our lives there is a Truth that can set us free, emotionally, from the problem. The problem may still be there, but the anxiety related to it is gone. Below are some common lies we sometimes believe. From the lies below, I will pick one randomly to read, and speak, briefly, on how it hinders our happiness, and how the truth can set us free. I will choose lie number ____.**

1) God doesn't love me.
2) I could never get married.
3) I could never forgive that person.
4) I could never be healed physically.
5) I could never be happy with my spouse.
6) Nobody would want to be my friend.
7) I need to have a spouse to be happy.
8) I could never be happy in my job.
9) I need money or things to be happy.
10) I'll never progress past this level of success.
11) I need to be loved and accepted to be happy.
12) I could never break free from my addiction.
13) I'll never have what it takes to be gainfully employed.
14) My worrying about problems shows that I am responsible.
15) My past is so bad, I'll never recover from my emotional wounds.
16) I could never be happy without this person. (e.g. A loved one who passes away)
17) I need to change my bodily features to be happy and accepted. *(e.g. weight changes or cosmetic surgery.)*
18) I need to act a certain way to be happy and accepted. *(e.g. "I need to be the life of the party.")*

28 - Truth Speaker: By seeing these lies for what they are, and using the Truth of God's Word to renew our minds, we can be set free from these lies! Back to you, ___(Chairperson name)___.

29 - *Chairperson: Thank you, ___(Speaker name)___. Here to help us understand the importance of Love, is our Love Speaker, ___(Speaker name)___.*

30 - Love Speaker: Thank you, ___(Chairperson name)___. Love helps us respond properly to life's challenges. We may know *what* we should do, but it is Love that allows us to do it willfully and cheerfully. Love is not based on feelings, but on our commitments. Love is a decision we make each day and is proven by our actions. From the verses below, I will pick one randomly to read, and speak, briefly, on how it applies to the importance of Love. I will choose verse ____.

1) **Romans 13:8** "Owe no man any thing, but to love one another: for he that loveth another hath fulfilled the law."

2) **Matthew 5:43-45** "Ye have heard that it hath been said, Thou shalt love thy neighbour, and hate thine enemy. ⁴⁴ But I say unto you, Love your enemies, bless them that curse you, do good to them that hate you, and pray for them which despitefully use you, and persecute you; ⁴⁵ That ye may be the children of your Father which is in heaven: for he maketh his sun to rise on the evil and on the good, and sendeth rain on the just and on the unjust."

3) **1 Corinthians 13:3** "And though I bestow all my goods to feed the poor, and though I give my body to be burned, and have not charity, it profiteth me nothing."

4) **1 Corinthians 13:4** "Charity (love) suffereth long, and is kind; charity envieth not; charity vaunteth not itself, is not puffed up,"

5) **1 Corinthians 13:5** "(Love) Doth not behave itself unseemly, seeketh not her own, is not easily provoked, thinketh no evil;"

6) **1 Corinthians 13:6** "(Love) Rejoiceth not in iniquity, but rejoiceth in the truth;"

7) **1 Corinthians 13:7** "(Love) Beareth all things, believeth all things, hopeth all things, endureth all things."

8) **1 Corinthians 13:8** "Charity (Love) never faileth: but whether there be prophecies, they shall fail; whether there be tongues, they shall cease; whether there be knowledge, it shall vanish away."

9) **1 Corinthians 13:13** "And now abideth faith, hope, charity, these three; but the greatest of these is charity."

10) **Galatians 5:13** "For, brethren, ye have been called unto liberty; only use not liberty for an occasion to the flesh, but by love serve one another."

11) **Galatians 5:14** "For all the law is fulfilled in one word, even in this; Thou shalt love thy neighbour as thyself."

12) **Galatians 5:22,23** "But the fruit of the Spirit is love, joy, peace, longsuffering, gentleness, goodness, faith, ²³ Meekness, temperance: Against such there is no law."

13) **Ephesians 4:2** "With all lowliness and meekness, with longsuffering, forbearing one another in love;"

14) **1 Peter 1:2** "Seeing ye have purified your souls in obeying the truth through the Spirit unto unfeigned love of the brethren, see that ye love one another with a pure heart fervently:"

15) **1 Peter 4:8** "And above all things have fervent charity among yourselves: for charity shall cover the multitude of sins."

16) **1 John 4:7** "Beloved, let us love one another: for love is of God; and every one that loveth is born of God, and knoweth God."

17) **1 John 4:18** "There is no fear in love; but perfect love casteth out fear: because fear hath torment. He that feareth is not made perfect in love."

31 - Love Speaker: So Love is vital to living a happy fruitful life! Back to you, ___(Chairperson name)___ .

32 - *Chairperson:* *Thank you,* ____(Speaker name)____ . *Affirmations are designed to be spoken out loud, enabling us to use our own self-help resource, our tongue. Here to help us understand the importance of affirmations is our Affirmations Speaker,* ____(Speaker name)____ .

33 - Affirmations Speaker: Thank you, ____(Chairperson name)____ . As we hear truth spoken by our own mouth, our belief system begins to change. Positive beliefs spawn positive thoughts, and positive thoughts create and maintain happiness. This program offers both generic and Bible-based affirmations. You can even create your own affirmations, customized for situations you come up against. I will pick a Generic Affirmation to read, and share, briefly, how it helps us. The affirmation I choose is ____ .

<u>Generic Affirmations</u>

1) "I am bigger than fear."
2) "I bounce back easily."
3) "I live my life effortlessly."
4) "My job is easy."
5) "I handle change easily."
6) "I love a challenge."
7) "Self-discipline is my strong point."
8) "I always see a silver lining."
9) "I see myself as a peaceful, loving person."
10) "You can't upset me. (I won't let you.)"
11) "I see myself as a winner before I see my victory."
12) "I forgive everybody immediately after they hurt me."
13) "God can bring good out of any of my mistakes."
14) "I see my prayers getting answered before I see the actual answer to my prayers."
15) "I see myself as healed in my body before I see and feel the changes I desire."

34 - Affirmations Speaker: I will now choose one of the Bible-based Affirmations below, in which we will all read 3 statements from. The Affirmation I choose is number _____ .

<u>Bible-Based Affirmations</u>

1) "I Do Not Fear" Affirmation (Page 173)
2) "I Am Strong" Affirmation (Page 176)
3) "I Flow in Harmony and Love" Affirmation (Page 179)
4) "I Only Speak Right Words" Affirmation (Page 181)
5) "I Only Think Right Thoughts" Affirmation (Page 183)
6) "I Am Happy Because…" Affirmation (Page 186)

35 - Affirmation Speaker: Positive affirmations spoken boldly, define what we believe is true. Doing so positions us to receive more from God and from life! So speak boldly! Back to you, ____(Chairperson name)____ .

36 - *Chairperson:* *Thank you,* ____(Speaker name)____ . *Slogans are thought-provoking statements that challenge us to respond to life's problems positively. To tell us more on Slogans is our Slogans Speaker,* ____(Speaker name)____ .

37 - Slogans Speaker: Thank you, ___(Chairperson name)___. From the slogans below, I will pick one randomly to read, and share, briefly, on how it helps us. The slogan I choose is number____.

1) "Sleep on it."
2) "Don't enable."
3) "I play to win!"
4) "You can start again."
5) "Knowledge is power."
6) "My job is to believe."
7) "Every day's a good day."
8) "Say it until you believe it."
9) "Respond rather than react."
10) "God is bigger than the facts!"
11) "We live by faith, not by sight."
12) "When we're in a battle, we fight!"
13) "Stop running and start confronting."
14) "It's not my problem, it's God's problem."
15) "Positive believing produces positive thinking."
16) "Faith is a lifestyle I can learn."
17) "Anger can be a sign that you are judging."
18) "God responds to faith, seldom to need."
19) "Don't make their problem, your problem.
20) "Problems are opportunities to see God move."
21) "The best *Defense* is a strong Offense."
22) "There is a stress-cancelling response to every problem."
23) "Don't focus on what you lost, focus on what you gained!"
24) "Life is 10% what happens to you, 90% how you respond to it."
25) "Problems are inevitable, the stress is optional."

38 - Slogans Speaker: Slogans are quick reminders of the truth. Say them often! Back to you, ___(Chairperson name)___.

39 - *Chairperson: Thank you, ___(Speaker name)___. There's an easy way to keep our thinking in check. Here to tell us more on that is our Beliefs Speaker, ___(Speaker name)___.*

40 - Beliefs Speaker: Thank you, ___(Chairperson name)___. Our thinking is influenced by our beliefs. Positive beliefs help us keep our responses to life's problems positive. We recommend adopting the following six Core Beliefs. The idea is to make these Core Beliefs the final word in our lives. No matter what our feelings say or what the circumstances try to tell us, these foundational beliefs are what we will use when thinking about ourselves, and when making decisions in our lives. For any belief that feels untrue, we simply say the scriptures associated with that belief over and over until the belief feels true. I will choose a Core Belief to read 3 verses from. The core belief I choose is number ____.

<u>Core Beliefs</u>

1) "I Believe God loves me, and that I am valuable." (Pg 195)
2) "I Believe Christ's crucifixion paid for my sin." (Pg 199)
3) "I Believe God wants me to live in perfect peace." (Pg 204)
4) "I Believe I have an enemy – Satan." (Pg 208)
5) "I Believe I have another enemy – my fleshly appetites." (Pg 216)
6) "I Believe God wants me to enjoy good physical health." (Pg 218)

41 - Beliefs Speaker: So, adopting and developing this Core Belief will help us with _____. Back to you ____(Chairperson name)____.

42 - *Chairperson:* *Thank you, ____(Speaker name)____. Our unhappiness can sometimes be easily diagnosed by pinpointing what the hindrance is. Here to talk to us about hindrances to happiness is our Hindrance Speaker, ____(Speaker name)____.*

43 - Hindrance Speaker: Thank you, ____(Chairperson name)____. There are many hindrances to happiness. From the hindrances below, I will pick one randomly to read, and speak, briefly, how it affects our happiness. The Hindrance I choose is number ____.

<u>Hindrances</u>

1) Self-pity "If only…"
2) Having an unthankful heart
3) Ostracized by community
4) Double-mindedness
5) Lack of purpose
6) Believing lies
7) Guilt (real or imagined)
8) Entitlement mentality
9) Sin, or sinful thinking
10) Unforgiveness
11) Debt
12) Shame
13) Anger
14) Isolation
15) Perfectionism
16) Lack of patience
17) Physical tiredness
18) Doubt and Unbelief
19) A Rebellious Heart
20) Mourning a loss
21) Pouting "I want it my way!"
22) Having an unthankful heart
23) Leaning on your own intellect
24) Being judgmental toward people.
25) Enabling abusive or poor behavior

44 - Hindrance Speaker: Let's live free of hindrances so we can brightly shine God's love in everything we do! Back to you, ____(Chairperson name)____.

45 - *Chairperson:* *Thank you, ____(Speaker name)____. We'll now work with one of the Happiness Tips. The place we left off last time was Page #____.* [If the place isn't known, the Chairperson may choose any Tip, and when finished, bring the group back here.]

(After working a Tip.)

46 - Gospel Speaker: We believe it is important to have a relationship with God, and that this relationship can help us find healing in our emotions. Let's take turns reading the following statements in the order we've been using. [Chairperson prompts speakers in the existing order.]

1) The main purpose of the Bible is to show mankind their need of Jesus Christ.
2) God wants to fellowship with mankind, but He can't until the issue of their sin has been dealt with.
3) Throughout the Bible there are prophecies about Jesus, and there are stories about Jesus.
4) All of these are there to show us the importance of Jesus.
5) Because of our tendency to sin, we need someone who would pay the penalty of our sin. And that was Jesus.
6) **John 3:16** says, "For God so loved the world, that he gave his only begotten Son, that whosoever believeth in him should not perish, but have everlasting life."

7) **Romans 1:16** says, "For I am not ashamed of the gospel of Christ: for it is the power of God unto salvation to every one that believeth; to the Jew first, and also to the Greek."

8) **Romans 6:23** says, "For the wages of sin is death; but the gift of God is eternal life through Jesus Christ our Lord."

9) **Romans 5:8** says, "But God commendeth his love toward us, in that, while we were yet sinners, Christ died for us."

10) Jesus, God's Son, came to earth to show us how to live, and to pay the penalty for our sin by dying on the cross.

11) Once we personally receive forgiveness for our sin, and ask Jesus to guide our lives, we find New Life! And we become part of God's family.

12) **John 3:3** says, "Jesus answered and said unto him, Verily, verily, I say unto thee, Except a man be born again, he cannot see the kingdom of God."

13) So, we must be born again. Is there anyone here who would like to become born again? And find New Life! And find forgiveness for their sins and become a part of God's family?

47 - *Chairperson: Please read along as I say the invitational prayer below.*

"Dear God, I see the sins that I have committed. I believe Jesus paid the penalty for my sin by His crucifixion. I receive your forgiveness for my sin. And I ask you to come into my life, and help me to live the rest of my life in a way that pleases you. Amen."

48 - *Congratulations! If you've prayed this prayer sincerely, you are now born again! You are now a part of God's family! And we, as a group, will help you learn how to live a happy, fruitful life in Christ. Welcome to God's family!*

49 - *Chairperson: For those of us who are already born again, God asks us to tell the world that they can be born again. Here are some verses that bear this out. Let's take turns reading these verses out loud.*

14) **Mark 16:15** (Jesus tells us) "Go ye into all the world, and preach the gospel to every creature."

15) **2 Corinthians 5:20**, "Now then we are ambassadors for Christ, as though God did beseech you by us: we pray you in Christ's stead, be ye reconciled to God."

16) **2 Corinthians 5:18**, "And all things are of God, who hath reconciled us to himself by Jesus Christ, and hath given to us the ministry of reconciliation;"

17) **2 Corinthians 5:14**, "For the love of Christ constraineth (compels) us; because we thus judge, that if one died for all, then were all dead:"

18) **2 Corinthians 3:6**, "Who also hath made us able ministers of the new testament; not of the letter, but of the spirit: for the letter killeth, but the spirit giveth life."

50 - *So let's challenge ourselves to tell the Good News of Jesus wherever we go this week. May God help us!*

51 - *We would like to take time now to pray for each other's needs.* *[Chairperson asks each person individually if they have any prayer requests, writing each one down, then asks who would like to pray for each person. Then the Chairperson goes back through the list asking each person who offered to pray to do so.]*

52 - *Does anyone have any final words before we conclude our meeting?*

53 - *I will now offer a closing prayer...*

54 - *Our meetings are held* *[tell days/times]*.

Meeting Options

Occasionally, Chairpersons may elect to have someone give their testimony of how God help them recover from a mental health condition. Another option is to add a segment in the meeting devoted to sharing The Lord's Supper with everyone.

Affirmation #1
"I Do Not Fear"

****

Throughout your day, try to recite out loud, the "I Do Not Fear" Affirmation.

Prayer of Dedication: "Father, I dedicate myself to live a life free of all fear. I now speak these Bible-based statements out loud to build in me a rock solid faith that keeps me at peace all day long."

The extra commas make the words more meditative and impactful. It also helps people read in unison during conference calls.

****

1) It is the Lord, who goes before me, He is with me, He will not leave me, nor fail me. I do not fear, nor am I dismayed. Based on Deuteronomy 31:8.

2) No one is able, to stand before me, all the days of my life. As God was with Moses, He is with me; He will never fail me, nor forsake me. Based on Joshua 1:5.

3) I am strong, and courageous, I am careful to obey, all the laws of God, I do not turn from it, to the right, or to the left, and I will prosper, wherever I go. Based on Joshua 1:7.

4) I am strong, and courageous. I am not afraid, nor dismayed, for the Lord my God, is with me, wherever I go. Based on Joshua 1:9.

5) I listen to God, and I dwell safely, I am quiet from fear of evil. Based on Proverbs 1:33.

6) I walk in my way safely, my foot does not stumble. Based on Proverbs 3:23.

7) When I lie down, I will not be afraid, when I lie down, my sleep is sweet. Based on Proverbs 3:24.

8) I am not afraid of sudden fear, nor the desolation of the wicked, the Lord is my confidence, He keeps my foot, from being taken. Based on Proverbs 3:25-26.

9) The fear of man, brings a snare, but because I put my trust, in the Lord, I am safe. Based on Proverbs 29:25.

10) The Lord is a shield for me, He lifts up my head. Based on Psalm 3:3.

11) I lie down and sleep. I wake again, because the Lord sustains me. Based on Psalm 3:5.

12) I am not afraid, of tens of thousands of people, who have set themselves against me, all around. Based on Psalm 3:6.

13) My enemies come up against, me but they stumble and fall. Based on Psalm 27:2.

14) The LORD is my light, and my salvation, whom shall I fear? The Lord is the strength of my life, of whom shall I be afraid? Based on Psalm 27:1.

15) Though an army encamps against me, my heart will not fear; though war rises against me, even in this will I be confident. Based on Psalm 27:3.

16) For in my time of trouble, He will hide me in His pavilion; In the secret of His tabernacle, do I hide. He sets me upon a rock. Based on Psalm 27:5.

17) My head is lifted up, above the enemies, all around me; At His tabernacle, will I sacrifice, with shouts of joy; I sing praises to the LORD. Based on Psalm 27:6.

18) Though my father and mother forsake me, the LORD will take me up. Based on Psalm 27:10.

19) I wait for the LORD; I am of good courage, He strengthens my heart, I wait on the LORD. Based on Psalm 27:14.

20) I sought the Lord, and He heard me, and delivered me, from all my fears. Based on Psalm 34:4.

21) I stop myself, from being angry, I forsake my wrath, I do not fret, for any reason, to do evil. Based on Psalm 37:8.

22) There is no reason for my soul to be cast down, or disquieted. My hope is in God, And I praise Him, He is the health, of my countenance, and my God. Based on Psalm 42:11.

23) I dwell in the secret place, of the Most High, and I abide, in the shadow of the Almighty. Based on Psalm 91:1.

24) I say of the Lord, "He is my refuge, and my fortress, my God, in him do I trust." Based on Psalm 91:2.

25) Surely God delivers me, from the fowler's snare, and from the noisome pestilence. Based on Psalm 91:3. (Noisome means "harmful.)

26) God covers me, with His feathers, under His wings I trust, His truth is my shield, and buckler. Based on Psalm 91:4. **(Buckler means Protector.)**

27) I do not fear the terror of night, nor the arrow that flies by day, nor the pestilence that stalks in the darkness, nor the destruction that destroys at midday. Based on Psalm 91:5-6. (Pestilence means deadly disease.)

28) A thousand falls at my side, ten thousand at my right hand, it does not come near me. Based on Psalm 91:7.

29) With my eyes, I see the reward of the wicked, because I make the Lord, who is my refuge, my dwelling place. Based on Psalm 91:8,9.

30) No evil befalls me, neither any plague comes near my home. Based on Psalm 91:10.

31) God commands His angels charge over me, to keep me, in all my ways. They bear me up, in their hands, so I do not dash my foot, against a stone. Based on Psalm 91:11-12.

32) I tread upon the lion, and the adder. The young lion, and the dragon, I trample under my feet. Based on Psalm 91:13. (Adder means snake)

33) Because I set my love on God, He delivers me, God sets me on high, because I know His name. Based on Psalm 91:14.

34) I call upon God, and He answers me. He is with me in trouble, and He delivers me, and honours me. Based on Psalm 91:15.

35) God is my salvation; I trust, and I am not afraid. The Lord Jehovah, is my strength, and my song. He is my salvation. Based on Isaiah 12:2.

36) I strengthen my hands, and I confirm my knees, I say to my heart, "Be strong! Do not fear! My God, will come through, with vengeance. He comes! and saves me!" Based on Isaiah 35:3-4. (Confirm means steady)

37) I do not fear, God is with me. I am not dismayed, God is my God, You strengthen me, You help me, You uphold me, with your right hand of righteousness. Based on Isaiah 41:10.

38) I do not fear, for the Lord my God, holds my right hand. It is He who says, "Fear not, I am the one who helps you." Based on Isaiah 41:13.

39) I do not fear, for He says, "Fear not, for I have redeemed you; I have called you by name, you are mine." Based on Isaiah 43:1.

40) I do not fear, for He says, "When you pass through the waters, I will be with you; and through the rivers, they shall not overflow you; when you walk through the fire, you shall not be burned, neither shall the flame, kindle upon you." Based on Isaiah 43:2.

41) God has given me power, to trample on snakes, and scorpions, over all the power of the enemy. Nothing harms me! Based on Luke 10:19.

42) I am not afraid, for it is God my father's, good pleasure, to give me the kingdom. Based on Luke 12:32.

43) I have not received, the spirit of bondage, to fall back into fear, but the spirit of adoption, as sons, so I cry "Abba Father!" Based on Romans 8:15.

44) Because God is for me, I do not fear those against me. Based on Romans 8:31.

45) I stand fast, in one spirit, with one mind, striving together, for the faith of the gospel, without being terrified, by my adversaries. Based on Philippians 1:27-28.

46) I do not overly care, about anything, but in everything, by prayer and supplication, with thanksgiving, I make my requests to God. And the peace of God, which passes all understanding, keeps my heart, and my mind, in Christ Jesus. Based on Philippians 4:6-7. (Supplication means petition)

47) God has not given me, a spirit of fear, but a spirit of power, of love, and of a sound mind. Based on 2 Timothy 1:7.

48) God has said to me, "I will never leave you, nor forsake you." Based on Heb. 13:5.

49) I boldly say, "The Lord is my helper, I do not fear, what man can do to me? Based on Heb. 13:6.

50) I do not fear, there is no fear in love. Perfect love, casts out all fear. God has made me perfect, in love. Based on 1 John 4:18.

51) I cast all my cares onto God, because He cares for me. Based on 1 Peter 5:7.

Let's go back to the Affirmation Speaker role.

Affirmation #2

"I Am Strong"

Throughout your day, try to recite out loud, the "I Am Strong" Affirmation.

Prayer of Dedication: "Father, I dedicate myself to live this day with a 'strength conscious' mindset. I now speak these Bible-based statements out loud to build in me a strong spirit that carries me victoriously through each challenge in my day!"

The extra commas make the words more meditative and impactful. It also helps people read in unison during conference calls.

1) No man is able, to stand before me, all the days of my life, as God was with Moses, He is with me, my God will not leave me, nor forsake me, I am strong, I have good courage. Based on Joshua 1:5.

2) For by God, I can run through a troop, and leap over a wall, Based on 2 Samuel 22:30.

3) God's Word is proven, He is a shield to me, because I trust Him. Based on 2 Samuel 22:31.

4) God is my rock, and my fortress, and my deliverer; my God my strength, in whom I trust; He is my buckler, the horn of my salvation, my high tower. Based on Psalm 18:2.

5) God arms me with strength, He makes my way perfect, He makes my feet, like hinds' feet, He sets me on high places, God teaches my hands to war, so that my arms, break a steel bow. Based on Psalm 18:32-34.

6) I pursue my enemies, I overtake them, I do not turn back, until they are destroyed, I wound them, so they cannot rise, they have fallen, under my feet. Based on Psalm 18:37,38.

7) God has armed me with strength, for the battle, God has subdued under me, those who rise against me. Based on Psalm 18:39.

8) I wait on the Lord; I have good courage, He strengthens my heart, I wait on the Lord. Based on Psalm 27:14.

9) The Lord is my strength, and my shield. Based on Psalm 28:7.

10) Because of Your favor, upon my life, You have made my mountain, to stand strong. Based on Psalm 30:7.

11) I have good courage, God strengthens my heart, as I hope in the Lord. Based on Psalm 31:24.

12) There is no reason, for my soul, to be cast down, or disquieted. My hope is in God. And I praise Him, He is the health of my countenance, and my God. Based on Psalm 42:11.

13) Through God, I push down my enemies, I trample those, who rise up against me. Based on Psalm 44:5.

14) God is in the midst of me, I shall not be moved: God helps me, and that right early. Based on Psalm 46:5.

15) God is my salvation, and my glory, the rock of my strength, and my refuge. Based on Psalm 62:7.

16) I publish god's Word! Kings of armies flee. I remain, and I divide the spoil. Based on Psalms 68:11,12.

17) God is the strength, of my heart, forever. Based on Psalm 73:26.

18) I dwell in the secret place, of the most High, and I abide in the shadow, of the Almighty. Based on Psalm 91:1.

19) I flourish like a palm tree, I grow like a cedar, in Lebanon, I am planted, in the house of the Lord, and I flourish, in the courts of my God. Based on Psalm 92:12 & 13.

20) God satisfies my mouth, with good things; so that my youth, is renewed like the eagles. Based on Psalm 103:5.

21) God increases me greatly, and has made them stronger, than my enemies. Based on Psalm 105:24.

22) God delivers my soul from death, my eyes from tears, and my feet from falling. Based on Psalm 116:8.

23) God strengthens me, according to His Word. Based on Psalm 119:28.

24) Because I trust in the Lord, I am like Mount Zion, which cannot be moved, I abide forever. Based on Psalm 125:1.

25) In the day, that I cry out to God, He answers me, and strengthens me, with strength in my soul. Based on Psalm 138:3.

26) God is the Lord of my strength. He teaches my hands to war, and my fingers to fight. Based on Psalm 144:1.

27) The Lord is my confidence, and keeps my feet, from being taken. Based on Proverbs 3:26.

28) Because I fear the Lord, I have strong confidence, and my children, have a place of refuge. Based on Proverbs 14:26.

29) I gird my loins, I strengthen my arms. (Loins means vulnerable areas.) Based on Proverbs 31:17.

30) Strength and honor, are my clothing, I rejoice, in the times to come. Based on Proverbs 31:25.

31) I am righteous through Christ, I hold to His ways, I have clean hands, I am getting stronger and stronger. Based on Job 17:9.

32) God gives power to the weak. To those who have no might, He increases strength. (My strength is increasing!) Based on Isaiah 40:29.

33) As I wait upon the Lord, I renew my strength. I mount up with wings as eagles; I run and do not grow weary, I walk and do not faint. Based on Isaiah 40:31.

34) No weapon formed against me, will prosper, every voice that rises against me, in judgment, God condemns. This is the heritage, of the servants of God. Based on Isaiah 54:17.

35) I know my God, I am strong, and I do exploits. Based on Daniel 11:32.

36) Jesus has given me power, and authority, over all demons, He has given me power, to cure diseases. Based on Luke 9:1, Mark 6:7,13 and Matthew 10:1,6, Matthew 28:18.

37) I go out, and preach everywhere, the Lord working with me, and He confirms His Word, with signs and wonders. Based on Mark 16:20.

38) Jesus has given me authority, to tread on serpents, and scorpions, and all power of the enemy, nothing shall hurt me. Based on Luke 10:19.

39) Jesus said I would receive power, when the Holy Spirit, has come upon me, I invite, the Holy Spirit, to enter my life, I believe, I have His power! Based on Acts 1:8.

40) With great power, I give witness, to the resurrection, of the Lord, great grace is upon me! Based on Acts 4:33.

41) In all things, I am more than a conqueror, through Christ, who loves me. Based on Romans 8:37.

42) I bear up under everything, I believe all things, I hope all things, I endure all things. Based on 1 Corinthians 13:7.

43) I am steadfast, immovable, always abounding, in the work of the Lord, and I know, that my labor, is not in vain, in the Lord. Based on 1 Corinthians. 15:58.

44) I watch, as if I am on guard; I stand fast, in my faith, I act like a man, I am strong! Based on 1 Corinthians 16:13.

45) I may be troubled, on every side, but I'm not distressed. I may be perplexed, but I'm not in despair, I may be persecuted, but I'm not forsaken; I may be cast down, but I'm not destroyed! Based on 2 Corinthians 4:8,9.

46) Christ's grace, is sufficient for me; His power is made perfect, in my weakness. Based on 2 Corinthians 12:9.

47) I am strong in the Lord, and in the power of his might. Based on Ephesians 6:10.

48) I can do all things, through Christ, who strengthens me. Based on Philippians 4:13.

49) The Lord makes me to increase in love toward others so that He establishes my heart as unblameable in holiness at the coming of my Lord with all His saints. Based on 1 Thessalonians 3:13.

50) The God of all grace, who has called me, into His eternal glory, by Christ Jesus, after a bit of suffering, makes me perfect, established, strengthened, and settled! Based on 1 Peter 5:10.

Let's go back to the Affirmation Speaker role.

AFFIRMATION #3
"I FLOW IN HARMONY AND LOVE"

****

Throughout your day, try to recite out loud, the "I Flow in Harmony and Love" Affirmation.

Prayer of Dedication: "Father, I dedicate myself to live this day with a love saturated mindset. I now speak these Bible-based statements out loud, to build in me a heart of love that is present in everything I think, say, and do."

(The extra commas make the words more meditative and impactful. It also helps people read in unison during conference calls.)

****

1) I am careful to remove the "plank," out of my own eye, before trying to remove the speck, out of my brothers (or sisters) eye. Based on Matthew 7:5.

2) When Jesus saw the crowds, He had compassion on them. I too have compassion, on all who are in my life. Based on Matthew 9:36.

3) I labor to support the weak, as I remember the words of the Lord Jesus, it is more blessed to give than to receive. Based on Acts 20:35.

4) I do not think of myself more highly than I ought, but I think soberly, allowing others to have importance too. Based on Romans 12:3.

5) I am kindly affectioned to others, with brotherly love; in honor, preferring others. Based on Romans 12:10.

6) I distribute, to the necessity, of the saints, and I am given, to hospitality. Based on Romans 12:13.

7) I do not repay evil for evil, I provide all things honest, in the sight of all men. Based on Romans 12:17.

8) I am not overcome by evil, I overcome evil with good. Based on Romans 12:21.

9) I love my neighbor as myself. I never work ill, to my neighbor. When I love, I am fulfilling the law. Based on Romans 13:9,10.

10) I walk honestly, as in the day, never rioting, and drunkenness, never chambering, or wantonness, nor in strife, or envying. Based on Romans 13:13. (Chambering is acting impure, wantonness is maliciousness)

11) I follow after things, which make for peace, and after ways, that I can edify others. Based on Romans 14:19.

12) I please my neighbor, for His good, for His edification. Based on Romans 15:2.

13) God who gives me patience, and consolation, helps me to be likeminded, with other people, according to Christ Jesus. Based on Romans 15:5.

14) Father, your love, has been shed abroad, in my heart, by the Holy Spirit, I therefore suffer long, I endure long, I am kind, I do not envy, I do not vaunt myself. Based on 1 Corinthians 13:4. (Vaunt means exalt.)

15) I do not behave myself unseemly. I do not seek my own way. I am not easily provoked. I do not think evil. Based on 1 Corinthians. 13:5.

16) I do not rejoice in iniquity, I rejoice in the truth. Based on 1 Corinthians 13:6.

17) I bear up under all things, I believe the best about people, I'm very hopeful, I endure all things. Thus, I am very patient with people. Based on 1 Corinthians 13:7.

18) My love never fails. Based on 1 Corinthians 13:8.

19) I pursue love. And I desire spiritual gifts. Based on 1 Corinthians 14:1.

20) When I see a brother or sister, who has been overtaken by a fault, I restore such a person, in a spirit of meekness. Based on Galatians 6:1.

21) With all lowliness and meekness, and with patience, I forbear others in love. Based on Ephesians 4:2.

22) I endeavor, to keep the unity, of the Spirit, in the bond of peace. Based on Ephesians 4:3.

23) My conduct is worthy, of the gospel of Christ, I stand fast in one spirit, with one mind, striving together, for the faith of the gospel. Based on Philippians 1:27.

24) I fulfill Paul's joy, I am like-minded, having the same love, being of one accord, of one mind. Based on Philippians 2:2.

25) I let nothing be done, in strife or vainglory, but in lowliness of mind, I esteem others, as better than myself. Based on Philippians 2:3.

26) I don't only concern myself of my own needs, but of others too. Based on Philippians 2:4.

27) I do not neglect to do good and to share, for of such sacrifices God is well pleased. Based on Hebrews 13:16.

28) I have some of the world's goods, and when I see my brother in need, I do not close my heart from him, because God's love, abides in me. Based on1 John 3:17.

Let's go back to the Affirmation Speaker role.

AFFIRMATION #4
"I ONLY SPEAK RIGHT WORDS"

Throughout your day, try to recite out loud, the "I Only Speak Right Words" Affirmation.

Prayer of Dedication: "Father, I dedicate myself to live this day speaking only right words, words that are free of all negatives. I now speak these Bible-based statements out loud to remind me to keep all my words positive and faith-filled!"

(The extra commas make the words more meditative and impactful. It also helps people read in unison during conference calls.)

1) My words are as a honeycomb, sweet to the soul, and health to the bones. Based on Proverbs 16:24.

2) My words are like a wellspring of wisdom, and as a flowing brook. Based on Proverbs 18:4.

3) Because I keep my mouth, and my tongue, I keep my soul from troubles. Based on Proverbs 21:23.

4) Because I am righteous, my mouth speaks wisdom. Based on Psalm 37:30.

5) My heart thinks of good things. I speak things that help others. My words are like those, of a ready writer, recording good things. Based on Psalm 45:1.

6) I put away from me, a froward mouth, I put perverse lips, far from me. Based on Proverbs 4:24. (Froward means deceitful)

7) I speak God's Words, because they are life to me, they are health, to all my flesh. Based on Proverbs 4:22.

8) All the words of my mouth, are in righteousness; there is nothing froward, or perverse in them. Based on Proverbs 8:8.

9) I only speak excellent things, and the opening of my lips, are for right things only. My mouth speaks truth, and wickedness, is an abomination to my words. Based on Proverbs 8:6,7.

10) I have the mouth, of a righteous man, my words are like a well of life. Based on Proverbs 10:11.

11) Because I am just, my words are as choice silver. Based on Proverbs 10:20.

12) My lips are righteous, they feed many. Based on Proverbs 10:21.

13) Because I am righteous, my mouth brings forth wisdom, continually. Based on Proverbs 10:31.

14) Because I am righteous, my lips know, what is acceptable. Based on Proverbs 10:32.

15) I am satisfied with good, by the fruit of my words. Based on Proverbs 12:14.

16) Because I have God's wisdom, my tongue, brings me health. Based on Proverbs 12:18.

17) Because I keep my mouth, I keep my life. He that talks too much, invites destruction. Therefore I watch what I say. Based on Proverbs 13:3.

18) Because grievous words stirs up anger, I answer people softly. My soft answers turn away wrath. Based on Proverbs 15:1.

19) Because I have God's wisdom, I use knowledge aright. Based on Proverbs 15:2.

20) Because I have a wholesome tongue, my words bring forth, a tree of life. Based on Proverbs 15:4.

21) I have joy, in my proper answers, and because I speak words, in due season, they produce good! Based on Proverbs 15:23.

22) As I prepare my heart, each day with prayer, and the Word, I believe the answers, of my tongue, are from the Lord. Based on Proverbs 16:1.

23) Gold and jewels are valuable. My knowledgeable words are also valuable. Based on Proverbs 20:15.

24) My soft words, breaks a bone, (bone-like resistance, from others). Based on Proverbs 25:15.

25) Because I am wise, the words of my mouth, are gracious. Based on Ecclesiastes 10:12.

26) The Lord has given me, the words of a disciple. This helps me speak uplifting words to him who is weary. Based on Isaiah 50:4.

Let's go back to the Affirmation Speaker role.

Affirmation #5
"I Only Think Right Thoughts"

*****

Throughout your day, try to recite out loud, the "I Only Think Right Thoughts" Affirmation.

Prayer of Dedication: "Father, I dedicate myself to live this day thinking only right thoughts, thoughts that are free of all negatives. I now speak these Bible-based statements out loud to remind me to keep all my thoughts positive and faith-filled!"

(The extra commas make the words more meditative and impactful. It also helps people read in unison during conference calls.)

*****

1) I trust in the Lord, with all my heart, and I do not lean, on my own understanding. In all my ways, I acknowledge Him, and He directs my steps. Based on Proverbs 3:5-6.

2) I meditate, on God's Word, day and night, I am like a tree, planted by the rivers, that brings forth its fruit, in season. And my leaves, do not wither, in whatever I do, I prosper. Based on Psalm 1:2-3.

3) I pray every day, for God's help, to keep the words of my mouth, and the meditation of my heart, acceptable, in His sight. Based on Psalm 19:14.

4) I thank God, that he leads me, (and my thoughts), beside still waters, and he restores my soul, with good thoughts, and he leads me, on paths of righteousness, for His name's sake. Based on Psalm 23:2,3.

5) I am diligent, to hide God's Word, in my heart, so that I, might not sin, against Him. Based on Psalm 119:11.

6) I ask God, to search me every day, to know my heart, and try my thoughts, to see if there is, any wicked way in me. And to lead me, in the way, everlasting. Based on Psalm 139:23,24.

7) I keep my heart, (my thoughts), with all diligence, for out of it, are the issues of my life. Based on Proverbs 4:23.

8) I bring to God, the plans in my mind, and he helps me, to know which way to go. (This keeps my mind at rest.) Based on Proverbs 16:3.

9) I know that a merry heart, is good like medicine, so I keep myself happy, hopeful, and trusting in God. Based on Proverbs 17:22.

10) Because I keep my mind, stayed on God, I enjoy perfect peace. Based on Isaiah 26:3.

11) I forsake my old thoughts, I return to the Lord, He has mercy on me, He pardons me abundantly. Based on Isaiah 55:7.

12) I keep myself hopeful, because God has plans for my peace, He has plans that give me, an expected end. Based on Jeremiah 29:11.

13) I am diligent, to love God, with all my heart, with all my soul, with all my mind. Based on Matthew 22:37.

14) Jesus left His peace with me, Jesus gave me His peace. I stop my heart, from being troubled, I never let it be afraid. Based on John 14:27.

15) I am after the Spirit, I mind the things of the Spirit, not the flesh. Based on Romans 8:5.

16) I do not let myself, be conformed, to this world, but I allow myself, to be transformed, by the renewing of my mind. This way I am able to know the good, the acceptable, and the perfect will of God, for my life. Based on Romans 12:2.

17) The weapons that God has given me, are not carnal, but mighty through God, to the pulling down of strongholds, in my mind, I cast down, every imagination, and every high thing, that exalts itself, against the knowledge of God, and I bring into captivity, every thought, to the obedience of Christ. Based on 2 Corinthians 10:4,5.

18) As a person thinks, so are they. And because I am a Christian, saved by the sacrifice of Jesus, I have been Born Again. I am a new creature in Christ Jesus. I have traded my sin nature, for God's nature, And now God's nature, is in my thoughts, as I give my mind to God, and His Word. Based on Proverbs 23:7 & 2 Corinthians 5:17, Ephesians 4:22-24

19) This one thing I do, I forget those things which are behind, so I can reach for the things that are before me. Based on Philippians 3:13.

20) I make sure, I do not overly care about anything, but in everything, by prayer, and supplication, with thanksgiving, I let my requests, be made known to God, And the peace of God, which passes all understanding, keeps my heart, and my mind, through Christ Jesus. Based on Philippians 4:6,7.

21) My mind, is an amazing gift from God, and I use it only as intended. I use it to think on things that are true, just, pure, lovely, things that are of a good report, things that are virtuous, and worthy of praise. Based on Philippians 4:8.

22) I can do all things through Christ, including keeping my mind, on right thoughts. Based on Philippians 4:13.

23) I set my mind, on thoughts of God, Jesus, the Holy Spirit, and of heaven, not on the things of this life. Based on Colossians 3:2.

24) Because I keep my mind, on godly things, I am able to "Let the peace of Christ, rule in my heart." And I am thankful. Based on Colossians 3:15.

25) I thank God, that he has given me, a spirit that is powerful, and love-filled, and he has given me a mind, that is sound, in every regard, so all my thoughts, are faith-filled, and peace-filled. Based on 2 Timothy 1:7.

26) Because I consider, what the Apostle Paul says, the Lord gives me understanding, in all things. Based on 2 Timothy 2:7

27) I study, to show myself approved to God, I am a workman, who is never ashamed, This helps me to rightly divide, the word of truth. Based on 2 Timothy 2:15. (Divide means understand)

28) The Word of God in me, is quick and powerful, and sharper than a two-edged sword, it helps me to discern, negative thoughts, and the intentions of my heart, (so I can quickly uproot them). Based on Hebrews 4:12.

29) I stay close to God, so I am never a double-minded person, a person who is unstable in all their ways. Based on James 1:8.

30) Greater is He who is in me, than he who is in the world, Because God lives big in me, His Word lives big in my thinking, and triumphs over all my negative thoughts. Based on 1 John 4:4.

Let's go back to the Affirmation Speaker role.

AFFIRMATION #6
"I AM HAPPY BECAUSE..."

****

Throughout your day, try to recite out loud, the "I Am Happy Because..." Affirmation.

Prayer of Dedication: "Father, I dedicate myself to live this day rejoicing in the things you have given me. I now speak these Bible-based statements to remind me of all the good things I have because I am your child!"

(The extra commas make the words more meditative and impactful. It also helps people read in unison during conference calls.)

****

1) I am happy because, those who mourn, will be comforted! Based on Matthew 5:4.

2) I am happy because, I know how to glorify God, by letting my light shine, before men, by doing good works. Based on Matthew 5:16.

3) I am happy because, I don't have to have negative feelings, about my enemies, I love them, and I pray for them. Based on Matthew 5:44.

4) I am happy because, when I give, and pray, and fast, in secret, God rewards me openly. Based on Matthew 6:4,6.

5) I am happy because, all my needs are met, when I seek first God's kingdom, and His righteousness. Based on Matthew 6:33, Luke 12:31.

6) I am happy because, when I ask - I receive, when I seek - I find, when I knock - it is opened. Based on Matthew 7:7, Luke 11:10.

7) I am happy because, when I labor, and am heavy laden, Jesus bids me come, he gives me rest! Based on Matthew 11:28,29.

8) I am happy because, even a small amount of faith, can do so much. Based on Matthew 17:20.

9) I am happy because, when two people agree, in prayer, it will be done, by my Father in heaven. Based on Matthew 18:19.

10) I am happy because, where 2 or 3 believers are, Christ is in the midst. Based on Matthew 18:20.

Affirmations

11) I am happy because, all things are possible! Based on Matthew 19:26 & Mark 9:23.

12) I am happy because, when I give to the needy, I give to Christ! Based on Matthew 25:40.

13) I am happy because, Jesus can take, what little I have, and multiply it! Based on Mark 8:1-9.

14) I am happy because, Jesus lays out an easy way, to become great – become a servant of all. Based on Mark 9:35, 10:44

15) I am happy because, Jesus said, whatever I pray for, and believe I have received it, I shall have it! Based on Mark 11:24.

16) I am happy because, I don't have to worry, about saying the wrong things, Jesus said the Holy Ghost, will give me the words to say. Based on Mark 13:11.

17) I am happy because, Jesus doesn't care how little, my offering is, it's how much is left over that counts! Based on Mark 12:43,44.

18) I am happy because, God gives me purpose! Jesus said "Go into all the world, and preach the gospel, to all creation." That's my purpose! Based on Mark 16:15.

19) I am happy because, whoever believes, and is baptized, will be saved! Based on Mark 16:16.

20) I am happy because, Jesus said we can heal people, in His name! Based on Mark 16:18.

21) I am happy because, Jesus said those who weep now, will one day laugh! Based on Luke 6:21.

22) I am happy because, I don't have to care, when people dislike me, Jesus said to rejoice, for my reward, in heaven, will be great! Based on Luke 6:22,23.

23) I am happy because, when Jesus is around, things happen: the blind see, lepers are cleansed, deaf people hear, the dead are raised to life, and the poor hear the gospel! Based on Luke 7:22.

24) I am happy because, I don't have to care! When people reject the gospel, I just shake it off! Based on Luke 9:5.

25) I am happy because, even devils are subject to us! through Jesus's name. Based on Luke 10:17.

26) I am happy because, Jesus give us power, to tread on serpents! And scorpions! And over all power, of the enemy! And nothing shall hurt us! Based on Luke 10:19.

27) I am happy because, my name is written in heaven! Based on Luke 10:20.

28) I am happy because, God has numbered, the hairs on my head! Jesus said I have great value! Based on Luke 12:7.

29) I am happy because, if God feeds the ravens, He will certainly feed me, if God clothes the lilies, He will certainly clothe me. Based on Luke 12:24,28.

30) I am happy because, God says "whosoever"! God so loved the world, that He gave, His only beloved Son, that <u>whosoever</u> believeth in Him, should not perish, but have everlasting life! Based on John 3:16.

31) I am happy because, the water Jesus gives me, is a well of water, springing up, into everlasting life. Based on John 4:14.

32) I am happy because, Jesus tells me what to work for, I do not labor for food that perishes, I labor for food that endures, to everlasting life, which Jesus gives me. Based on John 6:27.

33) I am happy because, that Jesus is the bread of life, when I come to Jesus, I never hunger, and never get thirsty. Based on John 6:35.

34) I am happy because, Jesus is the light of my life, When I follow Him, I do not walk in darkness. I have the light of life! Based on John 8:12, 12:35,46.

35) I am happy because, it is truth, that sets me free! (So I keep searching for truth!) Based on John 8:32.

36) I am happy because, Jesus is my shepherd, I can learn His voice, Jesus lays down His life, for the sheep! Based on John 10:14-18,27.

37) I am happy because, Jesus give us an easy way, for people to know, we are His, when we love one another. Based on John 13:34,35.

38) I am happy because, I can keep my heart, from being troubled! Based on John 14:1,27.

39) I am happy because, Jesus is preparing, a place for me, in heaven! Based on John 14:2.

40) I am happy because, Jesus says who He is, "I am the way, the truth, and the life: no man comes to the father, but by me." Based on John 14:6.

41) I am happy because, Jesus tells us, the works that He does, we shall do also! And greater works! Based on John 14:12.

42) I am happy because, Jesus sends me, the Comforter, the Holy Spirit. And He never leaves me! Based on John 14:16.

43) I am happy because, Jesus leaves me His peace. Based on John 14:27, 20:21.

44) I am happy because, I bear fruit! Jesus says, as I abide in Him, and He in me, I will bear much fruit! Based on John 15:2,4,5,16.

45) I am happy because, Jesus says, if I abide in Him, and His Word abides in me, I will ask, whatever I will, and it'll be done for me! Based on John 15:7, 17:24.

46) I am happy because, Christ's joy remains in me, and my joy is FULL! Based on John 15:11. My joy is a joy, that no man, can take from me! Based on John 16:22.

47) I am happy because, Jesus calls me His Friend! not a servant, I am His friend, if I do whatsoever He commands. Based on John 15:14

48) I am happy because, Jesus says, I didn't choose Him, but He chose me! Based on John 15:16.

49) I am happy because, the Holy Spirit, teaches me all truth! Based on John 16:13.

50) I am happy because, I can rejoice, in my sufferings, because I know, my sufferings, produce perseverance, and perseverance character, and character hope! Based on Romans 5:3,4.

51) I am happy because, God shows me His love! While I was still a sinner, Christ died for me! Based on Romans 5:8.

52) I am happy because, God gives me eternal life! The wages of my sin, is death, but the gift of God, is eternal life, in Christ Jesus. Based on Romans 6:23.

53) I am happy because, my present sufferings, are not worth comparing, with the glory, that will be revealed, in me! Based on Romans 8:18

54) I am happy because, God works all things, for my good, because I love Him. Based on Romans 8:28.

55) I am happy because, if God is for me, who can be against me? Based on Romans 8:31.

56) I am happy because, in all my trials, I am more than a conqueror, through Christ, who loves me! Based on Romans 8:37.

57) I am happy because, I don't have to conform to the world, I'm being transformed, by the renewing, of my mind. Based on Romans 12:2

58) I am happy because, I am joyful! I'm joyful in hope, patient in affliction, and faithful in prayer. Based on Romans12:12.

59) I am happy because, I am enriched, by Christ, in all my speaking, and all my knowledge. Based on 1 Corinthians 1:5.

60) I am happy because, God uses my foolishness, to confound the wise, and He uses my weaknesses, to confound the mighty. Based on 1 Corinthians 1:27.

61) I am happy because, God has planned, amazing things, for me! in my after-life! Things human eyes can't see, human ears can't hear, nor things imagined. Based on 1 Corinthians 2:9.

62) I am happy because, I am important, even with my flaws! Based on 1 Corinthians 12:22,23.

63) I am happy because, God gives me victory! Based on 1 Corinthians 15:57.

64) I am happy because, God comforts me, in all my troubles. Based on 2 Corinthians 1:4.

65) I am happy because, God causes me, to always triumph! Based on 2 Corinthians 2:14.

66) I am happy because, I am a sweet smell of Christ, to those around me. Based on 2 Corinthians 2:15.

67) I am happy because, I'm an able minister, of the gospel! Based on 2 Corinthians 3:6.

68) I am happy because, I have strong hope! And use plain speech! Based on 2 Corinthians 3:12.

69) I am happy because, I have freedom! Because the Spirit, of the Lord, is in me. Based on 2 Corinthians 3:17.

70) I am happy because, I am transforming, into God's image, from glory to glory! Based on 2 Corinthians 3:18.

71) I am happy because, I'm being renewed, day by day! Based on 2 Corinthians 4:16.

72) I am happy because, I have glory! My light affliction, is working in me, an exceeding weight of glory! Based on 2 Corinthians 4:17.

73) I am happy because, I have a new home! My earthly "house", is dissolving, but I have a new home, that God is building, in the heavens! Based on 2 Corinthians 5:1.

74) I am happy because, I am righteous! God made Christ, to be sin for me, that I might have, Christ's righteousness! Based on 2 Corinthians 5:21.

75) I am happy because, I have great grace! God is able, to make all grace, abound to me, so that I, might abound, in every way! Based on 2 Corinthians 9:8.

76) I am happy because, God's grace is sufficient, When my life gets hard, Jesus tells me, His grace, will get me through! Based on 2 Corinthians 12:9a.

77) I am happy because, I can boast about my weaknesses, because that's when, Christ's power, comes in, and makes me strong! Based on 2 Corinthians 12:9b.

78) I am happy because, I know what's most important - Faith! And that it works by love. (I'm developing my faith!) Based on Galatians 5:6.

79) I am happy because, God calls me to be free! I use my freedom, to serve others, in love. Based on Galatians 5:13.

80) I am happy because, God gives me, the fruit of the Spirit, I have Love and joy, peace and patience, gentleness and goodness, faith and meekness, and self-control! Based on Galatians 5:22,23.

81) I am happy because, I can choose, to crucify my old nature, with its passions and desires. Based on Galatians 5:24.

82) I am happy because, I have help, in carrying my burdens, others are helping me, and I help them! Together, we fulfill, the law of Christ. Based on Galatians 6:2.

83) I am happy because, I never lose heart! I don't get weary, in well-doing, (I keep working, I keep helping, with God's help!) Based on Galatians 6:9.

84) I am happy because, God has chosen me, before creation, to be holy, and blameless, in His sight. Based on Ephesians 1:4.

85) I am happy because, of God's rich mercy! And for His great love, for me, even when I was dead, in my sins, He made me alive, in Christ, It is God's grace, that I have been saved. Based on Ephesians 2:4,5.

86) I am happy because, God has raised me up, with Christ, I am seated with Him, in heavenly places, in Christ. Based on Ephesians 2:6.

87) I am happy because, I am God's workmanship! created in Christ Jesus, to do good works, which He prepared, from the beginning, for me to walk, in them. Based on Ephesians 2:10.

88) I am happy because, I am a part of God's home! Together we are, a habitation, for God, by His of Spirit. Based on Ephesians 2:22.

89) I am happy because, I have access to God's wisdom! I have boldness, and I access, with confidence, to the wisdom of God, through Christ. Based on Ephesians 3:10,12.

90) I am happy because, God can do exceeding abundantly, above all I can ask, or think, according to His power, that's at work in me. Based on Ephesians 3:20.

91) I am happy because, I am a peace-maker! With God's help, I do my best, to keep the unity, of the Spirit, in the bond of peace. Based on Ephesians 4:3.

92) I am happy because, God didn't leave me on my own! He's given me, apostles and prophets, evangelists and pastors, and teachers, who help me grow, and serve, and be a blessing, to the Body of Christ. Based on Ephesians 4:11.

93) I am happy because, I have a new self! God tells me, to put on my new self, created to be, like God, in true righteousness, and holiness. Based on Ephesians 4:24.

94) I am happy because, I don't go to bed mad! I forgive everyone, before going to bed. Based on Ephesians 4:26.

95) I am happy because, I'm quick to forgive! just like God, who forgave me through Christ. Based on Ephesians 4:32.

96) I am happy because, God made me a singer! I sing to myself, psalms and hymns, and spiritual songs, singing and making melody, in my heart, to the Lord. Based on Ephesians 5:19.

97) I am happy because, God made me a great worker! I serve my boss, as if I'm serving the Lord. I know, whatever good I do, I will receive a reward, from God! Based on Ephesians 6:5-9.

98) I am happy because, God wants me strong! Every day, I wear the armor of God, so I can stand, against the tricks, of the devil. I put on, the belt of truth, the breastplate of righteousness, the shoes of the gospel, the shield of faith, the helmet of salvation, and the sword of the Spirit, which is the Word of God. Based on Ephesians 6:11-17.

99) I am happy because, I have confidence! I am confident that God, who began a good work, in me, will carry it through, to completion, until the day, of Christ Jesus. Based on Philippians 1:6.

100) I am happy because, I can stand firm! I stand firm, in one spirit, with one mind, striving together, with others, for the faith of the gospel, and I'm never terrified, by my adversaries. Based on Philippians 1:27,28.

101) I am happy because of humility! I no longer do things, with strife and vainglory, but in lowliness of mind, I esteem others, as better, than myself. [7] Jesus made Himself nothing, taking the nature, of a servant. (With God's help, I will do the same.) Based on Philippians 2:3,7.

102) I am happy because, I'm going to see every knee bow, and hear every tongue confess, that Jesus Christ is Lord! Based on Philippians 2:10,11.

103) I am happy because of purity, I do everything, without complaining, or arguing, and I choose, to be blameless, and pure, a child of God, without fault, in this crooked, and perverse generation, in which I shine, like a light in the world, holding forth, the Word of Life! Based on Philippians 2:14-16.

104) I am happy because, I can forget my past! And focus on what is ahead, I press toward the mark, for the prize, of the high calling of God, in Christ Jesus. Based on Philippians 3:13,14.

105) I am happy because, God wants me joyful! in Him, Always!, So I rejoice! Based on Philippians 4:4.

106) I am happy because, I've learned to be gentle! to everyone! Based on Philippians 4:5.

107) I am happy because, God wants me carefree! He tells me, not to be careful about anything, I just pray about what I need, with thanksgiving, and the peace of God, which passes all understanding, keeps my heart, and my mind, through Christ Jesus. Based on Philippians 4:6,7.

108) I am happy because, God gives me guidance, on how to think, I only think on things, that are true, honest and just, pure and lovely, things of good report, things that are virtuous, and worthy of praise. Based on Philippians 4:8.

109) I am happy because I'm content, I have learned to be content, in whatsoever state I'm in. Based on Philippians 4:11.

110) I am happy because, I can do all things through Christ, who strengthens me. Based on Philippians 4:13.

111) I am happy because, God promises to meet all of my needs! Based on Philippians 4:19.

112) I am happy because, I am being strengthened, with all might, according to His glorious power, unto all patience, and longsuffering, and joyfulness! Based on Colossians 1:11.

113) I am happy because, God qualifies me, to share in the inheritance, of His holy people, in the kingdom of light! Based on Colossians 1:12.

114) I am happy because, when I was dead in my sins, and in the uncircumcision of my sinful nature, God made me alive with Christ, He forgave me, all my sins, and He canceled the written code, that was against me, He took it away, nailing it to the cross! Based on Colossians 2:13,14.

115) I am happy because, God has disarmed the powers of evil! And made a show of them openly! Triumphing over them! Based on Colossians 2:15.

116) I am happy because, I have a new man! I have put off the old man, with its deeds, and I've put on the new man, which is being renewed, in knowledge, in the image of my creator. Based on Colossians 3:9,10.

117) I am happy because of my peace! I can let, the peace of Christ, rule in my heart! Based on Colossians 3:15.

118) I am happy because, God makes me diligent, I obey my boss, not just when he's watching. In singleness of heart, I focus on my tasks. Based on Colossians 3:22.

119) I am happy because, God wants my life to win respect, God says when I lead a quiet life, minding my own business, working with my hands, I win respect. Based on 1 Thessalonians 4:11.

120) I am happy because, Jesus is returning! The day is coming, when the Lord Himself, shall descend from heaven, with a shout, and the voice of the archangel, and the trump of God, and the dead in Christ, shall arise! Then we who are alive, shall be caught up together, with them in the clouds, to meet the Lord, in the air, and so shall we be, ever with the Lord! Based on 1 Thessalonians 4:16,17.

121) I am happy because of God's help! He gives me people, who comfort me, and edify me. And I return the favor. Based on 1 Thessalonians 5:11.

122) I am happy because, God is a God of peace. He's sanctifying my spirit, soul and body, so that I'll be blameless, at the coming of my Lord. Based on 1 Thessalonians 5:23,24.

123) I am happy because, my faith and love are growing, exceedingly. Based on 2 Thessalonians 1:3.

124) I am happy because, I can persevere in my faith, in spite of my persecutions, and tribulations. Based on 2 Thessalonians 1:4.

125) I am happy because, God is counting me worthy of His calling, through Jesus, He is fulfilling, all the good pleasure, of His goodness, toward me, and there is at work in me, great faith and power. Based on 2 Thess 1:11.

Affirmations

126) I am happy because, the name of the Lord Jesus Christ, is being glorified in me, as I am in Him, according to the grace of God, in Christ. Based on 2 Thessalonians 1:12.

127) I am happy because, God chose me to be saved, through the sanctifying work, of the Spirit, and through belief of the truth. Based on 2 Thessalonians 2:13.

128) I am happy because, God loves me and gives me, everlasting consolation, and good hope through grace. Based on 2 Thessalonians 2:16.

129) I am happy because, the Lord of peace Himself, gives me peace always, and by all means. Based on 2 Thessalonians 3:16.

130) I am happy because, the grace of our Lord to me, is exceedingly great. Based on 1Timothy 1:14.

131) I am happy because, God wants all men saved, and to come to the knowledge, of the truth. Based on 1Timothy 2:4.

132) I am happy because, my godliness profits me, in this life, and in the life to come. Based on 1Timothy 4:8.

133) I am happy because, nobody looks down on me, because I'm young, I am an example, to all believers, in my speech, in my life, in my love, in my faith, and in my purity. Based on Timothy 4:12.

134) I am happy because, I have great gain, because I have godliness, and contentment! Based on 1Timothy 6:6.

135) I am happy because, God did not give me a spirit of fear, but of love, of power, and a sound mind! Based on 2 Timothy 1:7.

136) I am happy because, Christ Jesus destroyed death! and has brought me life, and immortality! Through the gospel! Based on 2 Timothy 1:10.

137) I am happy because, I have no shame! I know in whom I believe, and I am convinced, that Christ is able to guard, what I've given Him, for that day. Based on 2 Timothy 1:12.

138) I am happy because, I am fully convinced, in the marvelous grace, that is given to me, in Christ Jesus. Based on 2 Timothy 2:1.

139) I am happy because, I've learned how to endure hardship, like a good soldier, of Christ Jesus. Based on 2 Timothy 2:3.

140) I am happy because, God tells me not to get entangled, in this life, so I can please Christ, who has chosen me, to be a soldier. Based on 2 Timothy 2:4.

141) I am happy because, God tells me not to quarrel, which leads to stress, but to be kind to everyone, able to teach, not resentful. Based on 2 Timothy 2:24.

142) I am happy because, all scripture is God-inspired, and is profitable in doctrine, reproof and correction, and instruction in righteousness. Based on 2 Timothy 3:16.

143) I am happy because, there is stored for me, a crown of righteousness, which Jesus will award me, on that day. Based on 2 Timothy 4:8.

144) I am happy because, God stands beside me, and gives me strength, so that through me, the gospel is preached, and Gentiles are being delivered, out of the mouth of lions. Based on 2 Timothy 4:17.

145) I am happy because, God rescues me, from every evil attack, He will bring me safely, home with Him. Based on 2 Timothy 4:18.

146) I am happy because, Christ gave Himself for me, to redeem me from all wickedness, to purify me for Himself, a peculiar person, zealous for good works. Based on Titus 2:14.

147) I am happy because, the Word of God is quick and powerful, sharper than any two-edged sword, revealing the difference, between my soul and spirit, and joints and marrow, it discerns my thoughts, and the intents of my heart. Based on Hebrews 4:12.

148) I am happy because of faith, I picture in my mind what I want, I am confident I will get it. Based on Hebrews 11:1.

149) I am happy because, I know what pleases God - faith! When I come to God, I believe He exists, and He rewards me, because I seek Him. Based on Hebrews 11:6.

150) I am happy because, I'm not alone! there's a heavenly crowd, watching me "run my race", so I lay aside every weight, and sin that hinders me, and I run with patience, the race set before me, looking unto Jesus, the author and finisher, of my faith. Jesus endured the cross, I can certainly, endure my trial. Based on Hebrews 12:1,2.

151) I am happy because, I count it all joy, when I fall into various temptations, because I know, the trying of my faith, develops patience, and I let my patience, have its perfect work, so that I am perfect, and entire, lacking nothing! Based on James 1:2-4.

152) I am happy because of humility! When I humble myself, before the Lord, He lifts me up! Based on James 4:10.

153) I am happy because of humility again! When I humble myself, under the mighty hand of God, He exalts me, in due season! Based on 1 Peter 5:6.

154) I am happy because, I can cast all my cares onto Christ, because He cares or me! Based on 1 Peter 5:7.

155) I am happy because, the God of all grace, who has called me, into His eternal glory, by Christ Jesus, after a bit of suffering, makes me perfect and established, strengthened and settled! Based on 1 Peter 5:10.

156) I am happy because, when I confess my sins, God is faithful and just, to forgive my sins, and purify me, from all unrighteousness. Based on 1 John 1:9.

157) I am happy because, there is no fear in love, rather perfect love, casts out fear! Based on 1 John 4:18.

158) I am happy because, he who has the Son has life! Based on 1 John 5:12.

Let's go back to the Affirmation Speaker role.

Core Beliefs

Choose Your Core Beliefs

Our thoughts are influenced by our beliefs. Positive beliefs help keep our thinking and our responses to life's problems positive.

The goal is to make these core beliefs the final word in our lives. No matter what our feelings say or what the circumstances try to tell us, these foundational beliefs are what we are going to use when thinking about ourselves, when making decisions in our lives, and when we are praying about our needs and wants.

If we come across a belief that we would like to adopt but seems untrue to us, read out loud the scripture verses associated with the belief. The truth of these verses will slowly sink into our minds and over time will become real in our hearts.

CORE BELIEF #1

"Based on the following scriptures, I believe God loves me, and that I am valuable."

Below are some scriptures that talk about God's love for humanity. The most notable way God showed His love for us is in the offering of His only Son, Jesus, to die on the cross for our sins. Indeed, His love for us is great.

Remember that this is a <u>Core Belief</u>. Unless we believe this to be true, our lives can seem meaningless and hopeless. So let's renew our minds to the truth that God loves us, and that He has an amazing plan for our lives!

1) **Nehemiah 9:17** "but thou art a God ready to pardon, gracious and merciful, slow to anger, and of great kindness, and forsookest them not."

2) **Psalm 17:7** "Shew thy marvellous lovingkindness, O thou that savest by thy right hand them which put their trust in thee from those that rise up against them."

3) **Psalm 25:7** "Remember not the sins of my youth and my rebellious ways; according to your love remember me, for you are good, O LORD."

4) **Psalm 36:7** "How excellent is thy lovingkindness, O God! therefore the children of men put their trust under the shadow of thy wings."

5) **Psalm 48:9** "We have thought of thy lovingkindness, O God, in the midst of thy temple."

6) **Psalm 52:8** "But I am like a green olive tree in the house of God: I trust in the mercy of God for ever and ever."

7) **Psalm 63:3** "Because thy lovingkindness is better than life, my lips shall praise thee."

8) **Psalm 86:15** "But thou, O Lord, art a God full of compassion, and gracious, long suffering, and plenteous in mercy and truth."

9) **Psalm 103:8** "The Lord is merciful and gracious, slow to anger, and plenteous in mercy."

10) **Psalm 103:11** "For as the heaven is high above the earth, so great is his mercy toward them that fear him."

11) **Psalm 109:26** "Help me, O Lord my God: O save me according to thy mercy:"

12) **Psalm 136:26** "O give thanks unto the God of heaven: for his mercy endureth for ever."

13) **Isaiah 34:6** "And the Lord passed by before him, and proclaimed, The Lord, The Lord God, merciful and gracious, longsuffering, and abundant in goodness and truth,"

14) **Isaiah 41:10** "Fear thou not; for I am with thee: be not dismayed; for I am thy God: I will strengthen thee; yea, I will help thee; yea, I will uphold thee with the right hand of my righteousness."

15) **Isaiah 41:13** "For I the Lord thy God will hold thy right hand, saying unto thee, Fear not; I will help thee."

16) **Isaiah 49:16** "Behold, I have graven thee upon the palms of my hands; thy walls are continually before me."

17) **Isaiah 54:10** "For the mountains shall depart, and the hills be removed; but my kindness shall not depart from thee, neither shall the covenant of my peace be removed, saith the Lord that hath mercy on thee."

18) **Jeremiah 29;11** "For I know the thoughts that I think toward you, saith the Lord, thoughts of peace, and not of evil, to give you an expected end."

19) **Jeremiah 31:3** "The LORD hath appeared of old unto me, saying, Yea, I have loved thee with an everlasting love: therefore with lovingkindness have I drawn thee."

20) **Zephaniah 3:17** "The Lord thy God in the midst of thee is mighty; he will save, he will rejoice over thee with joy; he will rest in his love, he will joy over thee with singing."

21) **Mark 10:21** "Then Jesus beholding him loved him, and said unto him, One thing thou lackest: go thy way, sell whatsoever thou hast, and give to the poor, and thou shalt have treasure in heaven: and come, take up the cross, and follow me."

22) **John 3:16** "For God so loved the world, that he gave his only begotten Son, that whosoever believeth in him should not perish, but have everlasting life."

23) **John 14:21** "He that hath my commandments, and keepeth them, he it is that loveth me: and he that loveth me shall be loved of my Father, and I will love him, and will manifest myself to him."

24) **John 15:9** "As the Father hath loved me, so have I loved you: continue ye in my love."

25) **John 16:27** "For the Father himself loveth you, because ye have loved me, and have believed that I came out from God."

26) **Romans 5:5** "And hope maketh not ashamed; because the love of God is shed abroad in our hearts by the Holy Ghost which is given unto us."

27) **Romans 5:8** "But God commendeth his love toward us, in that, while we were yet sinners, Christ died for us."

28) **Romans 8:35** "Who shall separate us from the love of Christ? shall tribulation, or distress, or persecution, or famine, or nakedness, or peril, or sword?"

29) **Romans 8:37** "Nay, in all these things we are more than conquerors through him that loved us."

30) **Romans 8:38,39** "For I am persuaded, that neither death, nor life, nor angels, nor principalities, nor powers, nor things present, nor things to come, Nor height, nor depth, nor any other creature, shall be able to separate us from the love of God, which is in Christ Jesus our Lord."

31) **Romans 15:30** "Now I beseech you, brethren, for the Lord Jesus Christ's sake, and for the love of the Spirit, that ye strive together with me in your prayers to God for me;"

32) **2 Corinthians 5:14** "For the love of Christ constraineth us; because we thus judge, that if one died for all, then were all dead:"

33) **2 Corinthians 13:11** "Finally, brethren, farewell. Be perfect, be of good comfort, be of one mind, live in peace; and the God of love and peace shall be with you."

34) **2 Corinthians 13:14** "The grace of the Lord Jesus Christ, and the love of God, and the communion of the Holy Ghost, be with you all. Amen."

35) **Galatians 2:20** "I am crucified with Christ: nevertheless I live; yet not I, but Christ liveth in me: and the life which I now live in the flesh I live by the faith of the Son of God, who loved me, and gave himself for me."

36) **Ephesians 2:4** "But God, who is rich in mercy, for his great love wherewith he loved us,"

37) **Ephesians 3:17-19** "That Christ may dwell in your hearts by faith; that ye, being rooted and grounded in love, [18] May be able to comprehend with all saints what is the breadth, and length, and depth, and height; [19] And to know the love of Christ, which passeth knowledge, that ye might be filled with all the fulness of God."

38) **Ephesians 5:1,2** "Be ye therefore followers of God, as dear children; [2] And walk in love, as Christ also hath loved us, and hath given himself for us an offering and a sacrifice to God for a sweetsmelling savour."

39) **Ephesians 5:25** "Husbands, love your wives, even as Christ also loved the church, and gave himself for it;"

40) **2 Thessalonians 2:16** "Now our Lord Jesus Christ himself, and God, even our Father, which hath **love**d us, and hath given us everlasting consolation and good hope through grace,"

41) **2 Thessalonians 3:5** "And the Lord direct your hearts into the love of God, and into the patient waiting for Christ."

42) **Titus 3:4** "But after that the kindness and love of God our Savior toward man appeared,"

43) **1 Peter 5:6,7** "Humble yourselves therefore under the mighty hand of God, that he may exalt you in due time: ⁷ Casting all your care upon him; for he careth for you.

44) **1 John 3:1** "Behold, what manner of love the Father hath bestowed upon us, that we should be called the sons of God: therefore the world knoweth us not, because it knew him not."

45) **1 John 3:16** "Hereby perceive we the love of God, because he laid down his life for us: and we ought to lay down our lives for the brethren."

46) **1 John 4:7,8** "Beloved, let us love one another: for love is of God; and every one that loveth is born of God, and knoweth God. ⁸ He that loveth not knoweth not God; for God is love."

47) **1 John 4:9** "In this was manifested the love of God toward us, because that God sent his only begotten Son into the world, that we might live through him."

48) **1 John 4:10** "Herein is love, not that we loved God, but that he loved us, and sent his Son to be the propitiation for our sins."

49) **1 John 4:11** "Beloved, if God so loved us, we ought also to love one another."

50) **1 John 4:16** "And we have known and believed the love that God hath to us. God is love; and he that dwelleth in love dwelleth in God, and God in him."

51) **1 John 4:19** "We love him, because he first loved us."

52) **Jude 1:21** "Keep yourselves in the love of God, looking for the mercy of our Lord Jesus Christ unto eternal life."

53) **Revelation 1:5** "And from Jesus Christ, who is the faithful witness, and the first begotten of the dead, and the prince of the kings of the earth. Unto him that loved us, and washed us from our sins in his own blood,"

The goal of speaking these verses out loud is to fully believe the truth that God loves us and that we have immense value. We need to become so convinced of this that nothing could convince us otherwise. Reading these scriptures over and over will help us make this truth more a reality in our hearts.

Let's turn back to the Beliefs Speaker role.

CORE BELIEF #2

****

"Based on the following scriptures, I believe Christ's crucifixion on the cross has paid the penalty for my sin, and that I am destined to live eternally with Christ."

****

Unless we are convinced that our sins are forgiven, we'll never reach full happiness. If need be, we can read out loud the following scriptures to renew our minds to adopt this vital Core Belief.

1) **John 3:16** "For God so loved the world, that he gave his only begotten Son, that whosoever believeth in him should not perish, but have everlasting life."

2) **John 3:17** "For God sent not his Son into the world to condemn the world; but that the world through him might be saved."

3) **Acts 13:38** "Be it known unto you therefore, men and brethren, that through this man is preached unto you the forgiveness of sins:"

4) **Acts 13:39** "And by him all that believe are justified from all things, from which ye could not be justified by the law of Moses."

5) **Acts 15:11** "But we believe that through the grace of the LORD Jesus Christ we shall be saved, even as they."

6) **Acts 16:30,31** "And brought them out, and said, Sirs, what must I do to be saved? [31] And they said, Believe on the Lord Jesus Christ, and thou shalt be saved, and thy house."

7) **Romans 1:16** "For I am not ashamed of the gospel of Christ: for it is the power of God unto salvation to every one that believeth; to the Jew first, and also to the Greek."

8) **Romans 3:22-24** "Even the righteousness of God which is by faith of Jesus Christ unto all and upon all them that believe: for there is no difference: [23] For all have sinned, and come short of the glory of God; [24] Being justified freely by his grace through the redemption that is in Christ Jesus:"

9) **Romans 3:25** "God hath set forth to be a propitiation through faith in his blood, to declare his righteousness for the remission of sins that are past, through the forbearance of God;"

10) **Romans 5:1** "Therefore being justified by faith, we have peace with God through our Lord Jesus Christ:"

11) **Romans 10:4** "For Christ is the end of the law for righteousness to every one that believeth."

12) **Romans 10:9** "That if thou shalt confess with thy mouth the Lord Jesus, and shalt believe in thine heart that God hath raised him from the dead, thou shalt be saved."

13) **Romans 10:12,13** "For there is no difference between the Jew and the Greek: for the same Lord over all is rich unto all that call upon him. [13] For whosoever shall call upon the name of the Lord shall be saved."

14) **1 Corinthians 6:11** "And such were some of you: but ye are washed, but ye are sanctified, but ye are justified in the name of the Lord Jesus, and by the Spirit of our God."

15) **1 Corinthians 15:3** "For I delivered unto you first of all that which I also received, how that Christ died for our sins according to the scriptures;"

16) **2 Corinthians 5:18** "And all things are of God, who hath reconciled us to himself by Jesus Christ, and hath given to us the ministry of reconciliation;"

17) **2 Corinthians 5:19** "To wit, that God was in Christ, reconciling the world unto himself, not imputing their trespasses unto them; and hath committed unto us the word of reconciliation."

18) **2 Corinthians 5:20** "Now then we are ambassadors for Christ, as though God did beseech you by us: we pray you in Christ's stead, be ye reconciled to God."

19) **Galatians 1:4** "Who gave himself for our sins, that he might deliver us from this present evil world, according to the will of God and our Father:"

20) **Galatians 2:16** "Knowing that a man is not justified by the works of the law, but by the faith of Jesus Christ, even we have believed in Jesus Christ, that we might be justified by the faith of Christ, and not by the works of the law: for by the works of the law shall no flesh be justified."

21) **Galatians 3:14** "That the blessing of Abraham might come on the Gentiles through Jesus Christ; that we might receive the promise of the Spirit through faith."

22) **Galatians 3:26** "For ye are all the children of God by faith in Christ Jesus."

23) **Ephesians 1:7** "whom we have redemption through his blood, the forgiveness of sins, according to the riches of his grace;"

24) **Ephesians 1:13** "In whom ye also trusted, after that ye heard the word of truth, the gospel of your salvation: in whom also after that ye believed, ye were sealed with that holy Spirit of promise,"

25) **Ephesians 2:4,5** "But God, who is rich in mercy, for his great love wherewith he loved us, [5] Even when we were dead in sins, hath quickened us together with Christ, (by grace ye are saved;)"

26) **Ephesians 2:8** "For by grace are ye saved through faith; and that not of yourselves: it is the gift of God:"

27) **Ephesians 2:13** "But now in Christ Jesus ye who sometimes were far off are made nigh by the blood of Christ."

28) **Ephesians 3:9** "And to make all men see what is the fellowship of the mystery, which from the beginning of the world hath been hid in God, who created all things by Jesus Christ:"

29) **Ephesians 4:32** "And be ye kind one to another, tenderhearted, forgiving one another, even as God for Christ's sake hath forgiven you."

30) **Colossians 1:14** "In whom we have redemption through his blood, even the forgiveness of sins:"

31) **Colossians 1:20-22** "And, having made peace through the blood of his cross, by him to reconcile all things unto himself; by him, I say, whether they be things in earth, or things in heaven. ^{21} And you, that were sometime alienated and enemies in your mind by wicked works, yet now hath he reconciled ^{22} In the body of his flesh through death, to present you holy and unblameable and unreproveable in his sight:"

32) **Colossians 1:27** "To whom God would make known what is the riches of the glory of this mystery among the Gentiles; which is Christ in you, the hope of glory:"

33) **Colossians 2:13** "And you, being dead in your sins and the uncircumcision of your flesh, hath he quickened together with him, having forgiven you all trespasses;"

34) **1 Thessalonians 1:10** "And to wait for his Son from heaven, whom he raised from the dead, even Jesus, which delivered us from the wrath to come."

35) **1 Thessalonians 5:9,10** "For God hath not appointed us to wrath, but to obtain salvation by our Lord Jesus Christ, ^{10} Who died for us, that, whether we wake or sleep, we should live together with him."

36) **2 Thessalonians 2:13** "But we are bound to give thanks alway to God for you, brethren beloved of the Lord, because God hath from the beginning chosen you to salvation through sanctification of the Spirit and belief of the truth:"

37) **1 Timothy 1:15** "Here is a trustworthy saying that deserves full acceptance: Christ Jesus came into the world to save sinners--of whom I am the worst."

38) **1 Timothy 1:16** "Howbeit for this cause I obtained mercy, that in me first Jesus Christ might shew forth all longsuffering, for a pattern to them which should hereafter believe on him to life everlasting."

39) **1 Timothy 2:5,6** "For there is one God, and one mediator between God and men, the man Christ Jesus; ^{6} Who gave himself a ransom for all, to be testified in due time."

40) **2 Timothy 1:9** "Who hath saved us, and called us with an holy calling, not according to our works, but according to his own purpose and grace, which was given us in Christ Jesus before the world began,"

41) **2 Timothy 1:10** "But is now made manifest by the appearing of our Savior Jesus Christ, who hath abolished death, and hath brought life and immortality to light through the gospel:"

42) **2 Timothy 2:10** "Therefore I endure all things for the elect's sakes, that they may also obtain the salvation which is in Christ Jesus with eternal glory."

43) **2 Timothy 3:15** "that from a child thou hast known the holy scriptures, which are able to make thee wise unto salvation through faith which is in Christ Jesus."

44) **Titus 2:14** "Who gave himself for us, that he might redeem us from all iniquity, and purify unto himself a peculiar people, zealous of good works."

45) **Titus 3:3-7** "For we ourselves also were sometimes foolish, disobedient, deceived, serving divers lusts and pleasures, living in malice and envy, hateful, and hating one another. ^{4} But after that the kindness and love of God our Saviour toward man appeared, ^{5} Not by works of righteousness which we have done, but according to his mercy he saved us, by the washing of regeneration, and renewing of the Holy Ghost; ^{6} Which he shed on us abundantly through Jesus Christ our Savior; ^{7} That being justified by his grace, we should be made heirs according to the hope of eternal life."

46) **Hebrews 7:25** "Wherefore he is able also to save them to the uttermost that come unto God by him, seeing he ever liveth to make intercession for them."

47) **Hebrews 9:12-15** "Neither by the blood of goats and calves, but by his own blood he entered in once into the holy place, having obtained eternal redemption for us. ^{13} For if the blood of bulls and of goats, and the ashes of an heifer sprinkling the unclean, sanctifieth to the purifying of the flesh: ^{14} How much more shall the blood of Christ, who through the eternal Spirit offered himself without spot to God, purge your conscience from dead works to serve the living God? ^{15} And for this cause he is the mediator of the new testament, that by means of death, for the redemption of the transgressions that were under the first testament, they which are called might receive the promise of eternal inheritance."

48) **Hebrews 9:28** "Christ was once offered to bear the sins of many; and unto them that look for him shall he appear the second time without sin unto salvation."

49) **Hebrews 10:10** "By the which will we are sanctified through the offering of the body of Jesus Christ once for all."

50) **Hebrews 10:12** "But this man, after he had offered one sacrifice for sins for ever, sat down on the right hand of God;"

51) **1 Peter 1:18-19** "Forasmuch as ye know that ye were not redeemed with corruptible things, as silver and gold, from your vain conversation (lifestyle) received by tradition from your fathers; ^{19} But with the precious blood of Christ, as of a lamb without blemish and without spot:"

52) **1 John 1:7** "But if we walk in the light, as he is in the light, we have fellowship one with another, and the blood of Jesus Christ his Son cleanseth us from all sin."

53) **1 John 1:9** "If we confess our sins, he is faithful and just to forgive us our sins, and to cleanse us from all unrighteousness."

54) **1 John 2:2** "And he is the propitiation for our sins: and not for ours only, but also for the sins of the whole world."

55) **1 John 2:12** "I write unto you, little children, because your sins are forgiven you for his name's sake."

56) **1 John 2:25** "And this is the promise that he hath promised us, even eternal life."

57) **1 John 4:9** "In this was manifested the love of God toward us, because that God sent his only begotten Son into the world, that we might live through him."

58) **1 John 4:10** "Herein is love, not that we loved God, but that he loved us, and sent his Son to be the propitiation for our sins."

59) **1 John 2:1** "My little children, these things write I unto you, that ye sin not. And if any man sin, we have an advocate with the Father, Jesus Christ the righteous:"

60) **1 John 5:11** "And this is the record, that God hath given to us eternal life, and this life is in his Son."

61) **Revelation 1:5** "And from Jesus Christ, who is the faithful witness, and the first begotten of the dead, and the prince of the kings of the earth. Unto him that loved us, and washed us from our sins in his own blood,"

62) **Revelation 5:9** "And they sung a new song, saying, Thou art worthy to take the book, and to open the seals thereof: for thou wast slain, and hast redeemed us to God by thy blood out of every kindred, and tongue, and people, and nation;"

The goal of speaking these verses out loud is to fully believe the truth that Christ's death on the cross paid the penalty of our sin. Our salvation happens when we ask God/Jesus to forgive our sins, and ask Him to guide us the rest of our lives.

We need to become so convinced of God's faithfulness to forgive us, that nothing could convince us otherwise. Reading these scriptures over and over will help us make this truth more a reality in our hearts.

Note

This Core Belief is about believing that the sacrifice that Jesus made on the cross has paid for our sin. Have you ever taken the step to ask God to forgive you for all your sins? Have you invited Him to come into your life? If not, and you'd like to, there is a prayer below you can pray to invite Him into your life:

Invitation Prayer

> **"Dear God, I see the sins that I have committed. I believe Jesus paid the penalty for my sin by his crucifixion. I receive your forgiveness for my sin. And I ask you to come into my life and guide me. Help me live out the destiny you have for me. In Jesus's name I pray. Amen."**

If you've prayed this prayer, call us. We'd love to hear from you, and to help you get a great start in your new found faith!

USA: 213-426-8223   Canada: 289-723-2420   Email: victorytipsprogram@gmail.com

Let's turn back to the Beliefs Speaker role.

CORE BELIEF #3

****
"Based on the following scriptures, I believe God wants me to enjoy perfect peace at all times."
****

If we don't believe this Core Belief, we'll always wonder when it is OK to be nervous. It's best to believe that peace is always available. And we overcome anything that tries to rob us of God's peace. The peace God gives us passes all understanding (Philippians 4:7) and should never be given up.

1) **Numbers 6:26** "The LORD lift up his countenance upon thee, and give thee peace."

2) **Psalm 4:8** "I will both lay me down in peace, and sleep: for thou, LORD, only makest me dwell in safety."

3) **Psalm 16:8** "I have set the LORD always before me: because he is at my right hand, I shall not be moved (shaken)."

4) **Psalm 23:1-3** "The LORD is my shepherd; I shall not want. ² He maketh me to lie down in green pastures: he leadeth me beside the still waters. ³ He restoreth my soul: he leadeth me in the paths of righteousness for his name's sake."

5) **Psalm 27:1** "The LORD is my light and my salvation; whom shall I fear? the LORD is the strength of my life; of whom shall I be afraid?"

6) **Psalm 29:11** "The LORD will give strength unto his people; the LORD will bless his people with peace."

7) **Psalm 37:11** "But the meek shall inherit the earth; and shall delight themselves in the abundance of peace."

8) **Psalm 37:37** "Mark the perfect man, and behold the upright: for the end of that man is peace."

9) **Psalm 85:8** "I will hear what God the LORD will speak: for he will speak peace unto his people, and to his saints: but let them not turn again to folly."

10) **Psalm 91:1** "Whoever dwells in the shelter of the Most High will rest in the shadow of the Almighty."

11) **Psalm 94:13** "That thou mayest give him rest from the days of adversity, until the pit be digged for the wicked."

12) **Psalm 125:1** "They that trust in the LORD shall be as mount Zion, which cannot be removed (shaken), but abideth for ever."

13) **Proverbs 1:33** "But whoso hearkeneth unto me shall dwell safely, and shall be quiet from fear of evil."

14) **Proverbs 3:17** "Her ways are ways of pleasantness, and all her paths are peace."

15) **Proverbs 3:23-24** "Then shalt thou walk in thy way safely, and thy foot shall not stumble. ^{24} When thou liest down, thou shalt not be afraid: yea, thou shalt lie down, and thy sleep shall be sweet."

16) **Isaiah 26:3** "Thou wilt keep him in perfect peace, whose mind is stayed on thee: because he trusteth in thee."

17) **Isaiah 32:17** "And the work of righteousness shall be peace; and the effect of righteousness quietness and assurance forever."

18) **Isaiah 32:18** "And my people shall dwell in a peaceable habitation, and in sure dwellings, and in quiet resting places;"

19) **Isaiah 48:18** "O that thou hadst hearkened to my commandments! then had thy peace been as a river, and thy righteousness as the waves of the sea:"

20) **Isaiah 54:10** "For the mountains shall depart, and the hills be removed; but my kindness shall not depart from thee, neither shall the covenant of my peace be removed, saith the LORD that hath mercy on thee."

21) **Isaiah 54:13** "And all thy children shall be taught of the LORD; and great shall be the peace of thy children."

22) **Isaiah 55:12** "For ye shall go out with joy, and be led forth with peace: the mountains and the hills shall break forth before you into singing, and all the trees of the field shall clap their hands."

23) **Isaiah 57:2** "He shall enter into peace: they shall rest in their beds, each one walking in his uprightness."

24) **Isaiah 57:19** "I create the fruit of the lips; Peace, peace to him that is far off, and to him that is near, saith the LORD; and I will heal him."

25) **Jeremiah 33:6** "Behold, I will bring it health and cure, and I will cure them, and will reveal unto them the abundance of peace and truth."

26) **Haggai 2:9** "The glory of this latter house shall be greater than of the former, saith the LORD of hosts: and in this place will I give peace, saith the LORD of hosts."

27) **Malachi 2:5** My covenant was with him of life and peace; and I gave them to him for the fear wherewith he feared me, and was afraid before my name."

28) **Mark 9:50** "Salt is good: but if the salt have lost his saltness, wherewith will ye season it? Have salt in yourselves, and have peace one with another."

29) **Luke 1:79** "To give light to them that sit in darkness and in the shadow of death, to guide our feet into the way of peace."

30) **Luke 2:14** "Glory to God in the highest, and on earth peace, good will toward men."

31) **Luke 21:19** "In your patience, possess ye your souls."

32) **John 14:27** "Peace I leave with you, my peace I give unto you: not as the world giveth, give I unto you. Let not your heart be troubled, neither let it be afraid."

33) **John 16:33** "These things I have spoken unto you, that in me ye might have peace. In the world ye shall have tribulation: but be of good cheer; I have overcome the world."

34) **John 20:19** "Then the same day at evening, being the first day of the week, when the doors were shut where the disciples were assembled for fear of the Jews, came Jesus and stood in the midst, and saith unto them, Peace be unto you."

35) **Acts 10:36** "The word which God sent unto the children of Israel, preaching peace by Jesus Christ: (he is Lord of all:)"

36) **Romans 2:10** "But glory, honour, and peace, to every man that worketh good, to the Jew first, and also to the Gentile:"

37) **Romans 5:1** "Therefore being justified by faith, we have peace with God through our Lord Jesus Christ:"

38) **Romans 8:6** "For to be carnally minded is death; but to be spiritually minded is life and peace."

39) **Romans 14:17** "For the kingdom of God is not meat and drink; but righteousness, and peace, and joy in the Holy Ghost."

40) **Romans 15:13** "Now the God of hope fill you with all joy and peace in believing, that ye may abound in hope, through the power of the Holy Ghost."

41) **1 Corinthians 1:3** "Grace be unto you, and peace, from God our Father, and from the Lord Jesus Christ."

42) **1 Corinthians 14:33** "For God is not the author of confusion, but of peace, as in all churches of the saints."

43) **2 Corinthians 1:2** "Grace be to you and peace from God our Father, and from the Lord Jesus Christ."

44) **2 Corinthians 7:4** "Great is my boldness of speech toward you, great is my glorying of you: I am filled with comfort, I am exceeding joyful in all our tribulation.

45) **2 Corinthians 13:11** "Finally, brethren, farewell. Be perfect, be of good comfort, be of one mind, live in peace; and the God of love and peace shall be with you."

46) **Galatians 1:3** "Grace be to you and peace from God the Father, and from our Lord Jesus Christ,"

47) **Galatians 5:22** "But the fruit of the Spirit is love, joy, peace, longsuffering, gentleness, goodness, faith, ^{23} Meekness, temperance: against such there is no law."

48) **Ephesians 2:14,15** "For he is our peace, who hath made both one, and hath broken down the middle wall of partition between us; ^{15} Having abolished in his flesh the enmity, even the law of commandments contained in ordinances; for to make in himself of twain one new man, so making peace;"

49) **Ephesians 2:16,17** "And that he might reconcile both unto God in one body by the cross, having slain the enmity thereby: ^{17} And came and preached peace to you which were afar off, and to them that were nigh."

50) **Ephesians 4:3** "Endeavouring to keep the unity of the Spirit in the bond of peace."

51) **Philippians 1:2** "Grace be unto you, and peace, from God our Father, and from the Lord Jesus Christ."

52) **Philippians 4:11,12** "Not that I speak in respect of want: for I have learned, in whatsoever state I am, therewith to be content. ^{12} I know both how to be abased, and I know how to abound: everywhere and in all things I am instructed both to be full and to be hungry, both to abound and to suffer need."

53) **Philippians 4:6,7** "Be careful for nothing; but in everything by prayer and supplication with thanksgiving let your requests be made known unto God. ^{7}And the peace of God, which passeth all understanding, shall keep your hearts and minds through Christ Jesus."

54) **Philippians 4:9** "Whatever you have learned or received or heard from me, or seen in me—put it into practice. And the God of peace will be with you."

55) **Colossians 1:2** "To the saints and faithful brethren in Christ which are at Colosse: Grace be unto you, and peace, from God our Father and the Lord Jesus Christ."

56) **Colossians 1:20** "And, having made peace through the blood of his cross, by him to reconcile all things unto himself; by him, I say, whether they be things in earth, or things in heaven."

57) **Colossians 3:15** "And let the peace of God rule in your hearts, to the which also ye are called in one body; and be ye thankful."

58) **1 Thessalonians 1:1** "Paul, and Silvanus, and Timotheus, unto the church of the Thessalonians which is in God the Father and in the Lord Jesus Christ: Grace be unto you, and peace, from God our Father, and the Lord Jesus Christ."

59) **1 Thessalonians 3:13** "To the end he may stablish your hearts unblameable in holiness before God, even our Father, at the coming of our Lord Jesus Christ with all his saints."

60) **1 Thessalonians 5:13** "And to esteem them very highly in love for their work's sake. And be at peace among yourselves."

61) **2 Thessalonians 2:2** "That ye be not soon shaken in mind, or be troubled, neither by spirit, nor by word, nor by letter as from us, as that the day of Christ is at hand."

62) **2 Thessalonians 2:17** "Comfort your hearts, and stablish you in every good word and work."

63) **2 Thessalonians 3:16** "Now the Lord of peace himself give you peace always by all means. The Lord be with you all."

64) **2 Timothy 1:2** "To Timothy, my dearly beloved son: Grace, mercy, and peace, from God the Father and Christ Jesus our Lord."

65) **Titus 1:4** "To Titus, mine own son after the common faith: Grace, mercy, and peace, from God the Father and the Lord Jesus Christ our Saviour."

66) **James 5:8** "Be ye also patient; stablish your hearts: for the coming of the Lord draweth nigh."

67) **2 Peter 1:2** "Grace and peace be multiplied unto you through the knowledge of God, and of Jesus our Lord,"

The goal of speaking these verses out loud is to fully believe the truth that God wants us peaceful at all times. We need to become so convinced of this that nothing could convince us otherwise. Reading these scriptures over and over will help us make this truth more a reality in our hearts.

Let's turn back to Beliefs Speaker

CORE BELIEF #4

****
"Based on the following scriptures, I believe I have an enemy - Satan."
****

In 1 Timothy 6:12, we read, "Fight the good fight of faith..." Here we see the Christian life is a battle, a continuous fight for our faith. If we keep our faith intact, then our minds are kept at rest. If we succumb to the plots of our enemy, Satan, who seeks to undermine our faith, then we lose the peace and happiness God has for us, and life becomes difficult. You may not have faith in God at this time; in that case, the enemy will try to steal your faith in yourself. He knows if he can take your self-confidence, he can pull you down in every other aspect of your life. So beware of your enemy! Here are some other scriptures that support this belief that we have an enemy - Satan.

1) **Genesis 3:1** "Now the serpent was more subtil than any beast of the field which the LORD God had made. And he said unto the woman, Yea, hath God said, Ye shall not eat of every tree of the garden?"

2) **Genesis. 3:4,5** "And the serpent said unto the woman, Ye shall not surely die: ⁵ For God doth know that in the day ye eat thereof, then your eyes shall be opened, and ye shall be as gods, knowing good and evil."

3) **Genesis 3:14** "And the LORD God said unto the serpent, Because thou hast done this, thou art cursed above all cattle, and above every beast of the field; upon thy belly shalt thou go, and dust shalt thou eat all the days of thy life:"

4) **Deuteronomy. 32:17** "They sacrificed unto devils, not to God; to gods whom they knew not, to new gods that came newly up, whom your fathers feared not."

5) **Job 1:6** "Now there was a day when the sons of God came to present themselves before the LORD, and Satan came also among them."

6) **Job 2:3-7** "And the LORD said unto Satan, Hast thou considered my servant Job, that there is none like him in the earth, a perfect and an upright man, one that feareth God, and escheweth evil? and still he holdeth fast his integrity, although thou movedst me against him, to destroy him without cause. ⁴ And Satan answered the LORD, and said, Skin for skin, yea, all that a man hath will he give for his life. ⁵ But put forth thine hand now, and touch his bone and his flesh, and he will curse thee to thy face. ⁶ And the LORD said unto Satan, Behold, he is in thine hand; but save his life. ⁷ So went Satan forth from the presence of the LORD, and smote Job with sore boils from the sole of his foot unto his crown."

7) **1 Chronicles 21:1** "And Satan stood up against Israel, and provoked David to number Israel."

8) **Matthew 4:1-11** "Then was Jesus led up of the Spirit into the wilderness to be tempted of the devil. ² And when he had fasted forty days and forty nights, he was afterward an hungred. ³ And when the tempter came to him, he said, If thou be the Son of God, command that these stones be made bread. ⁴ But he answered and said, It is written, Man shall not live by bread alone, but by every word that proceedeth out of the mouth of God. ⁵ Then the devil taketh him up into the holy city, and setteth him on a pinnacle of the temple, ⁶ And saith unto him, If thou be the Son of God, cast thyself down: for it is written, He shall give his angels charge concerning thee: and in their hands they shall bear thee up, lest at any time thou dash thy foot against a stone. ⁷ Jesus said unto him, It is written again, Thou shalt not tempt the Lord thy God. ⁸ Again, the devil taketh him up into an exceeding high mountain, and sheweth him all the kingdoms of the world, and the glory of them; ⁹ And saith unto him, All these things will I give thee, if thou wilt fall down and worship me. ¹⁰ Then saith Jesus unto him, Get thee hence, Satan: for it is written, Thou shalt worship the Lord thy God, and him only shalt thou serve. ¹¹ Then the devil leaveth him, and, behold, angels came and ministered unto him.

9) **Matthew 4:24** "And his fame went throughout all Syria: and they brought unto him all sick people that were taken with divers diseases and torments, and those which were possessed with devils, and those which were lunatick, and those that had the palsy; and he healed them."

10) **Matthew 8:28-33** "And when he was come to the other side into the country of the Gergesenes, there met him two possessed with devils, coming out of the tombs, exceeding fierce, so that no man might pass by that way. ²⁹ And, behold, they cried out, saying, What have we to do with thee, Jesus, thou Son of God? art thou come hither to torment us before the time? ³⁰ And there was a good way off from them an herd of many swine feeding. ³¹ So the devils besought him, saying, If thou cast us out, suffer us to go away into the herd of swine. ³² And he said unto them, Go. And when they were come out, they went into the herd of swine: and, behold, the whole herd of swine ran violently down a steep place into the sea, and perished in the waters. ³³ And they that kept them fled, and went their ways into the city, and told every thing, and what was befallen to the possessed of the devils." (See Mark 5:2-20 for same story)

11) **Matthew 10:1** "And when he had called unto him his twelve disciples, he gave them power against unclean spirits, to cast them out, and to heal all manner of sickness and all manner of disease."

12) **Matthew 12:22** "Then was brought unto him one possessed with a devil, blind, and dumb: and he healed him, insomuch that the blind and dumb both spake and saw."

13) **Matthew 12:24** "But when the Pharisees heard it, they said, This fellow doth not cast out devils, but by Beelzebub the prince of the devils."

14) **Matthew 12:43-45** "When the unclean spirit is gone out of a man, he walketh through dry places, seeking rest, and findeth none. ⁴⁴ Then he saith, I will return into my house from whence I came out; and when he is come, he findeth it empty, swept, and garnished. ⁴⁵ Then goeth he, and taketh with himself seven other spirits more wicked than himself, and they enter in and dwell there: and the last state of that man is worse than the first. Even so shall it be also unto this wicked generation."

15) **Matthew 13:19** "When any one heareth the word of the kingdom, and understandeth it not, then cometh the

wicked one, and catcheth away that which was sown in his heart. This is he which received seed by the way side."

16) **Matthew 13:38,39** "The field is the world; the good seed are the children of the kingdom; but the tares are the children of the wicked one; ³⁹ The enemy that sowed them is the devil; the harvest is the end of the world; and the reapers are the angels."

17) **Matthew 17:14-18** "And when they were come to the multitude, there came to him a certain man, kneeling down to him, and saying, ¹⁵ Lord, have mercy on my son: for he is lunatick, and sore vexed: for ofttimes he falleth into the fire, and oft into the water. ¹⁶ And I brought him to thy disciples, and they could not cure him. ¹⁷ Then Jesus answered and said, O faithless and perverse generation, how long shall I be with you? how long shall I suffer you? bring him hither to me. ¹⁸ And Jesus rebuked the devil; and he departed out of him: and the child was cured from that very hour." (Same story in Mark 9:17-29, Luke 9:37-42)

18) **Matthew 25:41** "Then shall he say also unto them on the left hand, Depart from me, ye cursed, into everlasting fire, prepared for the devil and his angels:"

19) **Mark 1:23-26** "And there was in their synagogue a man with an unclean spirit; and he cried out, ²⁴ Saying, Let us alone; what have we to do with thee, thou Jesus of Nazareth? art thou come to destroy us? I know thee who thou art, the Holy One of God. ²⁵ And Jesus rebuked him, saying, Hold thy peace, and come out of him. ²⁶ And when the unclean spirit had torn him, and cried with a loud voice, he came out of him."

20) **Mark 3:11** "Whenever And unclean spirits, when they saw him, fell down before him, and cried, saying, Thou art the Son of God."

21) **Mark 3:22-26** "And the scribes which came down from Jerusalem said, He hath Beelzebub, and by the prince of the devils casteth he out devils. ²³ And he called them unto him, and said unto them in parables, How can Satan cast out Satan? ²⁴ And if a kingdom be divided against itself, that kingdom cannot stand. ²⁵ And if a house be divided against itself, that house cannot stand. ²⁶ And if Satan rise up against himself, and be divided, he cannot stand, but hath an end."

22) **Mark 6:7** "And he called unto him the twelve, and began to send them forth by two and two; and gave them power over unclean spirits;"

23) **Mark 7:25-30** "For a certain woman, whose young daughter had an unclean spirit, heard of him, and came and fell at his feet: ²⁶ The woman was a Greek, a Syrophenician by nation; and she besought him that he would cast forth the devil out of her daughter. ²⁷ But Jesus said unto her, Let the children first be filled: for it is not meet to take the children's bread, and to cast it unto the dogs. ²⁸ And she answered and said unto him, Yes, Lord: yet the dogs under the table eat of the children's crumbs. ²⁹ And he said unto her, For this saying go thy way; the devil is gone out of thy daughter. ³⁰ And when she was come to her house, she found the devil gone out, and her daughter laid upon the bed."

24) **Mark 9:38** "And John answered him, saying, Master, we saw one casting out devils in thy name, and he followeth not us: and we forbad him, because he followeth not us."

25) **Mark 16:9** "Now when Jesus was risen early the first day of the week, he appeared first to Mary Magdalene, out of whom he had cast seven devils."

26) **Mark 16:17** "And these signs shall follow them that believe; In my name shall they cast out devils; they shall speak with new tongues;"

27) **Luke 4:2,6** "Being forty days tempted of the devil. And in those days he did eat nothing: and when they were ended, he afterward hungered. 6 And the devil said unto him, All this power will I give thee, and the glory of them: for that is delivered unto me; and to whomsoever I will I give it."

28) **Luke 10:18** "And he said unto them, I beheld Satan as lightning fall from heaven."

29) **Luke 4:33-35** "And in the synagogue there was a man, which had a spirit of an unclean devil, and cried out with a loud voice, 34 Saying, Let us alone; what have we to do with thee, thou Jesus of Nazareth? art thou come to destroy us? I know thee who thou art; the Holy One of God. 35 And Jesus rebuked him, saying, Hold thy peace, and come out of him. And when the devil had thrown him in the midst, he came out of him, and hurt him not."

30) **Luke 4:41** "And devils also came out of many, crying out, and saying, Thou art Christ the Son of God. And he rebuking them suffered them not to speak: for they knew that he was Christ."

31) **Luke 8:27,28** "And when he went forth to land, there met him out of the city a certain man, which had devils long time, and ware no clothes, neither abode in any house, but in the tombs. 28 When he saw Jesus, he cried out, and fell down before him, and with a loud voice said, What have I to do with thee, Jesus, thou Son of God most high? I beseech thee, torment me not."

32) **Luke 10:17** "And the seventy returned again with joy, saying, Lord, even the devils are subject unto us through thy name."

33) **Luke 11:14,15** "And he was casting out a devil, and it was dumb. And it came to pass, when the devil was gone out, the dumb spake; and the people wondered. 15 But some of them said, He casteth out devils through Beelzebub the chief of the devils."

34) **Luke 13:16** "And ought not this woman, being a daughter of Abraham, whom Satan hath bound, lo, these eighteen years, be loosed from this bond on the sabbath day?"

35) **Luke 22:31** "And the Lord said, Simon, Simon, behold, Satan hath desired to have you, that he may sift you as wheat:"

36) **John 8:44** "Ye are of your father the devil, and the lusts of your father ye will do. He was a murderer from the beginning, and abode not in the truth, because there is no truth in him. When he speaketh a lie, he speaketh of his own: for he is a liar, and the father of it."

37) **John 10:20** "And many of them said, He hath a devil, and is mad; why hear ye him?"

38) **John 13:2** "And supper being ended, the devil having now put into the heart of Judas Iscariot, Simon's son, to betray him;"

39) **Acts 5:3** "But Peter said, Ananias, why hath Satan filled thine heart to lie to the Holy Ghost, and to keep back part of the price of the land?"

40) **Acts 5:16** "There came also a multitude out of the cities round about unto Jerusalem, bringing sick folks, and them which were vexed with unclean spirits: and they were healed every one."

41) **Acts 8:7** "For unclean spirits, crying with loud voice, came out of many that were possessed with them: and many taken with palsies, and that were lame, were healed."

42) **Acts 13:10** "And said, O full of all subtilty and all mischief, thou child of the devil, thou enemy of all righteousness, wilt thou not cease to pervert the right ways of the Lord?"

43) **Acts 16:16-18** "And it came to pass, as we went to prayer, a certain damsel possessed with a spirit of divination met us, which brought her masters much gain by soothsaying: ^{17} The same followed Paul and us, and cried, saying, These men are the servants of the most high God, which shew unto us the way of salvation. ^{18} And this did she many days. But Paul, being grieved, turned and said to the spirit, I command thee in the name of Jesus Christ to come out of her. And he came out the same hour."

44) **Acts 19:12-16** "So that from his body were brought unto the sick handkerchiefs or aprons, and the diseases departed from them, and the evil spirits went out of them. ^{13} Then certain of the vagabond Jews, exorcists, took upon them to call over them which had evil spirits the name of the LORD Jesus, saying, We adjure you by Jesus whom Paul preacheth. ^{14} And there were seven sons of one Sceva, a Jew, and chief of the priests, which did so. ^{15} And the evil spirit answered and said, Jesus I know, and Paul I know; but who are ye? ^{16} And the man in whom the evil spirit was leaped on them, and overcame them, and prevailed against them, so that they fled out of that house naked and wounded."

45) **Acts 26:18** "To open their eyes, and to turn them from darkness to light, and from the power of Satan unto God, that they may receive forgiveness of sins, and inheritance among them which are sanctified by faith that is in me."

46) **Romans 16:20** "And the God of peace shall bruise Satan under your feet shortly. The grace of our Lord Jesus Christ be with you. Amen."

47) **1 Corinthians 7:5** "Defraud ye not one the other, except it be with consent for a time, that ye may give yourselves to fasting and prayer; and come together again, that Satan tempt you not for your incontinency."

48) **1 Corinthians 10:20,21** "But I say, that the things which the Gentiles sacrifice, they sacrifice to devils, and not to God: and I would not that ye should have fellowship with devils. ^{21} Ye cannot drink the cup of the Lord, and the cup of devils: ye cannot be partakers of the Lord's table, and of the table of devils."

49) **2Corinthians 2:11** "Lest Satan should get an advantage of us: for we are not ignorant of his devices."

50) **2 Corinthians 11:3** "But I fear, lest by any means, as the serpent beguiled Eve through his subtilty, so your minds should be corrupted from the simplicity that is in Christ."

51) **2 Corinthians 11:14** "And no marvel; for Satan himself is transformed into an angel of light. ^{15} Therefore it is no great thing if his ministers also be transformed as the ministers of righteousness; whose end shall be according to their works."

52) **2 Corinthians 12:7** "And lest I should be exalted above measure through the abundance of the revelations, there was given to me a thorn in the flesh, the messenger of Satan to buffet me, lest I should be exalted above measure."

53) **Ephesians 2:2** "Wherein in time past ye walked according to the course of this world, according to the prince of the power of the air, the spirit that now worketh in the children of disobedience:"

54) **Ephesians 4:27** "Neither give place to the devil."

55) **1 Thessalonians 2:18** "Wherefore we would have come unto you, even I Paul, once and again; but Satan hindered us."

56) **Ephesians 6:11-16** "Put on the whole armour of God, that ye may be able to stand against the wiles of the devil. ^{12} For we wrestle not against flesh and blood, but against principalities, against powers, against the rulers of the darkness of this world, against spiritual wickedness in high places. ^{13} Wherefore take unto you the whole armour of God, that ye may be able to withstand in the evil day, and having done all, to stand. ^{14} Stand therefore, having your loins girt about with truth, and having on the breastplate of righteousness; ^{15} And your feet shod with the preparation of the gospel of peace; ^{16} Above all, taking the shield of faith, wherewith ye shall be able to quench all the fiery darts of the wicked."

57) **1 Thessalonians 3:5** "For this cause, when I could no longer forbear, I sent to know your faith, lest by some means the tempter have tempted you, and our labour be in vain."

58) **2 Thessalonians 2:9** "Even him, whose coming is after the working of Satan with all power and signs and lying wonders,"

59) **1 Timothy 1:20** "Of whom is Hymenaeus and Alexander; whom I have delivered unto Satan, that they may learn not to blaspheme."

60) **1 Timothy 3:6, 7** "Not a novice, lest being lifted up with pride he fall into the condemnation of the devil. ^{7} Moreover he must have a good report of them which are without; lest he fall into reproach and the snare of the devil."

61) **1 Timothy 4:1** "Now the Spirit speaketh expressly, that in the latter times some shall depart from the faith, giving heed to seducing spirits, and doctrines of devils;"

62) **1 Timothy 5:15** "For some are already turned aside after Satan."

63) **2 Timothy 2:26** "And that they may recover themselves out of the snare of the devil, who are taken captive by him at his will."

64) **Hebrews 2:14** "Forasmuch then as the children are partakers of flesh and blood, he also himself likewise took part of the same; that through death he might destroy him that had the power of death, that is, the devil;"

65) **James 2:19** "Thou believest that there is one God; thou doest well: the devils also believe, and tremble."

66) **James 4:7** "Submit yourselves therefore to God. Resist the devil, and he will flee from you."

67) **1 Peter 5:8,9** "Be sober, be vigilant; because your adversary the devil, as a roaring lion, walketh about, seeking whom he may devour: ^{9} Whom resist stedfast in the faith, knowing that the same afflictions are accomplished in your brethren that are in the world."

68) **1 John 2:13** "I write unto you, fathers, because ye have known him that is from the beginning. I write unto you, young men, because ye have overcome the wicked one. I write unto you, little children, because ye have known the Father."

69) **1 John 3:8** "He that committeth sin is of the devil; for the devil sinneth from the beginning. For this purpose the Son of God was manifested, that he might destroy the works of the devil."

70) **1 John 3:10** "In this the children of God are manifest, and the children of the devil: whosoever doeth not righteousness is not of God, neither he that loveth not his brother."

71) **1 John 3:12** "Not as Cain, who was of that wicked one, and slew his brother. And wherefore slew he him? Because his own works were evil, and his brother's righteous."

72) **1 John 5:18** "We know that whosoever is born of God sinneth not; but he that is begotten of God keepeth himself, and that wicked one toucheth him not."

73) **Jude 1:9** "Yet Michael the archangel, when contending with the devil he disputed about the body of Moses, durst not bring against him a railing accusation, but said, The Lord rebuke thee."

74) **Revelation 2:9-13** "I know thy works, and tribulation, and poverty, (but thou art rich) and I know the blasphemy of them which say they are Jews, and are not, but are the synagogue of Satan. ^{10} Fear none of those things which thou shalt suffer: behold, the devil shall cast some of you into prison, that ye may be tried; and ye shall have tribulation ten days: be thou faithful unto death, and I will give thee a crown of life. ^{11} He that hath an ear, let him hear what the Spirit saith unto the churches; He that overcometh shall not be hurt of the second death. ^{12} And to the angel of the church in Pergamos write; These things saith he which hath the sharp sword with two edges; ^{13} I know thy works, and where thou dwellest, even where Satan's seat is: and thou holdest fast my name, and hast not denied my faith, even in those days wherein Antipas was my faithful martyr, who was slain among you, where Satan dwelleth."

75) **Revelation 2:24** "But unto you I say, and unto the rest in Thyatira, as many as have not this doctrine, and which have not known the depths of Satan, as they speak; I will put upon you none other burden."

76) **Revelation 3:9** "I will make those who are of the synagogue of Satan, who claim to be Jews though they are not, but are liars--I will make them come and fall down at your feet and acknowledge that I have loved you."

77) **Revelation 9:20** "And the rest of the men which were not killed by these plagues yet repented not of the works of their hands, that they should not worship devils, and idols of gold, and silver, and brass, and stone, and of wood: which neither can see, nor hear, nor walk:"

78) **Revelation 12:9-12** "And the great dragon was cast out, that old serpent, called the Devil, and Satan, which deceiveth the whole world: he was cast out into the earth, and his angels were cast out with him. ^{10} And I heard a loud voice saying in heaven, Now is come salvation, and strength, and the kingdom of our God, and the power of his Christ: for the accuser of our brethren is cast down, which accused them before our God day and night. ^{11} And they overcame him by the blood of the Lamb, and by the word of their testimony; and they loved not their lives unto the death. ^{12} Therefore rejoice, ye heavens, and ye that dwell in them. Woe to the inhabiters of the earth and of the sea! for the devil is come down unto you, having great wrath, because he knoweth that he hath but a short time."

79) **Revelation 20:1-10** "And I saw an angel come down from heaven, having the key of the bottomless pit and a great chain in his hand. ^{2} And he laid hold on the dragon, that old serpent, which is the Devil, and Satan, and bound him a thousand years, ^{3} And cast him into the bottomless pit, and shut him up, and set a seal upon him, that he should deceive the nations no more, till the thousand years should be fulfilled: and after that he must be loosed a little season. ^{4} And I saw thrones, and they sat upon them, and judgment was given unto them: and I saw the souls of them that were beheaded for the witness of Jesus,

and for the word of God, and which had not worshipped the beast, neither his image, neither had received his mark upon their foreheads, or in their hands; and they lived and reigned with Christ a thousand years. ⁵ But the rest of the dead lived not again until the thousand years were finished. This is the first resurrection. ⁶ Blessed and holy is he that hath part in the first resurrection: on such the second death hath no power, but they shall be priests of God and of Christ, and shall reign with him a thousand years. ⁷ And when the thousand years are expired, Satan shall be loosed out of his prison, ⁸ And shall go out to deceive the nations which are in the four quarters of the earth, Gog, and Magog, to gather them together to battle: the number of whom is as the sand of the sea. ⁹ And they went up on the breadth of the earth, and compassed the camp of the saints about, and the beloved city: and fire came down from God out of heaven, and devoured them. ¹⁰ And the devil that deceived them was cast into the lake of fire and brimstone, where the beast and the false prophet are, and shall be tormented day and night for ever and ever."

The above scriptures show us that Satan is a real entity.

Let's turn back to the Beliefs Speaker role.

CORE BELIEF #5

***

"Based on the following scriptures, I believe I have another enemy - my fleshly appetites."

***

In 1 Timothy 6:12, we read, "Fight the good fight of faith...". Here we see that the Christian life is a battle, a continuous fight for our faith. If we keep our faith intact, our minds are kept at rest. If we succumb to the plots of our enemy, Satan, to undermine our faith, then we lose the peace and happiness God has for us, and life becomes difficult. Another enemy of the Christian can be the fleshly appetites of the physical body. They can crave things that are not good and can be a distraction taking our focus off of Christ and His plan for our lives. Allowing our fleshly appetites to have their way negatively in our lives will lead us toward anxiety and defeat.

1) **Romans 6:13** "Neither yield ye your members as instruments of unrighteousness unto sin: but yield yourselves unto God, as those that are alive from the dead, and your members as instruments of righteousness unto God."

2) **Romans 7:5** "For when we were in the flesh, the motions of sins, which were by the law, did work in our members to bring forth fruit unto death."

3) **Romans 7:18** "For I know that in me (that is, in my flesh,) dwelleth no good thing: for to will is present with me; but how to perform that which is good I find not."

4) **Romans 8:1,2** "There is therefore now no condemnation to them which are in Christ Jesus, who walk not after the flesh, but after the Spirit. ²For the law of the Spirit of life in Christ Jesus hath made me free from the law of sin and death."

5) **Romans 8:3** "For what the law could not do, in that it was weak through the flesh, God sending his own Son in the likeness of sinful flesh, and for sin, condemned sin in the flesh:"

6) **Romans 8:4** "That the righteousness of the law might be fulfilled in us, who walk not after the flesh, but after the Spirit."

7) **Romans 8:5** "For they that are after the flesh do mind the things of the flesh; but they that are after the Spirit the things of the Spirit."

8) **Romans 8:8** "So then they that are in the flesh cannot please God."

9) **Romans 8:9** "But ye are not in the flesh, but in the Spirit, if so be that the Spirit of God dwell in you. Now if any man have not the Spirit of Christ, he is none of his."

10) **Romans 8:10,11** "And if Christ be in you, the body is dead because of sin; but the Spirit is life because of righteousness. ¹¹ But if the Spirit of him that raised up Jesus from the dead dwell in you, he that raised up Christ from the dead shall also quicken your mortal bodies by his Spirit that dwelleth in you."

11) **Romans 8:12** "Therefore, brethren, we are debtors, not to the flesh, to live after the flesh."

12) **Romans 8:13,14** "For if ye live after the flesh, ye shall die: but if ye through the Spirit do mortify the deeds of the body, ye shall live. ¹⁴ For as many as are led by the Spirit of God, they are the sons of God."

13) **Galatians 5:16** "This I say then, Walk in the Spirit, and ye shall not fulfil the lust of the flesh."

14) **Galatians 5:17-18** "For the flesh lusteth against the Spirit, and the Spirit against the flesh: and these are contrary the one to the other: so that ye cannot do the things that ye would. ¹⁸ But if ye be led of the Spirit, ye are not under the law.

15) **Galatians 5:19-21** "Now the works of the flesh are manifest, which are these; Adultery, fornication, uncleanness, lasciviousness, ²⁰ Idolatry, witchcraft, hatred, variance, emulations, wrath, strife, seditions, heresies, ²¹ Envyings, murders, drunkenness, revellings, and such like: of the which I tell you before, as I have also told you in time past, that they which do such things shall not inherit the kingdom of God."

16) **Galatians 5:22-25** "But the fruit of the Spirit is love, joy, peace, longsuffering, gentleness, goodness, faith, ²³ Meekness, temperance: against such there is no law. ²⁴ And they that are Christ's have crucified the flesh with the affections and lusts. ²⁵ If we live in the Spirit, let us also walk in the Spirit."

17) **Ephesians 4:22-24** "That ye put off concerning the former conversation the old man, which is corrupt according to the deceitful lusts; ²³ And be renewed in the spirit of your mind; ²⁴ And that ye put on the new man, which after God is created in righteousness and true holiness."

18) **Colossians 3:5** "Mortify therefore your members which are upon the earth; fornication, uncleanness, inordinate affection, evil concupiscence, and covetousness, which is idolatry:"

19) **1 Peter 1:14-16** "As obedient children, not fashioning yourselves according to the former lusts in your ignorance: ¹⁵ But as he which hath called you is holy, so be ye holy in all manner of conversation; ¹⁶ Because it is written, Be ye holy; for I am holy."

20) **1 Peter 2:11** "Dearly beloved, I beseech you as strangers and pilgrims, abstain from fleshly lusts, which war against the soul;

21) **1 John 3:5-7** "And ye know that he was manifested to take away our sins; and in him is no sin. ⁶ Whosoever abideth in him sinneth not: whosoever sinneth hath not seen him, neither known him. ⁷ Little children, let no man deceive you: he that doeth righteousness is righteous, even as he is righteous."

The goal of speaking these verses out loud is to fully believe the truth that our fleshly appetites are at war with us. We need to become so convinced of this that nothing could convince us otherwise. Reading these scriptures over and over will help us make this truth more a reality in our hearts.

Let's turn back to the Beliefs Speaker role.

CORE BELIEF #6

"Based on the following scriptures, I believe God wants me to enjoy good physical health."

This belief can be difficult to adopt because so many people who pray for healing don't get healed. This is a mystery. However, we know that God responds to faith. Whenever Jesus healed someone, the scriptures say or imply that Jesus marveled at the person's faith. That is what we want Jesus to observe in us; we want Him to marvel at our faith. Thus, the purpose of saying these verses is to help keep our faith strong while we wait for God to move in our situation. As a side-benefit, we will enjoy peace of mind while we wait.

1) **Exodus 15:26** "And said, If thou wilt diligently hearken to the voice of the LORD thy God, and wilt do that which is right in his sight, and wilt give ear to his commandments, and keep all his statutes, I will put none of these diseases upon thee, which I have brought upon the Egyptians: for I am the LORD that healeth thee."

2) **Psalm 30:2** "O LORD my God, I cried unto thee, and thou hast healed me."

3) **Psalm 103:3** "Who forgiveth all thine iniquities; who healeth all thy diseases;"

4) **Psalm 107:20** "He sent his word, and healed them, and delivered them from their destructions."

5) **Proverbs 3:8** "It shall be health to thy navel, and marrow to thy bones."

6) **Proverbs 4:20-22** "My son, attend to my words; incline thine ear unto my sayings. ²¹ Let them not depart from thine eyes; keep them in the midst of thine heart. ²² For they are life unto those that find them, and health to all their flesh."

7) **Proverbs 10:27** "The fear of the LORD prolongeth days: but the years of the wicked shall be shortened."

8) **Isaiah 53:4-5** "Surely he hath borne our griefs, and carried our sorrows: yet we did esteem him stricken, smitten of God, and afflicted. ⁵ But he was wounded for our transgressions, he was bruised for our iniquities: the chastisement of our peace was upon him; and with his stripes we are healed."

9) **Jeremiah 17:14** "Heal me, O LORD, and I shall be healed; save me, and I shall be saved: for thou art my praise."

10) **Jeremiah 30:17** "For I will restore health unto thee, and I will heal thee of thy wounds, saith the LORD; because they called thee an Outcast, saying, This is Zion, whom no man seeketh after."

11) **Jeremiah 33:6** "Behold, I will bring it health and cure, and I will cure them, and will reveal unto them the abundance of peace and truth."

12) **Hosea 6:1** "Come, and let us return unto the LORD: for he hath torn, and he will heal us; he hath smitten, and he will bind us up."

13) **Malachi 4:2** "But unto you that fear my name shall the Sun of righteousness arise with healing in his wings; and ye shall go forth, and grow up as calves of the stall."

14) **Matthew 4:23-24** "And Jesus went about all Galilee, teaching in their synagogues, and preaching the gospel of the kingdom, and healing all manner of sickness and all manner of disease among the people. ^{24} And his fame went throughout all Syria: and they brought unto him all sick people that were taken with divers diseases and torments, and those which were possessed with devils, and those which were lunatick, and those that had the palsy; and he healed them."

15) **Matthew 8:7** "And Jesus saith unto him, I will come and heal him."

16) **Matthew 8:13** "And Jesus said unto the centurion, Go thy way; and as thou hast believed, so be it done unto thee. And his servant was healed in the selfsame hour."

17) **Matthew 8:15-17** "And he touched her hand, and the fever left her: and she arose, and ministered unto them. ^{16} When the even was come, they brought unto him many that were possessed with devils: and he cast out the spirits with his word, and healed all that were sick: ^{17} That it might be fulfilled which was spoken by Esaias the prophet, saying, Himself took our infirmities, and bare our sicknesses. "

18) **Matthew 9:35** "And Jesus went about all the cities and villages, teaching in their synagogues, and preaching the gospel of the kingdom, and healing every sickness and every disease among the people."

19) **Matthew 12:10** "And, behold, there was a man which had his hand withered. And they asked him, saying, Is it lawful to heal on the sabbath days? that they might accuse him."

20) **Matthew 12:13** "Then saith he to the man, Stretch forth thine hand. And he stretched it forth; and it was restored whole, like as the other."

21) **Matthew 12:15** "But when Jesus knew it, he withdrew himself from thence: and great multitudes followed him, and he healed them all;"

22) **Matthew 12:22**"Then was brought unto him one possessed with a devil, blind, and dumb: and he healed him, insomuch that the blind and dumb both spake and saw."

23) **Matthew 14:14** "And Jesus went forth, and saw a great multitude, and was moved with compassion toward them, and he healed their sick."

24) **Matthew 15:28** "Then Jesus answered and said unto her, O woman, great is thy faith: be it unto thee even as thou wilt. And her daughter was made whole from that very hour."

25) **Matthew 15:30** "And great multitudes came unto him, having with them those that were lame, blind, dumb, maimed, and many others, and cast them down at Jesus' feet; and he healed them:"

26) **Matthew 19:2** "And great multitudes followed him; and he healed them there."

27) **Matthew 21:22** "And all things, whatsoever ye shall ask in prayer, believing, ye shall receive."

28) **Mark 1:34** "And he healed many that were sick of divers diseases, and cast out many devils; and suffered not the devils to speak, because they knew him."

29) **Mark 3:10** "For he had healed many; insomuch that they pressed upon him for to touch him, as many as had plagues."

30) **Mark 6:5-6** "And he could there do no mighty work, save that he laid his hands upon a few sick folk, and healed them. ⁶ And he marvelled because of their unbelief. And he went round about the villages, teaching."

31) **Mark 16:18** "And I say also unto thee, That thou art Peter, and upon this rock I will build my church; and the gates of hell shall not prevail against it."

32) **Luke 4:18** "The Spirit of the Lord is upon me, because he hath anointed me to preach the gospel to the poor; he hath sent me to heal the brokenhearted, to preach deliverance to the captives, and recovering of sight to the blind, to set at liberty them that are bruised,"

33) **Luke 4:40** "Now when the sun was setting, all they that had any sick with divers diseases brought them unto him; and he laid his hands on every one of them, and healed them."

34) **Luke 5:15** "But so much the more went there a fame abroad of him: and great multitudes came together to hear, and to be healed by him of their infirmities."

35) **Luke 6:17-19** "And he came down with them, and stood in the plain, and the company of his disciples, and a great multitude of people out of all Judaea and Jerusalem, and from the sea coast of Tyre and Sidon, which came to hear him, and to be healed of their diseases; ¹⁸ And they that were vexed with unclean spirits: and they were healed. ¹⁹ And the whole multitude sought to touch him: for there went virtue out of him, and healed them all."

36) **Luke 8:43,44,47,48** "And a woman having an issue of blood twelve years, which had spent all her living upon physicians, neither could be healed of any, ⁴⁴ Came behind him, and touched the border of his garment: and immediately her issue of blood stanched. ⁴⁷ And when the woman saw that she was not hid, she came trembling, and falling down before him, she declared unto him before all the people for what cause she had touched him, and how she was healed immediately. ⁴⁸ And he said unto her, Daughter, be of good comfort: thy faith hath made thee whole; go in peace."

37) **Luke 9:11** "And the people, when they knew it, followed him: and he received them, and spake unto them of the kingdom of God, and healed them that had need of healing."

38) **Luke 9:42** "And as he was yet a coming, the devil threw him down, and tare him. And Jesus rebuked the unclean spirit, and healed the child, and delivered him again to his father."

39) **Luke 13:11-16** "And, behold, there was a woman which had a spirit of infirmity eighteen years, and was bowed together, and could in no wise lift up herself. ¹² And when Jesus saw her, he called her to him, and said unto her, Woman, thou art loosed from thine infirmity. ¹³ And he laid his hands on her: and immediately she was made straight, and glorified God. ¹⁴ And the ruler of the synagogue answered with indignation, because that Jesus had healed on the sabbath day, and said unto the people, There are six days in which men ought to work: in them therefore come and be healed, and not on the sabbath day. ¹⁵ The Lord then answered him, and said, Thou hypocrite, doth not each one of you on the sabbath loose his ox or his ass from the stall, and lead him away to watering? ¹⁶ And ought not this woman, being a daughter of Abraham, whom Satan hath bound, lo, these eighteen years, be loosed from this bond on the sabbath day?"

40) **Luke 14:3-4** "And Jesus answering spake unto the lawyers and Pharisees, saying, Is it lawful to heal on the sabbath day? [4] And they held their peace. And he took him, and healed him, and let him go;"

41) **Luke 17:12-15** "And as he entered into a certain village, there met him ten men that were lepers, which stood afar off: [13] And they lifted up their voices, and said, Jesus, Master, have mercy on us. [14] And when he saw them, he said unto them, Go shew yourselves unto the priests. And it came to pass, that, as they went, they were cleansed. [15] And one of them, when he saw that he was healed, turned back, and with a loud voice glorified God,"

42) **Luke 22:50-51** "And one of them smote the servant of the high priest, and cut off his right ear. [51] And Jesus answered and said, Suffer ye thus far. And he touched his ear, and healed him."

43) **Acts 3:12** "And when Peter saw it, he answered unto the people, Ye men of Israel, why marvel ye at this? or why look ye so earnestly on us, as though by our own power or holiness we had made this man to walk?"

44) **Acts 4:29-31** "And now, Lord, behold their threatenings: and grant unto thy servants, that with all boldness they may speak thy word, [30] By stretching forth thine hand to heal; and that signs and wonders may be done by the name of thy holy child Jesus. [31] And when they had prayed, the place was shaken where they were assembled together; and they were all filled with the Holy Ghost, and they spake the word of God with boldness."

45) **Acts 10:38** "How God anointed Jesus of Nazareth with the Holy Ghost and with power: who went about doing good, and healing all that were oppressed of the devil; for God was with him."

46) **1 Corinthians 12:7-10** "But the manifestation of the Spirit is given to every man to profit withal. [8] For to one is given by the Spirit the word of wisdom; to another the word of knowledge by the same Spirit; [9] To another faith by the same Spirit; to another the gifts of healing by the same Spirit; [10] To another the working of miracles; to another prophecy; to another discerning of spirits; to another divers kinds of tongues; to another the interpretation of tongues:"

47) **James 5:14-16** "Is any sick among you? let him call for the elders of the church; and let them pray over him, anointing him with oil in the name of the Lord: [15] And the prayer of faith shall save the sick, and the Lord shall raise him up; and if he have committed sins, they shall be forgiven him. [16] Confess your faults one to another, and pray one for another, that ye may be healed. The effectual fervent prayer of a righteous man availeth much."

48) **1Peter 2:24** "Who his own self bare our sins in his own body on the tree, that we, being dead to sins, should live unto righteousness: by whose stripes ye were healed."

49) **3 John 1:2** "Beloved, I wish above all things that thou mayest prosper and be in health, even as thy soul prospereth."

The goal of speaking these verses out loud is to fully believe the truth that God wants us to enjoy good health. We need to become so convinced of this that nothing could convince us otherwise. Reading these scriptures over and over will help us make this truth more a reality in our hearts.

Let's turn back to the Beliefs Speaker role.

TYPES OF ABUSE

When most people hear the word "abuse" they usually think of something very extreme, such as punching or kicking. However, abuse can take non-physical forms too. The following is a list of 6 types of abuse.

Physical

- Any unwanted physical contact
- Kicking, punching
- Pulling, pushing
- Slapping, hitting
- Pulling hair
- Arm twisting
- Holding against wall
- Squeezing hand, arm
- Choking
- Shooting
- Locking in a room
- Standing too close
- Stopping from leaving
- Restraining in any way
- Picking them up
- Holding or hugging when unwanted
- Pointing finger, poking
- Murder
- Hitting with objects
- Tickling
- Spitting

Sexual

- Forcing sex (rape)
- Total lack of intimacy
- Forcing certain positions
- Total lack of intimacy
- Sleeping around
- Hounding for sex
- Intimidation by knowledge or reputation
- Retaliating by refusing sex
- Put downs
- Being rough
- Using sex as basis for argument
- Treating someone as a sex object
- Pornography
- Forcing people to have sex with others

Emotional/Verbal/Psychological

- Forcing people to have sex with others
- Refusing to do things with them
- Getting your own way
- Pressuring them
- Not coming home
- Real or suggested involvement with another person
- Manipulation
- Annoying mannerisms, e.g. snapping fingers
- Saying "Do you remember what happened last time"
- Making threats to them about you, e.g. killing yourself

Financial

- Withholding money
- Spending money foolishly or beyond means
- Not spending money on special occasions, e.g. their birthday
- Making the decisions in terms of how money is spent

Environmental

- Locking them in
- Taking the phones with you to work
- Slamming doors
- Breaking things
- Throwing objects
- Turning the stereo/TV up loud
- Harming pets
- Throwing their clothes out
- Ripping their clothes

Social

- Not taking responsibility for children
- Embarrassment in front of children
- Putting down or ignoring in public
- Accusing them of sleeping
- Not saying what is on your mind
- Never really forgiving
- Lying
- Accusing them of sleeping around
- Treating them as a child
- Putting them on a pedestal
- False accusations
- Raising your voice with them
- Agreeing with them even though you don't
- Making them fearful
- Putting them or their family down
- Starting arguments
- Not letting them see their friends
- Using a continual joke or putdown about them with others
- Choosing friends or family over them
- Using kids as a weapon
- Abusing children physically or sexually
- Not taking them out
- Keeping them busy in the kitchen, e.g. during a party
- Change of personality with others
- Not being nice to their friends
- Making a "scene"

Emotional/Verbal/Psychological

- Insulting
- Yelling
- Name calling
- Verbal threats
- Intimidation
- Playing "mind games"
- Overpowering their emotions
- Brainwashing
- Bringing up old issues and arguing with them
- Putting them down for things they have done in the past
- Inappropriate expression of jealousy
- Turning around a situation against them
- Laughing in their face
- Silence
- Walking away from them in a discussion
- Finding and verbalizing their faults
- Comparing them to others to conform to a role
- Overtly sarcastic or critical
- Lack of consideration for their opinion
- Trying to get last word in
- Pre-violence cues
- Isolation, e.g. not telling them what you are doing

Author's Message

Dear friend,

I hope this manual helps you realize that with effort you can achieve a life free of nagging anxiety and depression. I wish this manual existed 40 years ago when I needed it. It wasn't, so I had to stumble along in life - hurting, wasting time thinking about life, trying to figure out how to psyche myself up to face life every day, wasting time reading unhelpful books, wasting time and money seeing various counselors who didn't help me. I would like to think this will be the last self-help book you'll ever need, but I would never endorse that. It's important to stay hungry for truth. So buy as many books as you like, keep learning. Trust God to deliver you from anything that is hindering you, so you can become everything He wants you to be. Life is short, so live it to the full. Get well, not just for you, but for your family and friends. Most of all, get well so God can use you to help others who struggle.

"One life 'twill soon be past, only what's done for Christ will last." One way to really make an impact for Christ is by getting involved in helping people with their mental health challenges. This program is one way to do that. We offer you the opportunity to learn how to be a chairperson for a Victory Tips group. In the beginning it can be a conference call group. Then, as your confidence grows, you may want to lead a community group in a public venue where you live. It is exhilarating watching people transform into happy, healthy individuals. You will feel great knowing that you played a part in seeing these people get healed.

For the next 60 seconds, I am taking my focus off of this book, and I'm thinking about you. I am envisioning the potential that resides in you… and I'm thinking back in history at all the world-shakers that the church of Jesus Christ has ever produced, and I'm thinking, "I could be looking at another world-shaker, right here, right now –You!" It is sobering. Thus, my goal is to be there for you, and inspire you to seek God with everything you have. Make Him a priority in your life. I will run alongside you until you reach your goal of peace and happiness. And I will do whatever I can to help you become a world-shaker Christian. That is my commitment to you. I invite you to contact me and we will see where this leads. I'm hoping it leads to tens…, hundreds…, and even thousands more people being helped out of anxiety and depression. Wouldn't that be awesome? Let's see.

To your happiness and success,

Vince
289-723-2420 (Canada)
213-426-8223 (United States)
victorytipsvince@gmail.com

Message To The Strong

The problem of poor mental health in society is so staggering that it is going to require everyone pitching-in to help those who struggle emotionally. The Bible teaches that we who are strong ought to help those who are weak, and this includes those with mental health challenges.

a) **Romans 15:1** "We then that are strong ought to bear the infirmities of the weak, and not to please ourselves."

b) **1 Thessalonians 5:14** "Now we exhort you, brethren, warn them that are unruly, comfort the feebleminded, support the weak, be patient toward all men."

c) **Hebrews 12:12** "Wherefore lift up the hands which hang down, and the feeble knees;"

d) **Psalm 41:1** "Blessed is he that considereth the poor: the Lord will deliver him in time of trouble."

e) **Isaiah 35:3** "Strengthen ye the weak hands, and confirm the feeble knees."

Even if we are strong, and those in our family, and circle of friends are strong, our lives can be severely affected by a stranger who has a random outburst. Please consider what you can do to help those who struggle emotionally.

The Victory Tips Program makes it easy to lead a weekly support group. By using this program, or parts of it, you will be doing your part to reach out to those who struggle. Don't wait until a co-worker, or a classmate of one your children reacts out of deep anxiety or depression. Reach out today. Make a difference where you are. With everyone doing their bit, we can help eradicate desperate feelings and actions in our communities. You are stronger and more helpful than you think!

Occasionally, we meet someone who is head and shoulders above everyone else, spiritually. We may not realize it at the time. But years later, we will remember them and say what the two travelers who were on the road to Emmaus said, *"Did not our heart burn within us, while he talked with us by the way, and while he opened to us the scriptures?"* This unique person is 'gripped' with the gospel, sharing it, teaching it, praying for more of God in their life, and the lives of others. It permeates everything about them. They are marked *by* God, and *for* God. Almost like John the Baptist. It's just on them. They have a narrow focus, so they are unencumbered by life's problems. This makes them jovial and fun to be with. And it attracts others who want to be like them. When a person like that comes into our lives, we'll want to make room on our agenda and spend some time with them. Perhaps, some of the Spirit that is on them will rub off on us. And if nothing else, we'll get to watch a fire burn, and be warmed by it. It is these kinds of people who make the most impact for God, for their family, for their church, and for the world.

www.ingramcontent.com/pod-product-compliance
Lightning Source LLC
Chambersburg PA
CBHW081455040426
42446CB00016B/3248